Awakening at The End of Time

Awakening at the End of Time

The Death of the 3-D Human "Caterpillar" and The Birth of the Luminous Human "Butterfly"

Barry Martin Snyder
and
Karen Anderson

Luminous Self Media

First Edition, January 2019

Copyright © 2018 Barry Snyder and Karen Anderson
All Rights Reserved. No part of this book may be reproduced by any means or in any form whatsoever without written permission from the publisher, other than for "fair use" as brief quotations embodied in articles and reviews.

Luminous Self Media
http://www.luminousself.com

ISBN 978-0-9835990-7-4
Printed in the United States of America

Contents

Foreword
by Kiara Windrider

Introduction

Prologue

PART ONE
The Death of The 3-D Human "Caterpillar"

1 Economic Crises 1
2 Social And Political Crises 3
3 Ecological Crises 5
4 Energy Crises 7
5 Climate Change Crises 21
6 Abrupt Climate Change 29
7 Overshoot and Collapse 39
8 Sixth Great Extinction Ahead? 49
9 Facing and Embracing Apocalypse 59

PART TWO
The Birth of the Luminous Human "Butterfly"

Introduction
10 A Vaster Perspective 67
11 The Essential Evolution of Consciousness 75
12 The Gift of Facing Death 83
13 Prophesies of a Great Evolutionary Leap 89
14 Signs Of An Evolutionary Leap 95
15 Galactic Re-Seeding 109
16 The Birth of Homo Luminous 115
17 Visions of a Wave of Light 119
18 Understandings and Confirmations of the Visions 129
19 Approaching the Quantum Moment 137
20 Beyond the Quantum Moment 143

21 Many Futures 147
22 Visions of the New Earth 153
23 The End That Is The Beginning 159

PART THREE
Bringing It All Home

24 Embrace and Transcend 165
25 Dealing With Ego Resistance and Defense 169
26 The Essential Reframe 175
27 Faith and Surrender 179
28 Love and Acceptance 183
29 Finding Meaning and Purpose at the End of an Age 187
30 Beyond Hope and Hopelessness 191
31 The Path of Grace 197
32 The Deep, Dark Descent of Ego Death 201
33 Facing Death as the Ultimate Doorway to Awakening 217
34 The Coming of the Collective Avatar 221

Afterword
An Offer of Many More Resources 227

Foreword

by Kiara Windrider

There is a mystic, a poet, and a warrior awakening in each of our hearts.

How many of us have gazed up at the stars at night and contemplated the mysteries of space and time, pondering how this vast universe came into being, looking for our own place in this tapestry of infinity?

How many of us have surveyed the beauty of an ancient forest, the stillness of a mountain lake, or the vast restless ocean, and felt the unifying pulse of an immense web of life energizing and connecting all things?

And how many of us have felt the ache of despair, impotency and rage as we watched the disappearance of this incredible world of mystery and beauty in the fast onslaught of a human civilization gone out of balance, and out of control?

Is this all there is to existence, fading out with a whimper or else going out with the proverbial bang, as we move inexorably towards the precipice of what many have called the Sixth Extinction Event?

Or could there perhaps be an evolutionary purpose to all this, once we are able to align with it, that allows us to transform our aching despair into hope, our impotent rage into creative action, transforming our precious blue planet into a galactic jewel of light?

I first met Barry and Karen in Mt. Shasta, California, where I lived during the 90s, and remember endless walks through the mountains examining these inter-related issues. We bonded instantly in our common search for meaningful hope, speaking of galactic waves and coronal mass ejections, ancient history and geomagnetic reversals, evolutionary cycles and templates of creation that shape the worlds of apparent physical form.

We discussed the possibility that despite our technological and spiritual advances, we were still an incomplete species, and that we needed to go through an evolutionary crisis much as a caterpillar does on its journey towards becoming a butterfly.

We spoke about how there is a divine intelligence pervading the universe and within our cells which was shaping our biology and creating new species on Earth just as surely as the forces of death were tearing down our current state of human civilization, resting on the illusion of a personal ego existing separately from the rest of creation. We realized we were not separate from the divine intelligence that was continually oscillating between states of form and formlessness, birthing new forms of increasing complexity and creative awareness.

We considered how the Earth herself was a living conscious being with her own cycles of growth and evolution. We pondered Sri Aurobindo's mystical understandings that a *supramental descent* was taking place right now and that our current cataclysms were simply a response to this incoming cosmic light so that outdated forms could give way to the new.

In all of this we noted how important it was to keep our hearts and minds open to the voice of the living Earth, denying neither our current ecological and human realities, nor our ability to harness the forces of creation to collectively transform these realities. We realized that for those who have chosen to come to this Earth as warriors of light, these times of crisis were unprecedented opportunities to evolve further. And that a 'big picture' perspective was essential if we were to look beyond the outer realities of these times.

This meticulously researched book, an expansion of those earlier ideas, spans vast realms of scientific and metaphysical enquiry, as well as deeply personal stories, futuristic visions and spiritual encounters. It is unique in that it not only provides detailed, sometimes brutal, descriptions of the current state of our planet, including the political agendas, climate changes and ecological disasters that are increasingly affecting our very survival, but also provides perspectives and possibilities for emerging from this chaos into a glorious new cycle of human and planetary evolution.

We have managed to desecrate and pollute the Earth in innumerable ways that threaten her survival as a planet, and the survival of millions of her species, including our own. This is a fact that can no longer be denied. The most recent of these threats has to do with the largely unacknowledged ongoing contamination of sea-water from the Fukushima nuclear reactor, which has already turned a third of the Pacific Ocean into a virtual dead zone.

The truth of cataclysmic climate change can no longer be denied either. Increasingly severe bouts of heat, cold, floods, fires, earthquakes, hurricanes, volcanoes, droughts, food and water shortages are becoming a reality for many around the world. There is still ongoing debate whether these cataclysms are caused by global warming resulting from greenhouse emissions such as carbon dioxide and methane, as Barry and Karen tend to concur, or from the inflow of cosmic rays and terrestrial cooling resulting from decreased electrical activity within the Sun, similar to what was experienced during the 'little ice age' in 17th century Europe, which happens to be my own personal conviction.

Whatever the ultimate verdict, and this will become clear very soon, the fact remains that we are entering a period of unprecedented environmental catastrophe, food shortages, social disintegration, economic collapse, and political tension. We must prepare for this with awareness and courage. Relegating all this into the trashcan of 'doom and gloom' is to deny that we are already in a rather gloomy state of runaway doom.

However, is it possible to face these coming times not from a place of fear and denial but from a place of vision and hope? What would this look like? If we are witnessing, at the end of our current evolutionary cycle, the death of *caterpillar consciousness*, what would it mean to emerge as a *human butterfly*? Can we embrace our deep subconscious fears of death, and thus realize our identity as infinite beings of creativity and light? What are some perspectives and practices for achieving this?

Many spiritual traditions speak of moving out of an age of darkness into an age of light. What are some of these prophecies, and what does the journey of Self-realization mean in this context? How does this correlate with revelations emerging from modern seers, mystics, yogis and physicists? Is there such a thing as collective enlightenment or *quantum awakening*? What would this look like, and what are the planetary mechanisms and timing keys for achieving this?

Ultimately, what power for change do we possess as awakened souls consciously attuned to the Soul of the Earth? What happens when we begin to shift into higher dimensional timelines for the future? Can we transform the worst-case scenarios of 'doom and gloom', and consciously shape the next evolutionary cycle as members of a new, soul-oriented human species, *homo luminous*?

The answer is a resounding YES! But transformation can never happen as long as we resist or reject any aspects of ourselves, whether dark or light, whether held within our own psychological landscape or projected out into the world as global events. The path of awakening is not about transcending, denying or bypassing our current realities but about honoring and embracing them.

This is the path of alchemy. This is what the final section of this book is about. As we connect with the simple truth of who we are, in the midst of all our illusions, fears, pain and attachments, we open to the magic of grace, where human ego and divine soul merge together as one, and where the caterpillar discovers its own hidden face as the butterfly. Our deep fears around survival, ego dissolution and death become the doorway to a life divine.

Please join this masterful exploration with Barry and Karen as they guide us into an exciting renaissance of the human body and spirit, taking our place as stewards and protectors of a living Earth, pioneers of tomorrow, Sun-eyed children of a new dawn!

Kiara Windrider is a transpersonal therapist and author of 'Gaia Luminous: Emergence of the New Earth' and 'Homo Luminous: Manual for the Divine Human' (Kiarawindrider.net).

Introduction

When I began to awaken four decades ago, one of my first realizations was that I was not the human personality I thought I was, but a being from another world. There was a knowing that I had come here for a time when the Earth and humanity would go through a great crisis. Many of you may also know that this is part of your soul purpose and destiny.

During this long journey of awakening, there has been a continual deepening and expanding of my understanding of what is transpiring on this planet, and what might lie beyond the great transformation we face individually and as a species. This passion was always in the forefront of my spiritual journey, but waned after living through decades of failed predictions of financial collapse and great Earth changes. A few years ago, amidst the debate around climate change and the obviously deteriorating state of the ecological and financial systems, I found myself entering the stream of passionate investigation once again.

This time, it was not initially from a spiritual perspective, but from a pragmatic, left-brained exploration of what was unfolding on the economic, ecological, energy, and climate change fronts. A nearly two-year research project ensued, reflecting the perspective of the scientific mind of my undergraduate chemistry major studies. The results were sobering indeed.

Even while this deep exploration of the third-dimensional, physical plane situation was occurring, major consciousness expansions were also taking place, accompanied by revelations on what lay ahead from a larger, extra-planetary and spiritual viewpoint. It became clear that both the material and spiritual aspects are essential facets of what is unfolding, neither more important than the other.

Unlike most books, which tend to emphasize either the material or spiritual perspective, this book traverses the entire scale of reality. Part One takes a serious look at the physical dimensions of where we are as a species, diving deeply into scientific data and projections on where the myriad crises of climate change, financial and energy collapse, and ecosystem demise might be taking us. We explore the darker shadows of a potential extinction crisis in a grounded, factually documented way.

In Part Two, we shift our viewpoint to the highest levels, seeing what is occurring on Earth as an unfoldment of God/One/Source in its most primal impulse, which is to know and experience itself through its myriad souls embodied in the species Homo sapiens sapiens. We embrace and transcend any apparent paradoxes between these two perceptual lenses. In truth, the spiritual and material dynamics dance together in a story that we will not fully understand until we look back on it sometime in the future.

I do not present this book as **the truth**, but as a version of reality that I have come to, which will probably change even before *Awakening at the End of Time* is published. So much is being revealed day by day as we accelerate towards this climactic moment in planetary history. As you read this book, you will be taking in a lot of information on the many crises humanity faces. This may open the door to some difficult passages, as it has for the two of us at times.

Frankly, that is one of the purposes that motivated us to write the book. Through our awakening work with people, we have come to know the importance of facing and embracing whatever is occurring. We've found this to be essential if true awakening is to occur. The inner and outer changes will only accelerate in the days ahead, providing one evolutionary opportunity after another. Will we meet them with our full presence, or do our best to evade and avoid them?

What I do know beyond any doubt is that there is an omnipotent, infinitely loving and intelligent Source Presence that is presiding over and orchestrating all that is unfolding. Despite appearances, all that shall unfold will be based in the most loving possibility, and in the end all that we shall go through, individually and as a species, will be well worth it. What lies ahead beyond the time of the great changes is grander than any of us could possibly conceive of. And it is the will of the One that this shall come to pass.

We hope that through reading this book your mind will be stretched to new levels of understanding. And we hope you will also find yourself asking new questions, or returning to ones you haven't thought about in a while. On that note, Part Three addresses the all-important question of *What do I do with all the information and stimulation that I just experienced (in Parts One and Two)?* Here, we attempt to provide support and assistance on how to face and embrace the death of our human, third-dimensional "caterpillar identities," while we open up to the luminous unfoldment of our emerging, divine "butterfly Selves."

Throughout the book, many links are embedded in the text as underlining, for those who want to go deeper and to verify our information and conclusions. You'll also find links to our other resources — books, website, YouTube channel, and so on — at the end of the book. Go to https://www.luminousself.com/awakeendtime-book-links.html to download a pdf of all the live hyperlinks or access them directly. The links are listed in order by chapter, worded exactly as they appear in the book.

We hope that you and your awakening will be stimulated and catalyzed by the information and insights in *Awakening at the End of Time*. More importantly, we hope that you experience a journey of transformation and awakening through reading this book. May that journey increase your awareness of the immense potential for awakening and Self-realization that is present on Earth at this time. And may you consecrate your life to that!

NOTE: The "I" voice of this book is that of Barry, and the research that informs it was done by him. Although Karen has contributed significantly to the book's creation, her primary role has been that of a ghostwriter, editing and polishing everything Barry wrote. She has also added content when prompted to do so. The totality of the book, like all that we do, reflects the **we** of our nearly 30-year partnership. We have come to understand that the co-creative communion we are blessed with works through the two us as one being, in a non-linear, unified manner that is beyond any personal attributions for what comes forth.

Prologue

As the second decade of the 21st century winds down, many of us are contemplating what the future might be like for the Earth and humanity. With so many crises increasingly impinging upon our everyday lives, we can't help wondering what the next decades will be like. Right alongside the growing specter of an extinction-level event, could the next steps in the evolution of our species also be occurring?

All of this has been front and center in my consciousness since I began to awaken four decades ago. I have found it helpful in answering these questions to look at the big picture, the long story of evolution. This has enabled me to see the invisible thread of grace that winds through it all.

Evolution on planet Earth is a mysterious process in which the seeming opposites of death and transcendence endlessly dance together to create the new. High drama typically ensues, as the One continually dissolves outmoded life forms and re-sculpts them into more complex and conscious forms that ever more fully embody and reflect its true, eternal nature. For the great desire of the One is to reside more completely — and more magnificently — within its myriad manifestations.

Often, the evolution of a species seems to be flowing along just fine. It may spend centuries or even millennia flourishing in its own particular way, when out of the blue it encounters an evolutionary precipice. Suddenly, that species has reached the limits of its existing capacities and/or its ability to thrive within its environment. Extinction may seem imminent, when an inexplicable breakthrough happens. A miraculous "something" — totally unexpected and previously inconceivable — occurs. Call it what you want, attempt to define it in relative, physical terms if you like, but the highest understanding of what is going on may be that it is a movement of Grace.

Well-known futurist and visionary Barbara Marx Hubbard often refers to "Our Story" — the long journey of ensoulment within life forms during the last 4.5 billion years on Earth, from the first organisms all the way up to us, homo sapiens. Her video, "Humanity Ascending", offers a fascinating glimpse into this eons-long process. To fully understand "Our Story" as human beings, we must travel back to one of the very first lifeforms, the prokaryotes, single-celled organisms that had no nuclei or other organelles. These tiny beings were as basic as life could be, and their existence was confined to drifting around in the primal oceans, gobbling up whatever floated by. They had no competition, so they multiplied until they reached the limits of what their environment would support. When that point came, a mass die-off seemed certain. Would one of the first attempts to express the evolutionary impulse on Planet Earth fail?

At that moment, magic happened. Grace descended. In her wonderful TED Talk, "How a Single-Celled Organism Almost Wiped Out Life on Earth", (Remember to go to https://www.luminousself.com/awakeendtime-book-links.html to download a pdf of all the live hyperlinks or access them directly) Anusa Willis tells the story. Not long after the Earth was formed, the atmosphere was largely made up of nitrogen, methane, and carbon dioxide, with very little of the oxygen we depend on to live. In fact, oxygen was toxic to the first organisms, the prokaryotes, which were anaerobic. And the oxygen that was present was chemically bound within molecules, as in water, not floating around in the air in the amounts that sustain human life today. The prokaryotes flourished for quite some time, as mentioned above, until they became so numerous that they exhausted their food supply. Their doom seemed assured.

But sometime between 2.5 and 3.5 billion years ago, the grace of evolutionary magic happened. One of the types of prokaryotes called cyanobacteria spontaneously developed the capacity we now call photosynthesis. Their cell membranes grew structures to turn carbon dioxide into simple sugars, which they then used for energy. Catastrophe had been averted!

Since Sunlight and carbon dioxide were virtually unlimited, the cyanobacteria population exploded. Instead of an extinction event, a whole new chapter of life unfolded as these more complex life-forms flourished. Is it any surprise that cyanobacteria soon became a dominant species?

A byproduct of their photosynthesis process was oxygen, which was released into the atmosphere. Soon there were so many cyanobacteria that the composition of the atmosphere became increasingly rich in oxygen. Since oxygen was toxic to anaerobic bacteria, a massive extinction event, called the Great Oxygen Catastrophe, ensued. Almost all single-celled life on Earth perished, but the new transformational capacity of the cyanobacteria allowed them to thrive.

Yet their very survival wasn't the only repercussion of the cyanobacteria's evolutionary leap into photosynthesis. The Earth's atmosphere, which had previously been very rich in methane, changed in the presence of the additional oxygen. The methane reacted with the oxygen, forming carbon dioxide and water. Methane is a greenhouse gas that is eighty times more potent than carbon dioxide, so as its insulating effect lessened, more and more heat was released from the atmosphere into space. A massive global cooling resulted in the Huronian Glaciation, which covered most of the Earth with ice for 300 million years.

Once again, just when it appeared that this great evolutionary experiment might fail and life would end on Earth, another movement of Grace arrived. Whereas oxygen had been poisonous to the initial life-forms on the planet, a new, aerobic organism appeared; it could ingest oxygen and use it as a superior energy source. This evolutionary leap in turn catalyzed the development of many other more complex organisms. As the cyanobacteria were ingested by larger microbes, a process called endosymbiosis was set into motion. Just as the cyanobacteria had become capable of rudimentary photosynthesis, the organisms that ate them developed organelles capable of photosynthesis, too. This key evolutionary leap set the stage for the entire plant kingdom to eventually come into being.

This basic story has repeated countless times during the evolution of life-forms on planet Earth. A species reaches its evolutionary limits in its current form. Extinction may seem inevitable, as the sustainability of the organism overshoots the support it receives from its environment. Or seemingly unrelated external factors such as asteroids, vulcanism, or changes in the Earth and Sun trigger the death and rebirth process. But in the midst of scenarios of doom, an inexplicably benevolent, creative event occurs. While many species meet a rapid and cataclysmic end, at least one new, higher-order life-form emerges.

If scientists had been on the planet when prokaryotes faced extinction, they almost certainly would have examined the situation and concluded that evolution appeared at a dead end. No one had ever heard of photosynthesis. There would have been no known mechanism that could catalyze an evolutionary leap into a new life-form that transcended the limitations of the prokaryotes.

How did that leap happen, and where did it come from? This is the mystery of evolution, and not even the brightest scientists can answer these questions. Nor can Darwin's theory of natural selection explain such immense evolutionary leaps. In virtually all cases, there is no discernible link from a failing species to the new organism that thrives in the same environment that brought death to its predecessor. This leads many of us to conclude that only the Grace emanating from an unfathomably intelligent, loving and powerful beingness can adequately explain this mystery.

Fast forward a few billion years to the second decade of the 21st century AD. Wherever we look, we humans seem to be facing an analogous situation to the one our little friends the cyanobacteria encountered eons ago. Our species has flourished to the point where we have overshot the Earth's capacity to support us. Increasing numbers of scientists agree that the Sixth Great Extinction Event has begun. Our story is entering a critical chapter, the most pivotal in its multi-billion-year journey. This time, we are the species that is front and center in the evolutionary drama.

PART ONE

✧ ✧ ✧

The Death of The Third-Dimensional Human "Caterpillar"

✧ ✧ ✧

Introduction

For millions of years, human beings have been living like caterpillars, crawling around on the planet's surface. We've been happy to pretend that this level of reality is the only one there is, as we grub around for food, safety, and a modicum of comfort on this often scary world full of threats to our very existence. Only recently have we managed to lift into the air; a very few have even left the womb of our biosphere. Little did anyone guess that these flights into the ethers unwittingly presaged our next evolutionary leap.

While most caterpillar humans seem happy with whatever they are able to grab within this dimension of reality, some sense the need to expand beyond the limitations of their earthbound existence. *There must be more to life than this*, they intuit. *I'm tired of inching around on the ground. I'm ready to soar, even if I don't have a clue how to do that!*

Beneath the surface of their caterpillar way of life, these beings are feeling their future butterfly nature beginning to stir. These edge-dwellers reach out and stretch toward what is next, even while they wonder what that might be. Deep within them lies the evolutionary programming that will someday propel them into a radically different way of being. But like the prokaryotes, they have no conscious idea of what that might look like or how they will survive the challenges that seem to besiege them from all sides.

Challenges? That's putting it mildly. In fact, what we human caterpillars are facing resembles nothing so much as impending catastrophe. Any number of disasters might well cause all Earthling caterpillars to die before we even have a chance to mutate into our butterfly potential. The big question facing us all is *Will we willingly submit to the evolutionary death and rebirth process that appears necessary if we are to become human "butterflies"?* Or will we resist what that might entail — and all that it may well ask of us — because we are too attached to our little caterpillar identity to give it up?

Unfortunately, our limited, materialistic sense of self is using up the planet's resources faster than we can say the word "caterpillar." Like certain kinds of garden pests, we human caterpillars have an insatiable appetite for **more, better, and different** things in the external, material world. The inability to curb our appetites puts us in imminent danger of out-consuming the Earth's capacity to support life. We may be not only ensuring our own demise through our greedy gobbling, but also the end of countless other species.

The prokaryotes found themselves in a similar dilemma eons ago. Like those early single-celled organisms, we face a potential extinction event. Just as they did, we have all but outstripped our life support system's capacity to sustain us. What makes our evolutionary crisis different from that of the prokaryotes is this: We are a much more complex species, whose mental capacities allow us to have a far greater impact on our world. Thus, many of the crises we face are of our own creation. They are also more complicated and multifaceted than anything the prokaryotes faced.

But unlike the prokaryotes, we humans have the ability to take stock of what is unfolding all around us. We can gather our courage and examine the many signs and symptoms of the death of this cycle of human evolution. In this section of the book, we will explore what is going on from a third-dimensional, concrete perspective. Later, we will expand our awareness to include far more.

The intensive research that has informed the first part of this book arose out of a strong impulse to get grounded in what is really occurring and what might happen next if things continue in the direction they are currently going. In this exploration, I allowed my higher mental capacities and inner guidance to intuitively lead me to those whom I strongly sensed are closest to perceiving our current situation as it truly is. As in any scientific inquiry, diverging viewpoints abound. I'll attempt to briefly address some of these perspectives, but debating theories is not the purpose of this book. I've come to my conclusions for reasons that make sense to me; most importantly, they feel like truth in my soul. I'll do my best to present the evidence I feel most resonant with here, as well as the conclusions I have reached.

Ultimately, everything you are about to read is intended to serve as "grist for the mill" of your own inner journey of truth discovery. It's important to remember that even hard data gathered from scientific sources and the conclusions of some of the brightest, most informed minds on the planet are still not 100% accurate, much less the absolute truth. Nonetheless, these perspectives may offer us the most grounded, reliable clues we have to ascertain not only where we are, but where we might be going.

As you read the following material, it's important to remember that no one knows how this will all work out. The script is still being written, and the human mind can never know or encompass all of the "facts." All projections on what might happen are possible or probable futures, not the final word on What Is or What Will Be. Projections are based on analyzing and interpreting third-dimensional, physical information; they do not reference any input from other levels of reality. Linear causality, from past to future, is assumed and inherent in this perspective, and does not include influences and factors that transcend linear time-related projections. Future timelines that seem to makes sense within 3-D become questionable, if not invalid, when we shift beyond third-dimensional, linear time. We will deeply explore the implications of this in the second part of the book.

I have presented what may seem like an overabundance of "crunchy" data and information, along with extensive links to support my conclusions. I did this for those who want to explore all of this in as great a depth as I did. If this much information obstructs the flow of your reading, or if you feel you already know most of what you need to know, feel free to skim-read what is familiar, and delve more deeply into information that is new to you. **Note:** If you are reading a paperback edition of this book, please go to our website and download the free pdf document of all links included in the book. This will enable you to consult the links as you read.

Even if you find this first section difficult reading, we encourage you to keep going. The rest of this book will take you on a journey that goes far beyond the earth-plane possibilities Part One presents. It might help to remember that buried within the seemingly irresolvable crises we face lie the gifts of grace they have come to reveal to us. For when we finally face and embrace our situation, we come into alignment with life as it is. We leave the emotional eddies and cul-de-sacs of sleep and denial and re-enter the ever-flowing stream of life, which, in its infinite love and wisdom, unfailingly carries us through and beyond the crises.

Surrendering into that unceasing flow is the focus of later sections of this book. For now, we will investigate what is happening on third-dimensional planet Earth during the second decade of the 21st millennium, emphasizing several major facets: economic, sociopolitical, ecological, and energy. What you read in this section of the book may be difficult for you to take in. It might stimulate challenging emotional responses within you. We encourage you to be with whatever arises as you read the material in this section. Observe the mind's futile strategies to evade the hard parts or point out why the presentation is flawed or limited. Beware of any tendencies to judge and separate from what is being said. Be present to any painful feelings that arise, giving them as much loving compassion as you can. **And if your feelings become overwhelmingly challenging, turn to Part Three for support in facing and even embracing them.** The very emotions that seem impossible to fully be with can serve as doorways to awakening, once we learn how to meet them with love and acceptance.

As spiritual teacher Byron Katie insists, reality is good and loving, no matter how horrendous it may seem at a human level. The Divine is concerned about the evolution of our souls far more than what happens to our physical forms. It knows that everything we create comes back to us to mirror the state of consciousness that created it. This is spiritual law; it is how we learn and grow. We are eternal souls that have inhabited many other forms prior to human embodiment, and will have other experiences after we leave Earth. This great play of third-dimensional life can appear to be a colossal tragedy, but nothing can ever harm, alter, or destroy us as eternal souls.

Researching this material over many years has presented me with one potent evolutionary catalyst after another. During my many passages through very dark moments of despair, grief, and fear as I faced what might unfold on Earth, I often heard a voice whispering reassurance from beyond: "The Universe is a very big place, and eternity is a very long time."

1

Economic Crises

Like so many individuals with significant credit card debt, our entire species has been living beyond our means, mortgaging the future. As a result, the world is deeply in debt. The total debt of all the world's nations is 217 trillion dollars, or 325% of what we produce annually. Think about that — we are spending more than three times what we collectively earn! And this figure does not include "exotic" financial instruments such as derivatives, which were estimated to be worth $1.2 quadrillion in 2016 and roughly $1.7 quadrillion in late 2017. All together, that comes out to more than $1.6 million of debt for each man, woman and child on this planet. How could this possibly make any kind of financial sense?

Virtually all the world's "developed" countries are bankrupt, when comparing combined corporate, banking, government and personal debt to future prospects for revenues. The likelihood that this debt will ever be repaid from future revenues is just about zero, barring a massive hyper-inflationary event. That would not only make the debt numbers worthless, it would also most likely result in a total collapse. Whether the debt unwinds in a deflationary event or explodes in hyper-inflation, financial collapse is the almost certain final destination.

It's tempting to read that and think, *People have been warning of collapse for decades. It's not going to happen anytime soon.* But financial realities belie this optimism. In 2008 the entire global financial system was within hours of total collapse. This was postponed not by things magically setting themselves aright, but by a massive infusion of money created out of thin air from the central banks in Europe, the US, and Japan. As a result, the

Federal Reserve in the US, the European Central Bank, and the Bank of Japan are now in the same desperate shape as were the corporate banks they saved in 2008. There is no one left to bail the system out, with the possible exception of the International Monetary Fund (IMF).

While the vast majority of humanity is living in poverty and/or deeply in debt, existing wealth is rapidly polarizing into the hands of a very few who are wealthy beyond all imagining. <u>The eight richest people in the world have half of the world's wealth</u>.

We've been mortgaging our collective economic future, borrowing massively to fund the infrastructure of a large, complex world culture. We've managed to grow way beyond our means by going ever more deeply into debt. We reached <u>"Peak Debt"</u> a decade or so ago; this is the point at which each dollar of <u>debt produced virtually no increase in global productivity</u>. The hard truth is that continuing to borrow simply won't create more growth, despite what governments and central banks are telling us. We are at the end of the financial manipulation game we've been playing for the last century.

Economic factors have an important effect on the next, critical portion of humanity's evolutionary journey, but even more pivotal issues deserve our attention.

2

Social And Political Crises

There are so many social and political issues, we won't even begin to list them. Instead, let's connect the larger social/political crises to their principal foundation, which is economic. Social and political issues generally don't reach crisis levels when basic human needs are being met. This is obviously not the case for at least half of the human beings living on planet Earth.

As mentioned above, wealth is very rapidly being concentrated into the hands of a handful of multi-billionaires. A small percentage of the super-wealthy, also known as the Global Elite, exert a great degree of power over the masses. Through their dominance of national central banks and the major multinational corporate banks, they largely control the global economy. They have the economic authority to determine who is elected to office, what news is broadcast, and which laws are passed. This will continue until the basics of the game are changed.

The Global Elite control virtually all first world countries, with the exception of Russia and, to a lesser degree, China and some of the BRICS nations. They also exert dominance in many lesser nations. This group foments social unrest and war all over the planet. There are many indications that <u>their plan is to instigate population reduction through various means</u>. The prospects of 7.5 billion people surviving, let alone thriving, on Earth are slim in light of resource and distribution issues, but appear nonexistent unless the global cabal is dethroned.

3

Ecological Crises

You already know that the planet is in ecological crisis, but touching in on some of the significant bellwether issues might provide a helpful reality check.

Water is the foundation of life, and <u>we are facing a major planetary water crisis</u>. (Remember to go to <u>https://www.luminousself.com/awakeendtime-book-links.html</u> to download a pdf of all the live hyperlinks or access them directly.) Eighty-five percent of the world's population lives in the driest half of the planet, and drought is being exacerbated by climate change. One out of every nine of us does not have access to safe drinking water. Fresh water may well be the next mega-crisis, before climate change and peak oil take center stage. Much of Asia gets its water from the Himalayas, which are rapidly losing their glaciers. Surface sources are rapidly becoming polluted, while aquifers are increasingly depleted from overuse.

Significant loss of farmland is upon us, and topsoil is being lost at an alarming rate. It takes *a thousand years* to create three centimeters of topsoil. Toxic factory farming practices are rapidly depleting and poisoning what remains. A third of the world's soil has been degraded; at current rates the <u>world's topsoil -- and with it, agriculture itself -- will be lost in 60 years</u>. Crop yields will almost certainly begin to decline long before then.

Species loss is soaring, all the way up and down the phylogenic tree. We are <u>losing species at a rate 1000 times faster than occurred during the pre-human era</u>, as the result of human impacts. More than 20,000 species are in danger of extinction. The loss of insect populations, and particularly bees, is especially alarming. A <u>recent study in Germany</u> measured the average biomass of insects between May and October over many years. It has steadily decreased, from 3.5 pounds per trap in 1989 to just 10.6 ounces in 2014. Beekeepers in the US lost 44 percent of their bees in one year, from 2015 to 2016. Neonictonoid pesticides seem to be a primary culprit in the losses worldwide. Much of our agriculture is dependent on bee pollination. Seventy to eighty-five percent of our crops require insect pollination. Insects also play an important role in controlling other pests and cleaning up waste materials.

The oceans aren't doing any better. More than 5 trillion pieces of plastic weighing a total of 250,000 tons are floating in the oceans, with more being added as you read this sentence. A 2015 study shows a 50% loss of marine life from 1970 to 2012. Ocean fish populations are in steep decline, with one study showing that populations of older, larger fish have dropped by 72% around Europe and the US. We'll deal with the bigger issues of ocean acidification and warming later in this section.

Coral reefs are the rainforests of the oceans. The largest, the Great Barrier Reef, may be in terminal decline. While silting from human activities is an issue, warming of the ocean is the chief factor causing the reef to rapidly bleach. A recent report claims the Great Barrier Reef can no longer be saved because climate change has not been adequately addressed. And the demise of this massive reef is not an isolated event; reefs all over the planet show signs of degradation for the same reasons. Most reefs will be bleached by 2050, and one study went so far as to project that the world's coral reefs could even be gone by that time.

In all kinds of ways, the world's ecological system appears to be on tilt. A new meme circulating among researchers concludes that the Holocene epoch, which began 11,500 years ago, is at an end. The Holocene is turning out to be the shortest of all epochs during which natural circumstances and events shaped planetary evolution. Now, humanity is the chief evolutionary force on Earth, catapulting us into the Anthropocene Age. The "wise" (perhaps "clever" is more appropriate) ape called Homo sapiens sapiens is now in charge, and by the looks of things the Anthropocene Age may be even shorter than the Holocene. It also may have a more dramatic conclusion, with far more species loss and environmental degradation than its predecessor.

4

Energy Crises

Energy: The Basis for Our World

How did we develop an amazingly complex planetary culture of 7.5 billion people? How have human beings managed to completely prevail over all other forms of life on Earth? The answers can be explained with one graph, shown below.

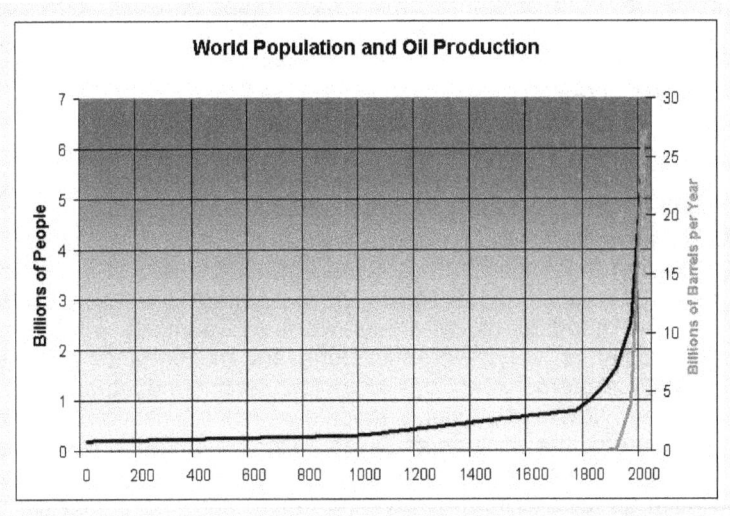

Humans clearly found a source of energy that allowed our species to flourish and dominate life on this planet. But we need to remember that within the 3-D level of reality, there is a force that opposes the building and continuance of all structures. The effects of the <u>Second Law of Thermodynamics</u> are inherent within the third-dimensional, physical level of reality. It states that all systems in the physical universe will always move toward greater entropy over time. Chaos and disorder will win in the end, but only at the 3-D level of energy-matter and most importantly, consciousness.

This law holds that to create and maintain any system in a constant state of order requires an input of energy equivalent to that lost through entropy. This explains why it takes so much effort to build anything new. It is also why the paint peels off a house after a few decades, and why the inside of the house doesn't stay clean once we have finally gotten around to cleaning it. The Second Law of Thermodynamics tells us why there is a certain life expectancy for all things material, and why we have repair shops for just about everything. It even explains why the face we see in the mirror never again looks as young and fresh as it did yesterday. This law not only predicts the aging and death of our physical bodies, it also accounts for the same processes on the macro-level of planets, Suns, and even galaxies. No matter how well we take care of ourselves and our belongings, the force of entropy will always resist and ultimately dismantle anything and everything within the third-dimensional realm. We may not like it, but this law is inviolable within the level of physical reality.

And that means we have a lot to lose. Think, for a moment, about the size and complexity of the many systems humans have developed across the planet. Virtually every country boasts major urban complexes, with all the intricate subsystems that keep them functioning. Myriad small towns and cities are linked by massive global transportation systems that carry everything we need to us, wherever we live. Countless producers, manufacturers, service organizations, and maintenance and distribution systems keep this complex, techno-industrial culture spinning. Now add in highly articulated communication/information systems that include satellites, telephones, radio, television, and the internet. These networks ceaselessly convey the information needed to keep everything functioning and enable us to stay in touch with one another.

Underneath it all, a benevolent Mother Earth just keeps giving and giving of herself. She never stops generating water, food, air, and innumerable other resources that allow us to maintain our way of life. The most critical of these resources is energy. In fact, to offset that Second Law of Thermodynamics, it's all about energy. It takes a massive amount of energy to maintain such an incredibly complex structure and prevent it from descending into chaos.

It's All About Fossil Fuels

So, if we are to more deeply understand our current situation, we need to learn as much as we can about where we stand regarding this all-important ingredient of modern life. To begin with, it's time to face an important fact: more than <u>two thirds of our global energy comes from fossil fuels</u>. This source of energy was created over millions of years, and gives us coal, natural gas, and petroleum products. Although we may wish fossil fuels would last forever, most humans know the remaining reserves will be used up at some point; the move to non-fossil fuel alternatives is already underway. Many people assume hydro, wind, and solar power will solve our problem, but will they satisfy our voracious appetite for energy? And can we make the transition in time? We'll return to these questions in a bit.

Meanwhile, when considering how to avoid an energy crisis, we must look to petroleum, because it is the densest, most transportable, and easiest-used of all the fossil fuels. It is also the one we are using up the quickest. Think about this: global transport, infrastructure, extraction and production of minerals and commodities (including all other energy sources — coal, renewables, nuclear, LPG, N-Gas), and the industrial food system are all utterly dependent on oil. Somewhere in the production and delivery chain of virtually all industrial processes, oil is required.

The industrial world spins on global transportation and petroleum is the axle it spins on. What would happen if we didn't have adequate energy to propel the trucks and trains that move all our consumer goods, never mind the resources, parts, and equipment for all our manufacturing? How would we get to work, go shopping or obtain the goods and services we need without our cars (or public transportation, where that is available)? What about the ships that function as the planetary conveyers of goods? How would our world be different without air travel? <u>One quarter of global energy production goes for transportation.</u>

Now consider global agriculture. Without petroleum products for the equipment in the fields, the fertilizers and pesticides deemed necessary to grow the crops, and the transportation to get the products to processors and distributors, we would all get very hungry very fast. Four hundred gallons of oil are used to feed each person in North America per year. Ten calories of fossil fuels are required for each calorie of food produced.

An ancient source of energy that took hundreds of millions of years to create is being used up within a few centuries. The moment of Peak Oil is reached when the world's consumption of oil outpaces its ability to produce it. Many believe humanity is already on the downslope from that pivotal moment; some theorize Peak Oil was reached in the 1970s. The fallout from this turning-point is not decades away in some nebulous future. Chris Martenson argues in "The Looming Energy Shock" that somewhere between 2018 and 2020, a severe energy depletion will impact our global industrial world.

The evidence, for those brave enough to look, is startling. Investment by oil and natural gas companies is plummeting. Starting in 2015, investment in exploration, plants and equipment has dropped 25% per year, a historic slump. Why would these companies stop investing? Oil discoveries have crashed to a 65-year low despite better exploration technologies. It's also taking a lot more energy and effort to get the new discoveries into production. The bottom line? It's much more costly and difficult, resource-wise, to produce a barrel of oil than it used to be. The easy-access sources were discovered and tapped into long ago. Today, oil companies are plunging deeper into the oceans and wilderness areas to find new reserves. The result is that it's getting harder for oil companies to make money. The statistics on new reserves don't take into account what is actually cost-effective to extract. The Bakken fields in North Dakota, for instance, are estimated to contain several hundred billion barrels, but only 10 billion, or less than 10%, are actually recoverable.

If petroleum products are increasingly difficult to extract, why can't the added costs be covered by higher prices? There are a number of interrelated reasons why this won't work. One is that the global economy hasn't been growing because we have gone deeply in debt (see Economic section above), and economic stimulus packages of more debt and cheaper interest rates aren't generating new growth. We have reached "Peak Debt" just as we have reached Peak Oil. Oil prices have dropped and oil companies can't make money at current prices. In fact, they are bleeding cash and going more deeply into debt. This is the path to bankruptcy.

In "End of the Oilocene" the Foundation for the Economics of Stability presents the case that the oil industry as we've known it is in demise. The world's oil companies are taking on debt and selling assets to deal with cash shortfalls. Not one new project that will make money below an $80 per barrel selling price has started producing. The vast majority need $100 a barrel or higher to function.

There appears to be a lot of unfounded optimism about future oil production, usually citing new sources such as offshore drilling, shale oil, and the north slope of Alaska. But as mentioned above, none of these will ever produce anything near estimated reserves. The reality is that more than half of global production comes from older fields which are declining rapidly. One percent of the fields produce around 60% of our petroleum. Most of these fields are at least 50 years old, and their production rates have declined by 6.5% per year. At that rate, production would fall by 50% in a little more than a decade. This rate of decline would be higher if it weren't for continuing advances in extracting more from the declining reserves. As these reserves become ever more difficult to extract, the rates of decline will accelerate.

These numbers match future production projections, which predict that the world will have to work with half the oil it currently uses per year by 2030. What would that mean for our way of life? The implications are clear.

The Energy Return On Investment (EROI) Trap

There's a deeper reason why oil production and consumption may be on a permanent, sharp decline, and happening faster than even the most conventional projections estimate. It's based in an understanding of EROI, or Energy Return On Investment; in short, the thermodynamics of petroleum as an energy source. You'll soon be hearing a lot more about EROI. Understanding what this is provides the illumining perspective necessary to perceive the rapidly approaching end of the petroleum era.

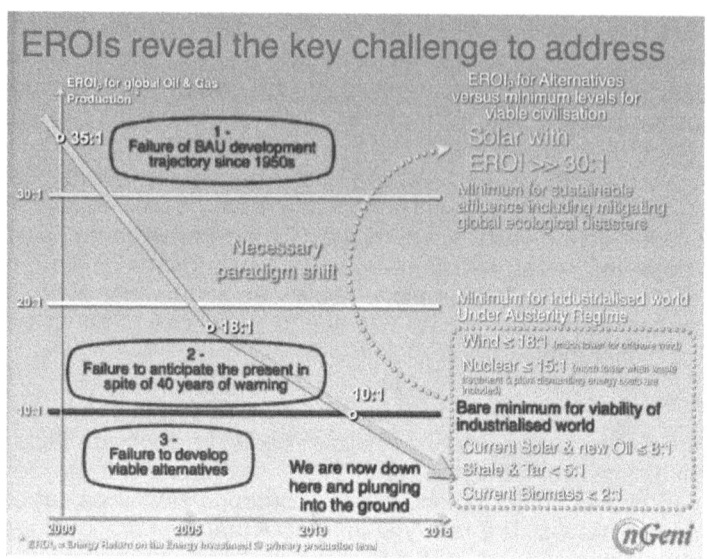

Simply stated, production isn't only about the amount of oil traded for a given price. It also has to consider the cost of each unit of energy we receive per unit of energy production. Energy Return On Investment (EROI) is basically the energy that is delivered to society divided by the energy expended to obtain that energy. The Second Law of Thermodynamics indicates the world needs sources of energy that produce in excess of the energy used to extract them. If it takes more energy to obtain a unit of energy, in this case a BTU, then it isn't practical or possible to use that energy source. The system of energy acquisition simply breaks down.

Several excellent resources explore the thermodynamic issues of rapidly declining EROI. Below, I'll briefly summarize the conclusions of the following reports, highly recommended for those wanting a deeper understanding.

A cutting-edge investigation on EROI and the future of petroleum has come out of the Hills Group, a collective of petroleum consulting engineers, professional project managers and PHDs who study the petroleum industry. The Hills Group has an astounding 99.5% accuracy rate in their projections of oil prices. In 2013, they began to warn about the crash that began in 2014.

Louis Arnoux has done some of the clearest, most accessible research on the EROI issue. His succinct, three-part article for Cassandra's Legacy, Some Reflections on the Twilight of the Oil Age, is loaded with supporting data and graphs that tell the story of a rapidly ending "Oilcene" era. If you prefer to listen, "Thermodynamic Oil Collapse" is a one-hour interview covering the same information. For the visually oriented who like lots of graphics, Tim Clarke summarizes the realities we face in "The Demise of the Global Oil Industry: We are rapidly heading towards a systemic global oil/financial shock."

Thinking that we will easily continue generating enough petroleum for our needs, even as it becomes harder and more expensive to access, is a little like deciding to live on celery alone. We probably couldn't consume enough celery to replace the energy it would take us to obtain it. So it goes with petroleum — it's taking ever more energy from oil to obtain an equivalent amount of new energy. When petroleum sources were close to the surface, easy to obtain, and of a high grade, EROIs were as much as a thousand to one, which means that using one barrel of oil energy equivalent produced a thousand barrels of oil to sell. This was clearly the Golden Age of oil extraction. By the 1950s, EROIs had already dropped to 100 to 1. That's still a workable ratio, allowing plenty of profits for the energy corporations and a decent prices for consumers, with a lot left over to invest in growth of our global industrial culture. But the ratio continued to fall; by 2000, we were getting only 35 barrels for each barrel invested.

Estimates differ, but some indicate that at least a 30 to 1 EROI is needed to maintain the continually growing industrial world culture as we know it. However, we descended below that average more than a decade ago. In 2006, average EROIs declined to 18 to 1, and in 2012 they fell to 12 to 1. Some sources estimate the bare minimum EROI to maintain our world is 20 to 1, and that collapse happens at 10 to 1. As an important example, our global agricultural system takes ten calories of energy to create one calorie of food, thus the need for the 10 to 1 EROI to keep us all fed. According to the Hills Group, oil production is already below this ratio. This is why the oil industry is in steep decline. It's also why it is in a rapidly deteriorating financial condition. We are falling off an energy cliff, as the following quote attests.

> *In 2012 the Global Oil Industry on average began to use more energy per barrel in its own processes (from oil exploration to transport fuel deliveries at the petrol stations) than what it delivers NET to the Global Economy.*
>
> Dr. Louis Arnoux, 2016

Projecting the rate of EROI decline, the zero point occurs in 2022-2026; for every barrel of oil used to obtain new petroleum, less than a barrel will be produced. If this theory is correct, the oil industry will succumb to a thermodynamic energy death. Simply stated, we will no longer get any net energy from petroleum. It will require more energy to produce it than it generates.

Are Renewables the Answer?

The hard, cold EROI facts naturally prompt a closer look at renewables as a possible solution. Some go so far as to insist that renewables ARE the energy future. *We're already moving in that direction,* these people argue, *so all we need to do is pour more money into research, development, and production. The fact that it takes too much oil to produce oil may be the sharp stick in the back that will get renewables happening more quickly.*

It's true that solar, wind, hydroelectric, and other forms of renewable energy are growing rapidly. They are also becoming ever more competitive in supplying our needs for electricity. In addition, costs of renewables have plunged. In the last 25 years, wind energy has declined from 40 cents/kilowatt hour to less than 5 cents. Solar has fallen from $1/kilowatt hour to 20 cents, and ethanol from $4/gallon to $1.20.

Some nations have committed to renewables in a big way, far outstripping what is happening in the US. Europe is way ahead of us in the transition process, at least in the area of providing electricity. At this point, Germany provides 25% of its electricity from renewables, and is targeting 80% by 2050. Spain produces more electricity with wind than with coal, nuclear and natural gas. Globally, electricity would be the easiest modality to switch; some estimate that up to 82% of all electricity could be supplied by renewables by 2050.

These successes with electricity turn the media spotlight on those who believe we can move from fossil fuels to renewables fast enough to avoid either a climate or an energy crisis. From this perspective, the transition to renewables looks easily attainable, especially considering our global electrical needs. For instance, a Stanford University research project was summarized in "A Road Map to 100 Percent Renewable Energy in 139 Countries by 2050" by Mark Jacobson, who headed the team. It proposed a detailed global plan to completely replace non-renewables with wind, water and solar by 2050, creating 25 million new jobs and reducing total energy needs by 42.5%.

This sounded promising until the criticisms began to surface. Shortly after publication, the report was strongly repudiated by 21 of the most respected energy experts in the prestigious *Proceedings of the National Academy of Sciences (PNAS)*. A simpler, more easily assimilable article in *Scientific American*, "Landmark 100 Percent Renewable Energy Study Flawed, Say 21 Leading Experts" presented evidence that Jacobson's analysis "used invalid modeling tools, contained modeling errors, and made implausible and inadequately supported assumptions." Thus, they conclude, Jacobson's findings on the cost-effectiveness and feasibility of a full transition to wind, water, and solar "are not supported by adequate and realistic analysis and do not provide a reliable guide to whether and at what cost such a transition might be achieved."

The article goes on to point out some of the major inaccuracies. The plan requires energy storage capacity double the entire current energy production capacities of all power plants in the US. Even if creating this much storage capacity were economically feasible, the technology to do so does not yet exist. The reason why so much storage is needed is that wind and solar electric power are intermittent; they will not provide a steady stream of energy 24/7/365, as do fossil fuels and nuclear plants. This has long been seen as one of the major Achilles heels of going 100% renewable.

Others criticized the unrealistic scale of the project. For one thing, it would require nearly every home, business, office building, hospital, school, and factory in the United States to have solar panels installed on its roof. This translates to the manufacture and installation of 2 trillion solar panels along with all necessary peripherals, including power controllers, inverters, and battery storage. We'd also need to come up with more than

2.5 billion wind turbines, in addition to all those solar panels. How likely does that sound? Will the commitment, will, government support, and resources — both natural and financial — to pull this off be there?

The Stanford report admits its goal would require a planetary effort at least as great as the one the US mobilized during WWII. This seems more than a little unlikely. So far, most countries haven't even agreed on a workable plan to cut carbon emissions, stymied by the high cost of doing so.

Delving more deeply into the requirements of transitioning from fossil fuels to renewables reveals major unresolved issues. For one, fossil fuels are still deeply embedded in our overall planetary energy picture. While renewables are growing rapidly, fossil fuels continue to dominate the US energy scene. For more than a hundred years, they have provided 80% of our energy needs. That's because fossil fuels are currently irreplaceable for transportation, which is our largest energy requirement. Petroleum is an extremely dense, easily transportable and distributable source of energy. It produces many times more usable energy than electricity, and is cheaper.

Even if we fully commit to a transition to renewables, it will take an enormous expenditure of time and resources to develop the infrastructure to replace oil. Research, development, and manufacturing facilities for solar, wind, and hydroelectric on the immense scale needed would take considerable time and resources to accomplish. Converting all transportation to run on electricity, hydrogen, or some other fuel is no small task. Developing the infrastructure to create, store and make that energy available, while appearing more and more possible technologically, also requires time and resources. Every piece of equipment on this planet with an internal combustion engine would need to be completely redesigned and remanufactured. In the real world of human culture, which tends to resist change, the hurdles are gigantic; so many issues could defeat the attempt to make the switch.

A concise, in-depth look at the possibilities and the challenges of moving to renewables appears in "The energy debate: Renewable energy cannot replace fossil fuels" by Toni Pyke. In this piece, Pyke questions the viability of utilizing the amount of land needed to accommodate the 46,480 solar PV plants envisioned for the US in the *100% Clean and Renewable Wind, Wa-*

ter and Sunlight (WWS) Vision. This enormous number of plants would require 650,720 square miles — almost 20% of the landmass of the lower 48 states. This approximates the areas of Texas, California, Arizona and Nevada combined. Producing the number of solar panels needed would take 929 years, assuming they could be built at the rate of one per second. The estimated total cost of the panels, battery modules, materials, electronic controls and transformers, land acquisition and equipment changes over 20 years is US $15.93 trillion.

Transitioning to biofuels is another popular option; however, the facts here are similarly daunting. To replace 54 million barrels per day (about 60%) of global oil production with corn ethanol, some estimate it would take a cornfield the size of the United States, China and India combined. Actually, this is an area larger than the currently used arable land in the world. Using this acreage to grow biofuels would eliminate that land for food production, and large portions of our species would starve.

When we investigate what it would require to completely convert to renewables globally by 2050, the economics and logistics appear formidable, if not impossible. One estimate is that it would cost $100 trillion, or $3,571 for every household on the planet. Even with this massive investment, which appears unlikely given the information presented above in the Economic section, how probable is it that humanity will accomplish the transition before 2050? Consider the full-on global commitment this would require, and then factor in the likelihood of its happening in light of our collective experience to this point. A major shift in consciousness would have to occur.

Assuming we magically find a way to create the financial resources and overcome all the logistics of making the transition, we still face some hard realities from an energy standpoint. We currently have no energy source that can completely replace petroleum; it is the only energy we can use to make the transition to renewables. Other forms of energy just don't produce the 30 to 1 EROI needed to keep our world functioning at its current level, let alone meet the increased requirements of a world attempting to transition fully to renewables. Wind has an 18/1 EROI, nuclear 15/1, solar and the new oil being produced are 8/1, and shale oil 5/1. For this systemic issue, there appear to be only two solutions. One: drastically reducing our overall energy consumption. This would almost certainly mean a major decline in not only our standard of living, but also human population. The other solution is Zero Point or Free Energy, discussed below.

We may have to face a hard reality: We probably have not responded soon enough to make the switch to renewables. As discussed above, a potential thermodynamic collapse of the oil industry may well occur by 2026, if not sooner. Our global industrial culture will decline and collapse as oil goes away, unless we have renewables to replace it. The most optimistic proposals for the transition target 2050, two and a half decades too late.

Let's assume that somehow, through an unprecedented, unified effort of all peoples, governments, and corporations on this planet, we focus on 2025 instead of 2050 as the end date of the transition. This would require an immense commitment of human time and resources, financial resources, and, of course, energy. We would need an enormous amount of the dwindling petroleum to make the shift. If renewables grow at a rate of only 7% per year, producing them will drain all the net energy from oil out of global oil production. If renewables grow 35% per year, which is what is required to avert global collapse within 10 years, the lack of available petroleum would still bring down our global industrial world. We would need all the petroleum that keeps the world functioning to make the switch; this in and of itself would cause the breakdown. All of this describes a condition known as overshoot and collapse, a concept we will define and discuss more fully later.

Free Energy: Our Savior?

But surely, even if it is impossible to transition to renewables in time to avert global catastrophe, free energy remains an option, doesn't it? Many of us have long hoped that zero point or free energy would allow us to escape our energy trap and stop putting carbon into the atmosphere. Certainly, zero point or other free energy devices would be an energy game-changer, and potentially buy us more time to solve the problems renewables present. Their use would drastically reduce air pollution and CO_2 emissions, which could have a huge, positive impact on climate change. Free energy would allow us to develop other technologies that could be immensely positive. It might even provide the energy necessary to translate our existing 3-D, material-based world into something of a higher and more sustainable order.

But free energy does not resolve all the issues around the potential for global collapse; in fact, it may make some even worse. Many of the resources that sustain our complex world culture are finite, such as the metallic ores and rare minerals used in advanced technologies. Others, although renewable, take time to replenish — think of fresh water supplies in aquifers, top soil, and forest products. If unlimited amounts of free energy were introduced into the global equation, the population and global economy would almost certainly grow. Without a commitment toward sustainability, this would accelerate the depletion of non-renewables and the renewables that require longer periods for regeneration.

Looking on the optimistic side, maybe we could hold per capita resource consumption stable and even generate less total pollution. Maybe we could recycle precious rare minerals and other hard-to-replace resources. Free energy would then, perhaps, offer a solution to the looming energy and global warming issues we face. It is certainly the one really bright spot on the horizon, if we are ready for all that it brings with it.

Imagine what would happen if, in our current state of awareness, we humans could suddenly and magically use free energy to produce all the material goods we wanted. Depletion of the resources needed in their manufacture would zoom off the scale. Again, a shift in consciousness is our only hope; otherwise, our current materialistic state of being would manifest ad infinitum, catapulting our species into oblivion. We have to assume there are good reasons why free energy is not yet available to human beings. Until we demonstrate that we are mature enough to handle it wisely, it will likely remain elusive.

Which brings us to the larger issue with free energy — another issue of consciousness. So far in human evolution, whenever we have discovered a new source of energy, we have quickly turned it into a weapon of war. Unless we evolve into a whole new dimension of consciousness that has transcended war as a means of settling conflicts, the unlimited energy of zero point or free energy would likely mean our demise. It seems that while our world is based in energy even more than matter, perhaps our state of consciousness is even more important and causal.

The material presented above has merely touched on the tremendous complexity and scope of what is involved in moving to a sustainable world, from a resource and energy standpoint. There is a lot here to digest and comprehend. I've spent months researching it all, and still feel like a beginner. As I delved ever more deeply into the subject, I came across a series of three short Youtube videos that clearly and succinctly put many of these pieces together. Rather than attempting to summarize this section, I invite you to devote a little more than half an hour to watching these videos.

There's No Tomorrow (Peak Oil Documentary) Part One

There's No Tomorrow (Peak Oil Documentary) Part Two

There's No Tomorrow (Peak Oil Documentary) Part Three

5

Climate Change Crises

A Quick Snapshot of Where We Are

While debate on the subject continues, compelling evidence indicates the Earth is warming, and warming quickly. Climate change is now a reality that most humans are experiencing through tangible, often dramatic changes right where they live. As I write this during the winter of 2017-2018, the wildfires that ravaged California during the fall of 2017 leave lingering shock and raise new concerns. Extreme fire behavior, rarely seen before, is becoming common. The fire season in my home state, California, is now *78 days longer* than it was a few decades ago. The five most destructive wildfires ever in California occurred this year, and in seven other countries as well. Extreme weather has escalated yet again as split polar vortexes cause wild fluctuations from normal temperatures over most of the Northern Hemisphere. As disasters related to global warming escalate, people all over the planet are talking about the changes they are witnessing. The time of denial is ending.

My own journey of considering and researching whether global warming could be anthropogenic — that is, human-caused — has taken me through many phases. I've watched myself segue from being a believer, to questioning whether other factors are really causing changes in the Earth's climate, to a new, deeper understanding that synthesizes many different factors and issues.

Here's what I now believe to be true. Yes, other factors are at work, and many believe they argue against human-made climate change. We will discuss some of these shortly. But in my view, humanity has been conducting the largest-ever experiment in climate engineering by pumping immense quantities of carbon — a scientifically proven greenhouse gas — into our atmosphere. The results of this are just beginning to make themselves known, and with increasing ferocity.

<u>Average global mean temperature has increased just shy of 1.2 °C</u>, based upon calculations of what are considered preindustrial levels in the mid-19th century. Similar data show up from non-US sources, such as the <u>Hadley research Center in the UK</u>. NOAA, NASA, Hadley and <u>Berkeley</u> report nearly identical data for global warming.

The rate of increase of warming is also on a sharp upward climb. The <u>27th annual State of the Climate report</u> published in August 2017 confirmed that 2016 was even warmer than 2015, the warmest year in 137 years of record-keeping. Atmospheric carbon dioxide was the highest ever, with the largest annual increase. Not only were global surface temperatures at an all-time high, average sea surface temperatures as well as the total upper ocean heat content were also the highest on record. The global sea level was the highest ever recorded, and Arctic sea ice was at or near record lows.

These and other signs indicate the planet is rapidly warming. For those who question the accuracy of this information, please note: the annual State of the Climate report is based on contributions from more than 450 scientists from nearly 60 countries across the planet. With so many contributors from so many countries, it would seem highly unlikely that all these scientists and/or their data could be manipulated.

What About the Growing Chorus Refuting Anthropogenic Warming?

As mentioned above, at certain points in my investigation of the state of the planet, I haven't been completely convinced that human beings are the primary cause of climate change. Many alternative viewpoints pointed to the Sun and the cyclical orbital changes of the Earth around it as the major factor. In addition, I had learned that even vaster phenomena in the solar system and galaxy might be causing the changes, at least to a greater degree than humans.

These extra-planetary factors are an issue, and it is also true that changes in the amount of solar energy the Earth receives drive the cyclical, large-scale mechanisms behind ice ages and extreme warming. But deeper investigation of the predominant scientific theories and the hard data on climate change has deepened my conviction that, indeed, human activity is by far the major driving force in climate change.

Some who deny the reality of global warming assert that an international conspiracy promotes the idea of global warming to forward the agenda of the Global Elite, who wish to control everyone and everything on planet Earth. Considerable evidence suggests that this behind-the-scenes control is going on, and that much of our news is literally "fake news" because this hidden group largely controls major corporations, government officials, media, and even academia to some degree. Awareness of the global domination agenda and its perceived connection to human-caused climate change theories is increasingly fueling the denial of anthropogenic global warming. Many view the UN 2030 agenda, which is a blueprint for sustainable development around the world, as <u>a Trojan horse designed to enforce laws that would enslave humanity</u>.

While there may be some truth to this assertion, many who feel sure that all information coming from governmental agencies and even academia is manufactured and false may have unconsciously created perceptual filters that prevent them from looking deeply and clearly at the overwhelming scientific data. Having studied it in depth, I believe this evidence clearly points towards human activities as the predominant cause of climate change.

The <u>process of gathering data on global temperatures</u> involves agencies and data-collection points all over the planet. As with the annual State of the Planet report, which relies on 450 scientists from 60 countries, it seems highly improbable that all these sources could be completely controlled, manipulated, and silenced in order to present an utterly fictitious story about something so deeply threatening to all life on planet Earth. As I researched some of the top proponents of human-caused global warming, it struck me that they were credentialed scientists, doing rigorous, peer-reviewed research. None seemed at all happy to relate what they were finding. Most of them appear to be sensitive human beings who are disturbed by what they are discovering, knowing that anthropogenic global warming (AGW) may be the greatest threat to humanity at this time. When I learned that *97% of the world's climate scientists agree* that global warming is real, the probability that this is not the case seems very, very small.

But just in case I might be missing something, I began to research the theories that refute human-caused climate change. One views the Sun as the primary driver of global climate change. Those who support this theory cite <u>Milankovitch cycles</u>, which last approximately 100,000 years, as a factor. During these cycles, the shape of Earth's orbit around the Sun changes due to the influence of gravitation from other planets. The result is that the total solar radiance (TSI) the Earth receives varies throughout this cycle, and these changes initiate periods of global cooling and glaciation as well as global warming.

There is truth to this, in that these cycles are affected by differing amounts of total solar energy reaching the Earth. But the mechanism involved is analogous to turning the ignition key and firing the starter in your car. The starter's job is to get the engine moving, but once the cylinders begin to fire, the real power that drives the car is activated. Long-term Earth temperature graphs do show these cycles of warming and cooling occurring at regular intervals. But the solar radiance serves only as the kickstart that sets into motion the other forces that are the primary drivers of climate change.

The real "engines" that drive global warming are greenhouse gases and the Earth's overall index or absorption of incoming solar energy. Changes in the total solar energy (solar irradiance) cased by the cyclical changes mentioned above cause the temperature to begin to rise. As this occurs, the oceans, which store enormous quantities of carbon dioxide, begin to warm. Since water is able to hold less gas as its temperature rises, the oceans begin to release this CO_2 into the atmosphere. Warming of the oceans and other bodies of water also causes more evaporation, for the warming atmosphere is able to hold more water vapor, which also acts as a powerful greenhouse gas.

As the primary climate drivers of CO_2 and water vapor are released from the oceans and increase the Earth's temperature, ice begins to melt all over the planet, particularly in the Arctic. This has a huge impact on the global climate situation, and here's why. Ice *reflects* 90% of the incoming solar energy, while seawater *absorbs* 90% of it. As ice melts, much more incoming solar energy is converted to heat by oceans, instead of being reflected back out to space by sheets of ice. The Arctic happens to warm more quickly than the rest of the planet, and as this occurs, it sets into motion an even greater driver of global warming, methane.

During previous major warmings, the vast quantities of methane trapped with the Arctic permafrost and in deposits called clathrates at the bottom of the Arctic Ocean became major factors. As land and water both warm, these frozen methane deposits begin to melt, releasing free methane gas into the atmosphere. Methane is an extremely potent greenhouse gas, 80-120 times more powerful than carbon dioxide on a short-term basis and 20 times more powerful over centuries. We may well have reached the point at which self-reinforcing feedback loops, involving temperature rise, warming oceans, melting ice, and methane releases, begin to kick in.

I've concluded, as have virtually all climate scientists, that the Sun is the kickstarter activating the primary climate drivers of albedo (the reflectivity of the Earth's surface) and greenhouse gases — the central factors propelling major climate cycles. But there is a growing argument that the Earth will cool or even enter a mini-ice age in the near future, due the cyclical changes in the solar energy we receive. The clear trend of decreasing Sunspot activity over the last decade or so may be coinciding with a cyclical trend toward lower Sunspot activity for at least a number of decades. Sunspot activity is one of the ways total solar energy or irradiance is measured, and it, too, has a cyclical relationship with global mean temperatures. Many climate watchers point to the very high solar and Sunspot activity of the last hundred years or so, prior to the past decade when they began to decline considerably, as the reason the Earth has been warming recently.

Sunspot activity occurs in cycles. The most commonly-known is the 11-year cycle, but longer patterns called grand minima and maxima can span hundreds of years. One of these minima occurred from the mid-1600s to the early 1700s, and is known as the Maunder Minimum. During this time solar activity was very low, Sunspots were almost nonexistent, and Europe and parts of North America had very cold winters. Scientists estimate that the chance of this happening again within the next forty years could be anywhere from 8% to 20%, based on the fact that the Sun's output has declined more rapidly recently than at any time over the last 10,000 years.

What might such a solar activity minimum do to global temperatures? When the parameters of a new Maunder Minimum were run through climate model programs, results indicated global average temperatures might be trimmed by about .12°C during the second half of this century. As occurred during the Maunder Minimum, effects could again be stronger in Europe and North America. These cooling effects would, though, be short-lived — possibly lasting several decades — after which solar activity would increase and even more rapid warming would kick in. Studies of the Maunder Minimum indicate that the average global temperature may have dropped by as much as 1°C for a number of decades, not the 4 or 5°C claimed by many proponents of a new Ice Age. During one or two anomalous years, sharp decreases occurred, but the average lowering was 1°C or less. Another strong argument against the idea of imminent cooling is that sunspot activity and total solar irradiance peaked around five decades ago, as increases in global temperatures began to accelerate. That means that global temperatures are increasing while they should be going in the opposite direction. This is seemingly impossible if the Sun is the primary driving force in climate change.

Could there be factors we don't yet understand that could potentially change our understanding of climate change and specifically AGW? Certainly, but the best information we have at present is pretty much consensual that AGW is the real issue.

There are far too many arguments against anthropogenic global warming to explore in this book. If you're interested in going deeper, Adapt 2030, Roy Spencer, John Casey, Valentina Sharkova and Dan Britt are some of the more popular websites forwarding this case. The Union of Concerned Scientists has published an article listing the principal organizations against AGW and why they and their theories are not credible. When I delved into the works of these anti-AGW authors, I simply wasn't convinced. Most of them are relatively lacking in credentials when compared to climate scientists who endorse AGW. There also appear to be major holes in their theories, along with omissions of important information. An article entitled "These are the best arguments from the 3% of climate scientist 'skeptics.' Really" looks at the organizations and their arguments against

AGW and points out the reasons they should be given little, if any, credibility.

Two websites dedicated to addressing virtually all of the theories against AGW use scientific data and reasoning that, in my opinion, debunk the human-caused global warming debunkers. They are Skeptical Science and Reality Drop. As I considered the many arguments against AGW, read the responses on these websites, and followed the links and articles they cite, I became convinced that anthropogenic global warming is what is going on.

As mentioned above, events occurring with the Sun and even on a galactic level could potentially create immense implications for what happens next — not only to the Earth's climate, but also to the evolution of the Earth, humanity, and all other species who live upon the planet. We will dive into some of these subjects later in the book. Meanwhile, if all the data and research cited above aren't convincing enough, Life is presenting us with plenty of simple, grounded evidence that the planet is warming — confirmation every human being can directly experience and validate. Let's examine some of these irrefutable clues.

Glaciers are receding everywhere on Earth. The worldwide glacier monitoring service of the University of Zürich, in conjunction with other entities in 30 countries, has been compiling changes in glaciers over the past century. This service has collected more than 5,000 measurements of glacier volumes and changes in mass since 1850, and 42,000 records of variations in glaciers in France from records dating back to the 16th century. According to this information, there is no question that glaciers are disappearing everywhere on the planet, and at an accelerating rate. Interestingly, glaciers in the southern hemisphere are disappearing faster in some cases, such as in the Andes, than they are in the northern hemisphere. I had suspected they would be receding more slowly, since the rate of ice loss in Antarctica has been much slower than that of the Arctic.

The total volume of sea ice in both of the planet's hemispheres has dropped by 75% in the last half-century. Until recently, it was believed the Antarctic was in stasis or actually gaining some ice. Recent evidence concludes this is not true. Antarctica is losing ice just like everywhere else on the planet.

The bottom line is that ice is disappearing all over the planet, both from glaciers and in the oceans. For those who doubt the Earth is warming, this may prompt another look at their beliefs. It's a thermodynamic impossibility that ice would be melting everywhere if the planet were cooling, or even remaining steady in temperature. As children, most of us learned that it takes heat to melt ice. And the ice is melting, wherever it is found, so there must be more heat coming from somewhere to cause this to happen. Once again, the logical "somewhere" that seems to make scientific sense is anthropogenic global warming.

6

Abrupt Climate Change

During the last few years, it's become very apparent to those who are watching that a new dynamic in climate change is occurring. Many predicted changes are happening more quickly than expected, and increasing numbers of scientists are opening to the possibility that a whole new phenomenon — Abrupt Climate Change — is underway.

As mentioned above, each of the last three years has been the hottest on record, and some of the increases, as in 2016, have been dramatic. It is compelling to realize that the 20 warmest years on record have occurred since 1995. This, as we have seen, is mirrored in the accelerated rate of loss of sea and land surface ice; the increase in sea-surface temperatures, leading to bleaching of coral reefs all over the planet; and increased incidence and severity of extreme weather events, among other indicators.

The Arctic — the Key Indicator Of Runaway Warming

The Arctic is warming about twice as fast as the rest of the planet; temperatures as high as 36°F above normal are being recorded. The Greenland ice sheet is also melting very quickly. This is critical information, because the ice at both poles constitutes the planetary refrigeration system that is responsible for keeping our climate in balance. The Arctic is the key to the potential for an ever-increasing probability of runaway global warming. It is the linchpin in the climate system stabilization mechanism, with the potential to trigger numerous other warming feedback loops that could easily cause runaway warming.

On the near horizon, the big fear haunting climate scientists is the specter of an ice-free Arctic. Some thought this would have occurred by now; many predict an ice-free Arctic summer within the next 20 to 30 years. Recent evidence from some of the top Arctic experts indicates it could happen much sooner — around 2020, or shortly thereafter.

It is becoming more widely known that what is happening in the Arctic is of critical importance to us all, but let's delve more deeply into what an ice-free Arctic really means. The stability of our global weather is dependent on a stable distribution of thermal energy. As mentioned above, the ice at the planet's north and south poles is the global air-conditioning system that maintains the heat, or thermodynamic, balance of the entire Earth. How does that work?

Ice is an enormous heatsink, capable of absorbing vast quantities of energy. When water changes phase from ice to liquid, the energy required to turn each gram of ice into water is 80 calories. This is called the latent heat of fusion, or the energy required to create a change in the phase state. It's important to understand *there is no change in the temperature of the water* when it melts. Ice is 32°, or 0°C, as is the ice water created when it melts. But if we took the resulting gram of water and applied the same 80 calories of heat, the temperature of the water would soar to 80°C, only 20°C below boiling. That's quite a differential! So, as the Arctic ice melts, each volume of ice lost equals a corresponding loss of the heat sink that has been buffering sea temperatures by a factor of 80. This, along with the increasing conversion of light into heat, explains why the disappearance of Arctic ice is such a critical factor. As it goes, the heat energy will push up water and air temperatures dramatically.

And that's not the whole story — as the Arctic warms, many other feedback loops will begin to kick in. Of the many climate scientists reporting on this, probably none is more accomplished than Peter Wadhams. He is professor of Ocean Physics and head of the Polar Ocean Physics Group in the Department of Applied Mathematics and Theoretical Physics at the University of Cambridge. Peter is not just an academic, he is also an in-the-field researcher, having led forty polar expeditions. He was the founder of the Arctic Methane Emergency Group.

After reviewing a large number of papers, articles, and books on the subject, I believe some of the most cogent information on the Arctic situation is presented in Peter's article, The Global Impacts Of Rapidly Disappearing Arctic Sea Ice, published by the Yale School of Environmental Studies, and his recent book *A Farewell To Ice*. The article should be more than sufficient for a basic understanding of the issue; if you're interested in diving deeper into the subject, *A Farewell to Ice* is excellent.

Wadhams began studying ice in the Arctic Ocean in the early 1970s, when there was considerably more ice to study. In the article linked above, Wadhams points out Arctic ice volume is in steep decline; he believes it could disappear by as early as 2020. He states there has been "a more than 50% drop in extent in summer, and an even steeper reduction in ice volume. Just a few decades ago, ice 10 to 12 feet thick covered the North Pole, with sub-surface ice ridges in some parts of the Arctic extending down to 150 feet. Now, that ice is long gone, while the total volume of Arctic sea ice in late summer has declined, according to two estimates, by 75% in half a century."

Wadhams succinctly summarizes the import of this situation:

> *Few people understand that the Arctic sea ice 'death spiral' represents more than just a major ecological upheaval in the world's far north. Decline of Arctic sea ice also has profound global climatic effects, with feedbacks that are already intensifying global warming and have the potential to destabilize the climate system. Indeed, we are not far from the moment when the feedbacks themselves will be driving the change every bit as much as our continuing emission of billions of tons of carbon dioxide annually.*

Wadhams and others base their warnings on the critical combination of the loss of the heat sink of the ice and the increasing conversion of incoming solar radiation into heat without the high reflectivity of the ice. Ice, as we've seen, *reflects* 80-90% of the incoming solar radiation back into space, while seawater — because it is darker in color — *absorbs* 80-90% of it, converting it to heat. If 10 units of solar energy strike the Earth, 8 to 9 of these are reflected back out into space by ice, while only

1 or 2 are converted into heat. The opposite is true of water: of the 10 units, 8 or 9 would be turned into heat, while 1 or 2 would be reflected. The decreasing albedo, or reflectivity, of seawater will cause 8 to 9 times the energy conversion to heat as ice does. That is obviously a huge impetus for much more rapid warming.

Now, combine this with loss of the heat sink as the ice disappears. Each unit of ice absorbs 80 times as much heat as an identical unit of water, so melting ice creates another very large boost to warming. As Arctic Sea ice disappears, albedo change and loss of the heat sink combine to catalyze an enormous amplification of warming.

The Greenland ice sheet is also melting quickly. As the ice vanishes, it exposes the underlying earth, which not only absorbs much more solar radiance than ice, but also converts it to heat. Greenland, too, is part of the Earth's air-conditioning system, as much of its surface is covered by a substantial amount of ice. As this ice melts, the immense heat sink that vanishes along with it will escalate temperature rise. This will contribute to the warming of the Arctic and create another challenge: the salinity in the upper northeast Atlantic will decrease.

Why is this decrease in salinity important? The northeast area of the Atlantic Ocean acts as a critical control point for the Earth's oceans. All the oceans of the world maintain their temperature balance by exchanging heat through cold and warm "rivers" or currents of water. What causes these rivers of heated or cooled water to flow is the salt or "haline" concentration differential found at the beginnings or ends of these currents. Salty water is heavier than fresh water. So, traditionally, when the warm Gulf Stream off the East Coast of the US flows north in the Atlantic, it eventually meets cooler, saltier, and denser water from the Arctic. This denser Arctic water sinks, pulling the warmer Gulf Stream water down with it. As the Gulf Stream sinks, it continues to pull more water up from the Caribbean, sustaining its flow. Until recently, this pattern of thermohaline circulation continued as it had for millennia.

How is this dynamic changing now? As it melts, the Arctic ice pack releases warmer, fresh water. When this water flows into the North Atlantic, it is no longer as cool, salty, and dense as it used to be. It therefore does not sink as rapidly, reducing the pull on the Gulf Stream. Over time, this will most likely result in another feedback loop for climate change. Scientists refer to it as the slowing and potential shutdown of the North Atlantic thermohaline circulation, also called Atlantic Meridional Overturning Circulation (AMOC).

The IPCC has long thought that this scenario was unlikely, but new research reveals previous models had major errors that led to an underestimate of sensitivity — that is, to what extent Arctic ice melt would affect the AMOC. One recent study predicts that if CO_2 were to double, the AMOC would shut down in 200-300 years. Another from Scripps Institute of Oceanography reports that it could be a serious near-term issue. The dean of climate science, James Hansen, agrees. Based on a study he conducted with eighteen other top climate experts, he believes substantial effects on AMOC could occur much more rapidly. This would result in multi-meter sea level rises and climate chaos, especially in countries bordering the North Atlantic. "All hell will break loose in the North Atlantic and neighbouring lands," says Hansen on loss of AMOC and its effects.

The Jet Stream Goes Wonky

During the last few years, the jet stream has gone through a major transformation. Its previous seasonal, predictable path and strength have probably changed more than any other indicator of abrupt climate change. Let's examine why this factors so significantly in the bigger picture.

The jet stream is caused by the intersection of the polar vortex, a stable dome of cold, dense air over the usually icebound polar areas, and the warm air rising up from the Equator. Where the warmer, lighter air meets the colder, denser polar vortex, the major air pressure changes result in strong winds high up in the atmosphere. Due to the spin of the Earth, these winds are deflected to the east in the northern hemisphere and the west in the southern half of the planet.

Our weather fronts are carried by the jet stream as it weaves its way around the planet. In the northern hemisphere, the jet stream tends to drift more northward in the summer, as increasing warm air pushes the polar vortex influence back. Conversely, during the winter the opposite happens, as the jet stream moves southward. The air on the north side of the jet stream is cold, due to the polar influence, and warm on the southern side due to the equatorial influence. During the summer months, we who live in the temperate latitudes are south of the jet stream, basking in the heat moving up from the south, while in the winter we are north of the jet stream, shivering from the cold air moving down from the Arctic.

There is usually little north-south undulation in the river of air that is the jet stream, and historically, this has kept our regional temperatures and weather fairly stable. The big changes have occurred seasonally, as the jet stream passes to the north or south of our location.

But during the past few years, that has all changed. As mentioned previously, the Arctic is heating much faster than the rest of the planet. This means that the dome of the polar vortex isn't as cold or dense as it once was. Thus, it no longer serves as the strong wall of high pressure that holds the jet stream in a relatively stable north-south position as it flows east to west (in the northern hemisphere). As a result, the jet stream is slowing and becoming wavy, undulating much further to the north and south than in the past. Large troughs are created as it moves much further south than normal, allowing the polar vortex to plunge down to latitudes it rarely got near in the past. Corresponding ridges or upward movements are also created, as much warmer-than-normal air from the south ventures into latitudes higher than it ever visited previously. The dips have become so severe that the jet stream has actually crossed the Equator, something that was not believed to be possible. This has caused some climate scientists to declare a global climate emergency.

As these undulating waves of air cross America, we experience extremes in temperatures and weather as we go from much colder or warmer than normal to exactly the opposite. In the eastern US, the polar vortex was largely responsible for recent winter temps that were much colder than normal. Often these wavy patterns stay in place for a much longer period than jet stream patterns did in the past, another effect of warming at the North Pole. While some cite recent severely cold winters as proof of global cooling, they are actually an unmistakable sign that the Arctic is warming extremely quickly. This is a sure indicator of global warming, one that has been predicted by almost all of the models.

The unusual jet stream activity discussed above is causing a powerful climate change feedback loop that is accelerating warming in the Arctic. The most dramatic wave of warm air to ever penetrate the Arctic circle occurred during the winter of 2017-2018, causing the polar vortex to fracture into two vortexes. Many climate scientists are in a state of alarm over this. Temperatures in Siberia, for example, soared to 35°C or 95°F. Seasoned observers have described what is happening as "crazy," "weird," and "simply shocking."

> "This is an anomaly among anomalies. It is far enough outside the historical range that it is worrying – it is a suggestion that there are further surprises in store as we continue to poke the angry beast that is our climate," said Michael Mann, director of the Earth System Science Center at Pennsylvania State University. "The Arctic has always been regarded as a bellwether because of the vicious circles that amplify human-caused warming in that particular region. And it is sending out a clear warning."

This is brand new territory we are exploring, with ramifications only time will reveal. One that seems certain is more extreme, erratic weather the world over. Another is an acceleration of warming in the Arctic, which we must remember is the major driver of global climate change.

The Arctic Methane Time Bomb

The biggest reason some researchers insist abrupt climate change is likely, if not inevitable, centers on the little-known gas called methane. Specifically, they see the potential for large releases of the methane that is stored in Arctic permafrost and in frozen deposits at the bottom of the Arctic Ocean. While many climate scientists do not believe a massive, catastrophic release of Arctic methane is likely, with each passing year evidence mounts that this is a potentially huge issue — the biggest in the entire climate change matrix.

Scientists have known for a very long time that a number of mass extinction events, including the Permian extinction, which occurred 250 million years ago, were triggered by the release of enormous quantities of methane hydrate that had been previously frozen in the Arctic. Methane hydrate is essentially trapped, frozen methane gas that is encapsulated in ice and snow and deposited during ice ages. During the Permian extinction, the planet began to rapidly warm through massive releases of carbon dioxide, purportedly from vulcanism, which then warmed the Arctic sufficiently to begin to release methane trapped in the permafrost. The CO_2 ultimately warmed shallow Arctic Ocean areas, especially near the East Siberian shelf, beneath which lie enormous deposits of methane hydrate.

As mentioned previously, compared to carbon dioxide — the gas everyone is worried about — methane is a greenhouse gas monster. On a short-term basis of a few decades, it can cause effects that are 80 to 100 times more potent than CO_2, and remains at least 20 times more influential even after a century. The Arctic methane situation is even more critical, since methane release does not tend to occur gradually. Once certain threshold temperature levels are reached in the shallow perimeter of the Arctic Ocean, the methane tends to come out rapidly. This has been labeled the Arctic Methane Time Bomb.

Some of the leading authorities on this subject are with the Russian Academy of Sciences,. Other researchers are adding their voices to this possibility. Natalia Shakova, a research professor at the University of Alaska, Fairbanks International Arctic Research Center, Dr. Igor Semiletov, of the Tomsk Polytechnic University in Russia, and Peter Wadhams, who founded the Arctic Methane Group, all believe this may be the most important issue in climate change. After monitoring changes in ice, water temperatures, and methane releases in the Arctic for decades, they have concluded that a 50-gigaton burst of methane from permafrost beneath the East Siberian Arctic shelf is possible at any time. As Shakova warns:

> "...methane releases from decaying frozen hydrates could result in emission rates that could change in order of magnitude in a matter of minutes, and that there would be nothing smooth, gradual or controlled about it." She described it as a "kind of release that is like the unsealing of an overpressure pipeline."

If this "burp" happens, the methane that could be released within a year or less is the equivalent of 1000 Gt of carbon dioxide. To provide some perspective on this, since 1850, humans have released 1475 Gt of carbon dioxide. When the <u>Arctic last released mass quantities of methane during the Permian extinction</u>, 90% of all species on the planet became extinct.

Why is that important to understand today? <u>A study at M.I.T. discovered that it may be critical to what is about to occur</u>. Dan Rothman, of the department of Earth, Atmospheric and Planetary Sciences (EAPS) at MIT, spells it out:

> The rate of injection of CO2 into the late Permian system is probably similar to the anthropogenic rate of injection of CO2 now. It's just that it went on for 10,000 years.

The crucial point here is that not only are similar levels of C02 release occurring — they are happening much, much faster. This indicates that the potential for near-term, catastrophic methane releases is much greater than many would like to think.

The reason most scientists did not believe this could happen is that the models were wrong. Most of the classic models, including that of the IPCC, were based on grossly inaccurate assumptions about the potential for massive Arctic methane releases. According to <u>a study conducted by Russian scientists at the Tomsk Polytechnic University</u>, the ocean bottom — the subsea permafrost — is melting faster than anyone previously believed. The study concluded that ocean warming has now reached a level at which seafloor sediments are melting at a rate that portends a massive methane release.

> New data obtained by complex biochemical, geophysical and geological studies conducted in 2011-2016 resulted in the conclusion that in some areas of the East Siberian Arctic Shelf the roof of the subsea permafrost had already reached the depth of hydrates' stability, the destruction of which may cause massive releases of bubble methane.

The potential for such methane releases is already becoming a fact. As early as the beginning of this decade, vast, <u>unprecedented plumes of methane began to bubble to the sur-</u>

face of the Arctic Ocean. "In an exclusive interview with *The Independent*, Igor Semiletov of the International Arctic Research Centre at the University of Alaska, Fairbanks, who led the eighth joint US – Russian cruise of the East Siberian Arctic seas, said that he has 'never before witnessed the scale and force of the methane being released from beneath the Arctic seabed. Earlier we found torch-like structures like this but they were only tens of meters in diameter. This is the first time we found continuous, powerful and impressive seeping structures more than 1000 meters in diameter. It's amazing.' He went on to add, 'I was most impressed by the sheer scale and the high density of the plumes. Over a relatively small area we found more than 100, but over a wider area there should be thousands of them.'"

Dr. Semiletov led another expedition into the Arctic in late September of 2016 to measure the current state of the methane emissions. The research team concluded the rate of emissions could boost global temperatures by 9°F or more by the end of the century.

Among climate researchers, all eyes are on the Arctic, and particularly the East Siberian continental shelf, to observe the size and quantity of the methane plumes being released. These seem to be the earliest flashing red lights signaling we're in the danger zone of possibly the most significant tipping point that could catapult the planet into uncontrolled global warming.

7

Overshoot and Collapse

Modeling the Future of Our World

When we attempt to project where humanity is headed in light of all the crises discussed above, their complexity and interconnectedness make predictions tentative at best. For example, think about the interrelatedness of energy effects, population trends, climate, the ecosystem, and economics. Burning more fossil fuels inevitably leads to more warming and greater pollution; it also impacts money flows throughout the global economy. If the planet continues to warm, that will affect food production, cause more desertification, and require ever more financial, energy and human resources to find new ways to feed people. To get a true, comprehensive picture of what might lie ahead, we somehow have to develop a synthesis of the major issues and their interconnections. But where do we even begin?

This was a consideration that continued to surface in my mind until I discovered that such a study of these interrelationships had already been done — nearly fifty years ago — and had been repeated twice since then. In 1970, Donella Meadows, Dennis Meadows and Jurgen Randers, M.I.T. research professors, were commissioned by the Club of Rome, an international group of high-level businessmen, statesmen and scientists, to lead a multi-disciplinary team to model our complex, techno-industrial culture and its impacts on the Earth's resources and biosphere. The project was funded by the Volkswagen Foundation, one of the largest, most influential research organizations on the planet. A two-year study at MIT developed a sophisticated computer model to investigate the long-term causes and consequences of growth in population, industrial capital, food production, resource consumption, and pollution. The computer model was called World 3.

This highly sophisticated model was developed by a multidisciplinary team of some of the leading experts in their fields. The most advanced understandings of the dynamics of all the different parts of our integrated global system were each modeled. Expectations for future growth patterns were determined, and the resulting data used to construct an empirical model.

This was the first time a truly thorough and comprehensive model had ever been developed to study the current state of our complex, dynamic human culture, and to project where it was most likely headed. The model also provided the basis for government and private research and planning groups to run simulations for the future, based upon proposed policies, laws, and regulations designed to positively redirect humanity's future where that seemed necessary.

Two years of focused research by some of the best in their fields were devoted to quantifying these variables. These researchers also did what had never been done before: they recognized the complex interrelationships that create feedback loops among the various components of human world culture and the planet. The World 3 model was almost certainly the most advanced computer simulation of its kind at that time. And it probably still is; since 1970, it's been updated a number of times.

To convey the depth and complexity of the model, take a moment to consider the facet of persistent pollution. Although this is merely one of the small-to-medium sized parts of the model, it contained 30 subcategories, including industrial material emissions factor, agricultural material toxicity index, desired persistent pollution index, policy time implementation, technology development delay, and many other factors. While these terms may not mean much without reading the study in depth, they provide some idea of what an amazingly comprehensive model this was, and still is.

The research team published their results in 1972 in their first book, *Limits to Growth*. The study clearly showed that "growth" is not and cannot be endless. A key finding:

If the present growth trends in world population, industrialization, pollution, food production, and resource depletion continue unchanged, the limits to growth on this planet will be reached sometime within the next hundred years. The most probable result would be a sudden, uncontrollable decline in both population, production, consumption and quality of life.

That is a stark statement. Along with many of the study's other conclusions, it resulted in a worldwide firestorm of dialogue, and harsh criticism by those who were unwilling to accept these findings. The study's results were vociferously debated by major governmental and scientific groups the world over. This landmark study had a huge impact, for the results of the model's various scenarios highlighted the need for a reversal of thinking from the accepted unlimited growth paradigms that predominated in corporate and governmental sectors worldwide. (Unfortunately, that reversal of thinking has yet to take place on a scale that would indicate true change is underway.)

Some praised the study for demonstrating the need for limits to the endless expansion that had become deified by those who made money from it. Others — including more than a few whose wealth and power depended on continued "growth" — attacked and vilified the study's conclusions.

Those conclusions, as articulated in *The Limits to Growth*, delivered a strong message that change was needed to ensure a viable future for all life on the planet. But the reported results were not intended as a message of gloom and doom. The authors took care to state that it was still possible to establish a stable and sustainable planetary culture — if significant changes were voluntarily made. And indeed, much that was beneficial blossomed out of this initial wake-up call. The environmental movement, along with the search for alternative energy sources, became two of the most notable efforts engendered by this report.

In 1990 the study was conducted again, with an updated World 3 computer model. The researchers entered all new data for the previous twenty years in order to make new projections. They developed a "standard run" which assumed status quo; that is, present trends would continue. The results of this study were even more dramatic — and less optimistic. It was clear that during the twenty intervening years, little had been done to institute the changes the 1970 study indicated were necessary to move toward sustainability. Instead, many of the trends had actually deteriorated. The model revealed that the global techno-industrial system was in a state of overshoot, which means that we had gone beyond the limits of what is sustainable. This inspired the name of the group's second book: *Beyond the Limits,* published in 1993.

What exactly did they mean by the term overshoot? Imagine driving through thick, opaque fog, unaware that the speed at which you are traveling requires a braking distance greater than your visibility. Peering through the fog, you are shocked to suddenly see a large boulder in the middle of the road. There is no way to avoid it, and no time to gradually slow down. You slam on the brakes, but unfortunately it is too late; the car simply will not stop before the collision. That was the state of the planet, according to the World 3 model in 1990.

The study was conducted again in 2000 and the results were published in 2004 in *The Limits to Growth: The 30-Year Update*. The conclusions were similar to those of the 1990 study. The "maintaining status quo projections" revealed that human population would crest and begin to decline around 2025. Industrial output would peak and decline a few years before that, as would life expectancy. The declines were precipitous in some cases, such as industrial output and consumer goods and services per person. This indicated that even as population began to decline, humans would be living under increasing poverty and hardship sometime around the second half of the second decade of this century.

In case you haven't done the math, that time is now. According to the World 3 model, human culture is essentially facing overshoot and collapse — not some distant day, but in the very near future. Once that stark prognosis was made, the next part of the study ran multiple scenarios to determine how we could change various components to bring human culture into a position of sustainability. For example, the researchers tried doubling the natural resource endowments input into the model, assuming that somehow we could find more resources through better exploration and extraction. When they ran the model with this change, population rose and continued steady a little further out into the future before it entered into an even steeper curve of collapse, as did all the other variables. Finding and using more

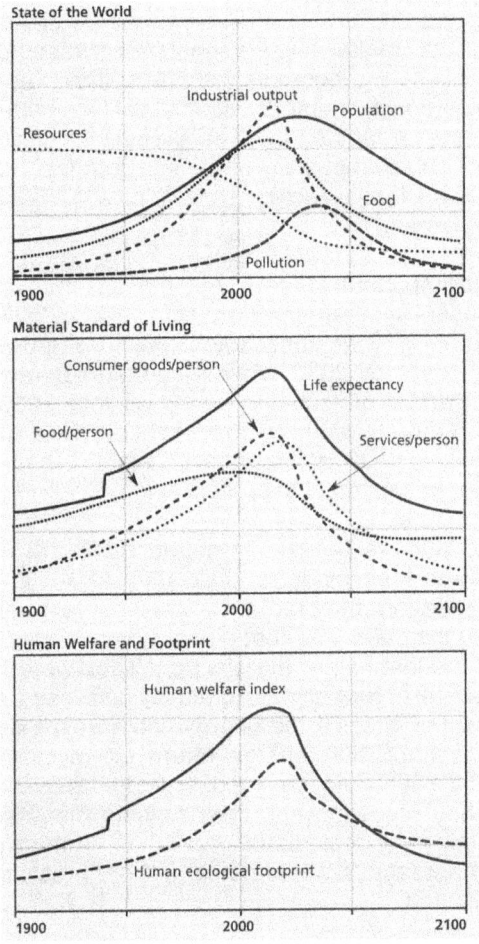

natural resources only postponed the moment when we peaked out, and then drastically accelerated the rate of decline.

The researchers did not give up. They ran numerous other scenarios, most of which were based on questionable, if not unreasonable expectations of what humanity might be able to do in the very best circumstances. Even with this optimistic basis, almost all the runs resulted in scenarios of some sort of overshoot followed by decline and/or collapse.

For those who were paying attention, the 1990 and 2000 studies popped the bubble of illusion that we could continue to grow, or for that matter sustain, population, resource consumption, and pollution generation without detrimental effects. The myth that we could prevail by simply being smarter and doing things better — a fantasy that many clung to then and still believe today — was empirically uprooted. Both the 1990 and 2000 studies showed that planetary overshoot and collapse was the most likely scenario.

It is important to note that the assumptions these researchers used to create their projections were *optimistic* at the time, based on what we know now. They projected world population to be 7 billion by 2030, when it had already reached 7.3 billion in 2017, and is projected to hit 8.6 billion in 2030. That figure is nearly 25% greater than the models used. They also predicted global growth in GDP of 3% when, in fact, it has been nearly stagnant and has recently been declining.

The authors repeatedly stated there are many factors not included in their models. While they took into account the ecological situation, they did not know how fast carbon dioxide levels would increase, and that global temperatures would begin to spike in the last half of this decade. They were not aware of the prospect of abrupt climate change, discussed above. They probably did not imagine the energy crisis we'd face, due to the rapidly declining EROI (energy return on investment) for petroleum. While it would be impossible to layer these into the models without updating and then running them all again, it is almost certain that declines in population, human welfare, and other important factors would be even more precipitous than the models predicted.

The *Limits to Growth* team concluded in 2000 that general awareness of our predicament was "hopelessly limited" and it would take a long time to obtain sufficient political support to bring the ecological footprint back into sustainability. The researchers were "much more pessimistic about the global future than we were in 1972. It is a sad fact that humanity has largely squandered the past thirty years with futile debates and well-intentioned, but halfhearted responses to the global ecological challenge. **We do not have another 30 years together.** (My emphasis) Much wants to change if the ongoing overshoot is not to be followed by collapse in the 21st century."

"Much wants to change," the World 3 modelers concluded in 2000. But will it? What else do we need to understand to evaluate the odds of that happening in time to avert global catastrophe?

The Importance of Grasping Exponential Functions

After reading that subtitle, if your mind is not particularly mathematically inclined you might be asking yourself, *What the heck are exponential functions?* A rebellious inner voice might even be adding, *And why should I care?* Well, it turns out they matter — a lot. Especially when it comes to imagining what lies ahead for humanity and the planet.

In college, I had a social sciences professor who, not once, but a number of times during the course, prophesied the demise of humanity. Why did he feel so sure our species wouldn't make it? Because he understood that even small, incremental increases in annual economic growth and consumption — say, in the 2 - 4% per year range — would eventuate in scenarios of doom. The minds of most human beings, this professor insisted, operate in a linear, concrete way; we are not innately wired to comprehend the dangers hidden in exponential growth functions. So we are unlikely to do anything to address the challenges such rates of growth present, because we are blind to them.

While I only dimly grasped what my professor was saying at the time, in recent years I often find myself thinking of his words as I digest all that is coming forth about the state of the planet. The World 3 studies in particular aimed a spotlight on the unexpected effects of exponential growth functions. In *The Limits to Growth: The 30-Year Update*, the authors used a French riddle to illustrate this.

> Suppose you own a pond. One day you notice that a single water lily is growing on your pond. You know that the lily plant will double in size each day. You realize that if the plant were allowed to grow unchecked, it would completely cover the pond in 30 days, choking off the other forms of life in the water. But initially the lily seems small, so you decide not to worry. You'll

deal with it when it covers half the pond. How much time have you given yourself to prevent the destruction of the pond?

You have left yourself just one day! On the 29th day the pond is half-covered. The next day — after one final doubling — the pond will be totally shaded. It initially seems reasonable to postpone action until the pond is half covered. On the 21st day, the plant covers just .02 percent of the pond. On the 25th, the plant covers just 3 percent of the pond. But again, that policy allows just one day to save your pond.

You can see how exponential growth, combined with response delays, can lead to overshoot. ... Exponential growth accumulates suddenly to produce a problem that is unmanageable.

Virtually all aspects of our highly complex, techno-industrial culture rely on non-linear rates of growth. When we hear about growth rates of 2 or 3% for the economy or food consumption, for instance, the numbers sound innocuous; we can't imagine such rates of expansion could present any threat to our way of life. But when even a few components of our incredibly complex system grow exponentially, and all the interrelationships of these pieces are factored in, we begin to grasp the inevitability of overshoot and collapse.

So far, though, few humans have been able to comprehend the potential for disaster that lies hidden within optimistic projections of neverending growth. It appears my long-ago professor was right. Are we reaching the 28th or 29th day of our species' cycle of expansion, as in the lily pond metaphor?

Skating Off the Seneca Cliff

Long ago, a philosopher named Lucius Seneca discovered an important characteristic of complex systems, which, in his honor, is called the Seneca Effect. They tend to grow and mature slowly, he found, but when their inevitable decline comes, such systems usually end in rapid collapse. This phenomenon has been termed the Seneca Cliff.

The World 3 model computer runs generated many graphs that display the Seneca Cliff. For a time, things seem to be going swimmingly, with a nice, steady pattern of growth symbolized by a gently curving ascending line on the graph. Suddenly, the subtle upward curve of the line on the graph veers downward. A convergence of factors causes an abrupt halt to the current rate of growth, followed by an often precipitous fall.

Why do complex systems tend to fall apart in such a sudden, drastic way? To understand why the Seneca Cliff so often occurs, we need to step back a bit and consider how systems work. As you would expect, every complex system is a network of subsystems, each a complete entity in itself. These sub-entities are often termed holons. Each subsystem is linked with all others to form the complex network of the entire macrosystem.

In the human body, for example, millions of cells link together to form tissues, which then network and combine to make organs, which in turn work together within organ systems, which themselves exist as subsets of the human body as a whole. As in the body, each aspect of the global techno-industrial culture is linked to all other subsets and sub-subsets of components in an unimaginably complex web of feedback loops. Energy is linked to population is linked to food production is linked to pollution, in an enormous spiderweb of interconnection. When any link becomes weak, every other link feels the effects, and if the perturbation is sufficiently strong, the entire network may be threatened with collapse.

Thus, if any one holon or subsystem becomes imbalanced, that distortion ripples like a wave throughout the whole system. Other holons are, in turn, stressed by the imbalance, weakening them and ultimately the totality. To some degree, this domino effect can be absorbed and mitigated by a healthy, intact system. But when a system is inherently unstable and out of balance, these interconnected effects can lead to more critical results.

As we learned in the Energy section, within third-dimensional, physical reality the Second Law of Thermodynamics, otherwise known as entropy, is always pulling any system toward disorder. The larger and more complex the system, the more resources — energy, financial, material, and human — are needed to maintain order and balance. The further the system moves away from sustainability, the more energy is required to get it back on track, and the stronger the entropic pull toward chaos and breakdown.

Here's the bottom-line fact that few want to face: on a planet with finite resources — a planet such as our own Earth — a forever expanding industrial, material culture that is becoming ever more complex is an impossibility. As resources grow more and more scarce, it gets ever more costly, in terms of energy and resource inputs, to keep the system stable, much less growing. Each of the system's components becomes more stressed as the imbalance grows. The larger and more complex the system, and the more unstable its fundamental support structure, the less it takes to trigger the destabilization of any one part of the system. As we've seen, this seemingly isolated impact is rapidly transmitted to all other interconnected parts, starting a downward spiral of disintegration and dissolution. In worst-case scenarios, this process accelerates until collapse — a Seneca Cliff — occurs.

Ugo Bardi explores the application of the Seneca Cliff to limits to growth in this excerpt from <u>The Seneca Effect: Why Growth is Slow but Collapse is Rapid</u>. Thanks to studies like those reported in *Beyond the Limits* and *Limits to Growth,* many of the world's leaders have been aware of the potential for a global Seneca Cliff for some time. Nearly a decade ago, Sir John Beddington, chief scientific advisor in the UK, <u>in a major speech to environmental groups and politicians</u>, foretold that the world was heading for major upheavals that are due to come to a head in 2030, if not sooner. In his words:

> A "perfect storm" of food shortages, scarce water and insufficient energy resources threaten to unleash public unrest, cross-border conflicts and mass migrations, as people flee from the worst-affected regions.

It is obvious we are already in the early stages of Beddington's "perfect storm," as climate refuges flee northern Africa and soon-to-be-submerged islands the world over. The many issues cited in previous chapters — the decline of the oceans, burgeoning pollution, a financially bankrupt world, emerging energy and climate crises — signal that we are rapidly approaching a Seneca Cliff.

8

Sixth Great Extinction Ahead?

Warning Cries From On High

One of the most significant signs that we are skating toward a Seneca Cliff is the recent apocalyptic warnings by some of the most respected and conservative scientific groups. During the last few years, the number of scientists willing to say that we face extremely serious, even dire, consequences as a result of our way of life is growing rapidly.

An extensive study published in 2013, Abrupt Impacts Of Climate Change, Anticipating Surprises, was sponsored by the National Oceanic and Atmospheric Administration, the National Science Foundation, and the National Academies. The report stated climate change was already in motion and disrupting the marine food web, animal habitats, stability of coastlines, and climate and weather patterns throughout the northern hemisphere. It predicts that climate change alone, without catastrophic methane release, could "crash coral reefs, the rainforests of our oceans, as early as 2060 and precipitate the collapse of the West Antarctic Ice Sheet." Interestingly, this study didn't even address the danger of abrupt methane release, considering it a long-term, less-important issue, a premise that now appears highly questionable.

The dean of climate change, James Hansen, isn't afraid to speak his truth. "We've got an emergency", Hanson states, adding that multiplying impacts and feedback loops will accelerate the changes:

"It will happen faster than you think." He warns that those in power aren't aware of how dire the situation is, and that even the few who are concerned "don't really get it." Hansen insists "we've only begun to feel the warming from the gases that are out there."

In a February 2018 speech at the University of Chicago, James Anderson, a professor of atmospheric chemistry at Harvard University, went on record predicting <u>humanity will be wiped out by climate change</u> unless we stop using fossil fuels within five years.

"The chance that there will be any permanent ice left in the Arctic after 2022 is essentially zero," Anderson said, with 75 to 80 percent of permanent ice having melted already during the last 35 years.

Recovery is all but impossible, he argued, without a World War II-style transformation of industry—an acceleration of the effort to halt carbon pollution and remove it from the atmosphere, and a new effort to reflect Sunlight away from the Earth's poles.

"This has to be done," Anderson added, "within the next five years."

Anderson is a very credible source, as he was responsible for the original ozone research that led to the global campaign to reduce ozone-depleting chemicals. His research is widely recognized and respected all across the planet.

In the summer of 2017, <u>the official national climate assessment</u>, a 600-page report on climate change in the US, was released in draft form by climate scientists working in thirteen US government agencies. The report emphatically stated:

"It is now certain that human influence has been a dominant cause of global warming. Without major reductions in emissions of greenhouse gases," the report continued, "annual temperatures could rise 9 degrees F or more, relative to pre-industrial times."

These scientists also produced detailed information on potential sea level rise, increasing ocean acidification, ever more powerful storms, and worsening droughts and flooding, all of which threaten food supplies. Echoing Hansen, the authors state that the AMOC, which keeps winters mild in the UK and western Europe, could weaken as much as 54% during this century, causing more climate changes. Recent studies have shown that a similar process is now beginning in the Antarctic. And increasing methane releases in the Arctic have the potential to spawn dire global consequences.

Possibly the most hard-hitting warning comes, for the second time, from the Union of Concerned Scientists. This illustrious group, which includes most of the world's Nobel laureates, recently updated their original, landmark alert issued in 1992 by more than 1700 scientists regarding the disintegrating state of the planet. In November 2017, this group released a new, dire "warning to humanity." This open letter to the people of the world has already won the support of more than 15,000 scientists from 184 countries, who offered their names as signatories. The report cites a familiar litany of problems, including catastrophic climate change, deforestation, mass species extinction, dead zones in the ocean, and lack of access to fresh water. It summarizes starkly: "Soon it will be too late to shift course away from a failing trajectory, and time is running out."

Even highly respected non-climate scientists are speaking up. In mid-2017, the late, renowned professor Stephen Hawking stated that he believed human beings have only 100 years left on Earth, and that we should be looking for off-planet habitation. Hawking added that he is not the only one who has come to this conclusion.

The recent spate of dire reports by large numbers of accredited scientists is unprecedented. Those who know the most about what is occurring on this planet are bluntly telling us we are in deep trouble. Scientists with reputations to protect tend to be very cautious about making statements like these; they are well aware of the impact they will have. Until recently, highly accredited scientists like those mentioned above have never come out so strongly, or in such large numbers, to deliver the truth as they see it. Most scientists with these kinds of credentials *understate* what is going on, to avoid creating alarm. They tend to be reticent to conjecture, and prefer to stick to what they can prove through repeated experiments, running them again and again to make sure they know their results are trustworthy. Because of this, accredited, peer-reviewed scientific information often lags behind other reports of what is really going on by years, if not decades. In the scientific world, many believe it is better to be too late and right than too early and wrong. In some cases this makes sense, but it could lead to potentially catastrophic results when the global situation is the area of study. In light of this tendency to err on the side of certainty before making any conclusions, reports like the widely circulated ones mentioned above cause us to wonder if the situation is, in fact, much worse than they are telling us.

Cassandras of Climate Change

This brings us to another group of scientists who seem compelled to speak more forcefully and openly about the possibilities of catastrophic climate change. I sense that these are souls who are human beings first and scientists second. Laying many of their personal and career concerns aside, they share the research insights and intuitions that lead them to believe abrupt, catastrophic climate change is now a reality.

Some of these scientists and academics express their perspectives via Arctic News, a blog through which they can speak out with more honesty than is normally acceptable. While all of the scientists are listed on the site, nearly every article is released under the pseudonym Sam Carana. This serves as a buffer to the negative feedback that much of what they publish generates.

In May 2017, Arctic News published an article entitled "Abrupt Warming – How Much and How Fast?" The unknown author lays out all the factors that can contribute to a 10°C or 18°F warming from the baseline in preindustrial 1750 to sometime between 2021-2026, by which time the planet's base temperature could theoretically have risen by this amount. When I first read these projections of major warming within a very short time frame, I must admit I was skeptical. But as I looked at the data behind these projections, I concluded that they were probably low-probability scenarios, but still possible. In light of recent accelerating changes in the Arctic, and remembering the human proclivity to underestimate exponential change, maybe they aren't as low probability as they initially seemed.

The Apollo–Gaia project headed by David Wasdell provides cutting-edge research into climate sensitivity, or how the many factors within the Earth's climatic system amplify the effects of anthropogenic emissions of greenhouse gases. The report "Climate Dynamics: Facing the Harsh Realities of Now" presents research findings on past climate sensitivities to atmospheric CO_2 changes, from the depths of the previous Ice Age to the present.

The Apollo-Gaia study reveals that current estimates of climate sensitivity are dangerously low. The rate at which global warming factors such as CO_2, water vapor, and methane concentrations amplify global temperature change is much higher than the IPCC models. For example, the amplification factor of CO_2's effect on temperature change is eight in the Apollo-Gaia research, while only three in the IPCC models. The Apollo-Gaia models predict an 8-12°C temperature increase based upon projected CO_2 concentrations, far higher than previous estimates.

Guy McPherson is another climate scientist who is becoming increasingly well-known for being vocal about catastrophic climate change. Some years ago, Guy realized the trajectory of anthropogenic climate change was catapulting us toward near-term human extinction. As he awakened to this stark possibility, Guy took the important psycho-spiritual step of facing the likely demise of the human species. This resulted in a complete transformation of his consciousness and his life. He left his secure professorship at the University of Arizona to lecture internationally on abrupt climate change, the resultant human extinction he believes is inevitable, and how we might deal with this mentally, emotionally, and spiritually. Guy presents extensive evidence for why he believes humanity is facing extinction in his "Monster Climate Change Essay," which provides detailed, frequently updated information to support his conjectures.

In his avowed certainty about near-term human extinction, Guy McPherson differs from virtually all other climate scientists. Yet he is saying essentially the same thing as the new batch of scientists who see abrupt, catastrophic climate change as increasingly likely: *We've reached a point at which self-reinforcing feedback loops are now taking over and will drive runaway climate change by themselves.* In simple terms, we overshot our margin for error and have now initiated a process similar to what happened during the rapid acceleration in global temperatures that resulted in previous mass die-off events.

Guy McPherson is often labeled an "extremist" and a "doom and gloomer." Granted, some of his predictions have not come true as rapidly as he thought — an ice-free Arctic did not happen by 2017, for instance. Yet much of the basis for his speculations about abrupt climate change is being confirmed as Earth's climate change saga unfolds.

I find it interesting when listening to Guy that he does not seem to be in an emotional state of "gloom and doom," but exudes tremendous peace and compassion as a human being. He does not peddle fear as part of his message, but rather insists that when we accept What Is and face the inevitability of our demise, which is certain from the moment we are born, we can find a new level of freedom. This is something that many great spiritual beings have told us for millennia. We'll talk a lot more about this in the second and third sections of this book.

Doomed by Denial of Doom and Gloom?

While the scientific evidence supporting abrupt climate change continues to mount, what goes on at a subtler level of reality may turn out to write the epitaph for much of humanity. Although many dismiss abrupt climate change as "gloom and doom" rhetoric, it is possible that the reverse may be true. Our reluctance to face reality as it is, especially when it appears bleak and threatening to our human selves, could be the shadow issue that leads to climate catastrophe. In "Our Aversion to Doom and Gloom is Dooming Us", John Atcheson shares his insights on this issue, which he repeatedly encountered during his 35 years of environmental work. Environmental and climate scientists continue to debate whether telling it like it is risks spreading "doom and gloom." Does sharing the facts as they are quell optimism and dampen initiative to work toward positive change?

So far, in most cases the choice has been made to downplay the more difficult aspects of our situation in order to present a more optimistic message. According to Atcheson, scientists tend to attack their peers who present information pointing to environmental apocalypse, believing they are creating "paralyzing" narratives of doom and hopelessness. Atcheson adds that the scientific community and especially the IPCC has avoided getting anywhere near addressing the worst-case scenarios. Yet compared to their models and previous forecasts, actual climate trends do not resemble midrange projections nearly as much as worst-case scenarios.

Some IPCC forecasts result in temperatures that would exceed 4°C by 2100, even if progress towards implementing climate treaties occurred. When we include the ignored IPCC feedback loops, increases of 6.5°C are more likely. This is the range discussed by the scientists at Arctic News and Apollo-Gaia, as well as by Guy McPherson, Paul Beckwith, and even James Hansen, of late.

As we can see, the truth has been hidden behind understated information, out of the fear that it will lead to widespread panic and hopelessness. As John Atcheson states, the real issue that may determine the future of humanity is our fear of doom and gloom, which may cause us to hypnotize ourselves into ignoring what is actually going on.

As I write this during early 2018, it appears we have entered the climatic overshoot and collapse phase first predicted by the original *Limits to Growth* team decades ago. The global climate system is breaking down much more rapidly than anticipated, as evidenced by increasing weather extremes caused by the immense distortions in and fragmentation of the jet stream, as well as the fracturing of the polar vortex. Recent weather events lend increasing credence to those who have endorsed abrupt climate change, and make the 10°C forecasts for this century seem more and more realistic. But what does that mean for our everyday life on Earth?

What a Difference a Degree (or Two) Makes

For years, when the IPCC talked about a degree or two of warming, most of us didn't take much notice. We might have thought, *One or two degrees...so what! That doesn't sound so terrible.* In fact, many of us relaxed, hearing those numbers, having feared our predicament was a lot worse.

It can be tempting to believe that much bigger temperature increases are not a big deal, either. Who among us hasn't had the following experience? You get up on a spring day and the temps are in the low 50s as you head outside. You feel perfectly comfortable wearing your light jacket. By late afternoon, the day has warmed by twenty degrees. Now the temperature is in the 70s, and you realize you don't need your jacket for the walk home. As evening falls, you comment to your family about what a nice spring day it was. Although the temperature rose by twenty degrees, you didn't experience the slightest discomfort, let alone a threat to your very existence. So why is everyone so concerned about a degree or two — or more — of global temperature rise?

When I first became aware of how important a degree or two can be, Karen and I were living in Arcata, California during the mid-1990s. Arcata is the home of Humboldt State University, one of the better schools in the country for environmental sciences. We "happened" to have a friend and client who had worked at their research lab, where she performed an in-depth study of the temperature sensitivity of the coast redwoods. The study revealed that a mean temperature change of between one and two degrees C would doom the giant coastal sequoias. This truly surprised me at the time. And, since we love to walk in the redwood forests, it brought up a lot of sadness for us both.

Today, study after study is revealing that changes of even a few degrees are likely to result in the dissolution of our global, techno-industrial culture. As it perishes, it will take with it some considerable portion of humanity, not to mention countless other species. A compelling article, <u>A Degree By Degree Explanation Of What Will Happen When the Earth Warms</u>, provides some rough projections of what might happen. The article begins by pointing out that six thousand years ago, the world was one degree warmer — and Nebraska was a desert. If that happens again, "the western United States once again could suffer perennial droughts, far worse than the 1930s. Deserts will reappear, particularly in Nebraska, but also in eastern Montana, Wyoming and Arizona, northern Texas and Oklahoma. As dust and sandstorms turn day into night across thousands of miles of former prairie, farmsteads, roads and even entire towns will be engulfed by sand."

Things get increasingly difficult, and then we hit the two to three degree range. At this point, mass starvation will occur. Sea levels will be 25 meters higher. At three degrees, the carbon cycle reverses; now, vegetation and soils emit it, rather than using or sequestering it, adding more greenhouse gases to the atmosphere. We have already seen that, due to human intervention, this is already occurring in the rainforests. At five degrees of warming, we are back to being hunters and gatherers. Civilization as we have known it has disintegrated. I won't divulge what happens beyond that. If you feel brave, please click the link and find out for yourself.

I became aware of the complexity, interdependency, and fragility of our worldwide, techno-industrial culture while I worked in banking many years ago. I discovered, for example, that the major automakers don't manufacture cars, they assemble them. At the time, GM had approximately 5,000 suppliers. If they couldn't get ball bearings for some part of the drivetrain, for example, no cars would roll off the assembly line. The situation is similar with so much of what we utilize every day.

The other thing most of us don't consider when faced with the possibility of a systemic collapse is what happens once it starts. This brings us back to the Seneca Cliff, and includes another important aspect of modern life that I seldom see mentioned. If the collapse begins and gains momentum, a lot of things we depend on simply won't get manufactured anymore. The GM ball bearing example above gets even more complex; since 1980, cars have become highly sophisticated and require computers to diagnose problems. They are no longer composed of many independent parts like ball bearings that can be replaced individually. Now, there are entire modules, especially in the engine, which can only be produced by a manufacturer. Tinkering with our cars in the backyard is no longer easy, if it is even possible. The same is true of many other things we use daily.

So much for the idea that, in a collapse scenario, we would simply repair what we have and make that work for as long as possible. If we don't have a way to repair most things, what do we do? We might start to wonder what would happen in the various areas of life as we've known it. Take transportation, for example. How will we get where we need to go? Do we go back to riding horses? How would that work out? And how will the goods we need get to us, in our far-flung locations? That is, if they are still being grown or manufactured. Suddenly, the scope of our lives is likely to shrink to encompass just a few miles from home.

Or think about agriculture. Without modern machinery and long-distance transportation, how will we grow and distribute enough food to feed us all? Does anyone remember how to make the equipment for horse-drawn farming, much less how to accomplish that? How many blacksmiths are still forging iron into implements?

Our global industrial culture developed over a couple of centuries, each new discovery dooming many others to obsolescence. Finding our way back to those pre-industrial methods of doing nearly everything presents countless challenges. The inventions that made our culture work in the past exist now only in museums. Few humans indeed have any idea how to resurrect them.

So where does this leave us? It seems to me that at a certain point we will reach a very steep Seneca Cliff, after which we may find ourselves living a simple agrarian or even hunter-gatherer lifestyle. The inevitable question that then arises is this: *If it comes to that point, how many humans would remain?*

9

Facing And Embracing Apocalypse

As we conclude our exploration of what might turn out to be the end of life as we've known it, you may want to take stock of where you are with what you have read and the inner experiences it has engendered. There are so many places this journey can take us. It's possible you already knew most of what you've just read. You may have felt little impact on your consciousness as you read the many crisis scenarios. Then again, you may be feeling deep sadness, grief, hopelessness, and despair over the world situation. You might be experiencing frustration, the heat of anger, or even rage. Or you might have arrived at a sense of acceptance and peace about it all. A combination of these emotions may also be present within you. Some of you will disagree with the information to one degree or another, finding my research faulty. Others believe human creativity will triumph over the myriad crises we face, just as it more or less has throughout history. Those who are spiritually inclined may put their faith and trust in divine grace, sensing that a collective awakening is in process. These readers may believe we will somehow transcend all the potential issues and scenarios discussed above.

You may be feeling deeply impacted at the core levels of being by what you have read. You might have had some inkling that all was not right with the world, but until now you had no real grasp of the many interconnected crises we face. Right now you may be sitting with some very challenging emotions. We've anticipated this and discuss some possible ways you might approach them in the third section of the book. **If you are having a difficult time proceeding, you may want to skip ahead to Part Three for help in finding peace and alignment with the journey this book is taking you on.** Please be gentle with yourself as you digest this challenging material. Give yourself plenty of empathy and compassion for whatever is going on within you.

It might help for you to know something about what it's been like for me to do this intensive research into a subject that encompasses all aspects of human life — and our very future as a species. I had considered humanity's future pretty much continuously with various levels of involvement since I began to awaken four decades ago. During that time, I have plunged into the depths and soared to the heights while researching and contemplating our species' future.

A couple of years ago, when I began the research that culminated in this section of the book, I had arrived at a pretty peaceful place with it all. I believed that, in the end, all things would work out for the best future for humanity, whatever that journey might put us through. I still believe that, but I didn't know that deep in the recesses of the subconscious, parts of the ego/personality self hadn't fully faced the physical realities of the precarious state of humanity and the planet. Diving into the research that resulted in the information you just read had a dramatic impact on my psyche. To my surprise, there have been some dark moments. Yet I see they also served to catalyze deeper levels of embodied awakening and understanding of what lies ahead for our species. In the end I came to see the perfection of where we are in the journey, collectively, and felt the assuredness that a larger, more loving hand is guiding this entire journey with absolute perfection into a far grander future.

To come to this knowing, we must ascend to a higher level of consciousness. This provides a larger perspective from which we can consider the possible extinction scenario we face. Viewing what is unfolding through the eyes that can see that bigger picture helps to bring all levels of ourselves to peace with it all, and engenders a hope not founded in the things of this current "world." I know with absolute certainty that all of this is going somewhere beyond what most of us could ever dream of as possible. In Part Two, I will tell you how I arrived at this conclusion, and share what has inspired me to see what is unfolding through very different eyes.

Remember the story about the prokaryotes that began this book? What appeared to be impending species death to the prokaryotes, floating in the ancient seas billions of years ago, was, in truth, the evolutionary catalyst that resulted in the leap to a new species. Thus, the photosynthetically capable cyanobacteria came into being, heralding a new era of evolution on planet Earth. Could something similar be underway right now? And could it be that we are a vital part of that new story? Could it be that the death of the caterpillar is aways the prelude to the birth of the butterfly?

PART TWO

✧ ✧ ✧

Birth Of The Luminous, Human "Butterfly"

✧ ✧ ✧

Introduction

In Part One we looked deeply into the apparent ending of the world as we have known it — a potential extinction event. While we may certainly be facing the ending of our third-dimensional, human "caterpillar" existence, we also know there is never an ending without a corresponding beginning just beyond it. What might it be? What could be next for humanity and planet Earth? What might the journey be like as we pass through and beyond the end of the Anthropocene into a new time we cannot imagine?

As the story becomes ever more compelling, it can be very tempting to limit our focus to the tangible particulars of what is unfolding on planet Earth. The nearly universal human tendency is to view the world through third-dimensional eyes and to form conclusions through our linear, concrete and intellectual minds. From that perspective, there IS nothing else to consider. What we see is what is happening — end of story.

But this way of viewing what is happening on Earth misses a lot. The desire to fully understand all that is going on compels us to shift to a larger context, a level of consciousness that includes and transcends our everyday, five-sensory perspective. It has often been said that no problem is solved at the level at which it exists. In order to grasp what is transpiring on our planet, wouldn't it be logical to shift to the largest context our consciousness can access?

10

A Vaster Perspective

Through A Higher-Dimensional Looking Glass

Third-dimensional evidence insists we have every reason to conclude that we are entering a season of great loss on planet Earth, an era that may even include the demise of the human species. Indeed, countless other species are already rapidly declining in number, if they are not threatened with extinction or already gone. Yet there is another story, one that can only be seen from a greatly expanded viewpoint. In this narrative, some species leave, while others go forward.

This, in fact, has been the saga of evolution on our planet for billions of years. From a Buddhist perspective, we might view this as the long story of the immutable reality of impermanence. If sadness is arising about the inevitable endings that accompany this tale, it might help to remind ourselves that even planets and Suns cease to exist, but the galaxies and universes that contain them go on.

To enter into the realm of this larger story, I'm going to ask you to take a big leap with me. We're going to hold hands and jump out into the unknown — beyond every one of the linear, matter-related phenomena we explored in Part One. Our destination is the biggest, most inclusive context and level of perception we can possibly leap into. How will it all look from out there?

Before we can begin to answer that question, we need to consider another one: What IS the biggest consciousness context we can expand into? Our physical senses and linear, concrete mind and intellect come in very handy here in 3-D, but they have no capacity to sense or experience anything beyond that level of reality. To do that, we need to embark upon an exploration that transcends third-dimensional limits. Throughout human history, religions and spiritual traditions have always reached out beyond what we can see and apprehend with our physical senses to encompass levels of experience that cannot be explained by third-dimensional laws. During recent decades, these metaphysical discoveries have been augmented by equally exciting revelations from quantum physicists, mathematicians, and brain researchers, who understand that the universe has many dimensions and that there may even be other universes. Using the most sophisticated technologies, researchers have microscoped down into the subatomic, quantum, and even subquantum worlds to find a highly articulated, complex reality that becomes less material until it dissolves into energy. Ultimately, it melts into a primal substratum that is more void or emptiness than substance.

Turning our gaze outward, we can peer out into the universe and explore the macro-world beyond our planet. As satellites hurtle toward the edges of the solar system, the images they send back to our tiny planet reveal a universe as boundless and multifaceted as the subatomic realms. Whether we look into the innermost minutiae of matter or out into the endless star fields of space, we encounter no end of mysterious phenomena that bring everything our scientific minds have thought was certain into question.

Cutting-edge scientific opinion and mathematical models tell us that even the immensity of all that we can perceive is but a fraction of what is out there. And that's not all. <u>For models of the universe to work, it must be multidimensional</u>. Superstring theory requires at least ten dimensions, while more recent theories need even more to explain how it all works.

While the still-predominant view of a mechanistic, material causation of the universes lingers, it is fast becoming an obsolete, dying paradigm. Having gone beyond the bounds of traditional science, some quantum and astrophysicists have come to the realization that there must be something -- call it God, Creator, Source, or whatever name resonates — that is the creative beingness behind the multi-verse. One of these is theoretical quantum physicist Amrit Goswami, a retired full professor at the

University of Oregon. In his article, "God Is Not Dead", he states his conviction that there is a God that is the creative source of the universe.

> The real questions, and these are all questions of science, are: (1) Is there causation in the world apart from material interactions? (2) Are there subtle non-material levels of reality? And (3) is there any scientific justification of ethics, which compels us to pursue Godliness in our lives?
>
> Most scientists today squarely say "No" in answer to these questions because they contradict their metaphysics of scientific materialism, according to which there is only matter and its interactions, nothing else is real. In my book, God Is Not Dead, I give answers also, and they are all in the affirmative. Yes, there is God. Because (1) there is an agent of causation apart from material interaction; (2) what we experience internally are subtle non-material worlds; and (3) not only should we pursue Godliness in our lives, our evolution is taking us toward better and better manifestations of Godliness. In my book I back up these assertions with both scientific theory and empirical evidence.

Like Amrit Goswami, other quantum physicists and astrophysicists have come to the same realization that mystics, shamans, and saints from all traditions have experienced since before human history was recorded — that there is an infinitely powerful, intelligent and creative "something" beyond it all that is simultaneously the source and the substratum or fabric of all of Creation. Call it God, Creator, Infinite Intelligence, Brahman, Source, or Allah, all are names given to this presence and beingness. We are not talking about an ancient, white-haired, bearded man in robes, but a "something/someone" so vast, so intelligent, and beyond multidimensional, that we are incapable of perceiving it with our minuscule third-dimensional senses and mind. It can only be apprehended when we transcend the limits of third-dimensional consciousness and enter into the realms of higher-dimensional creation, which are vaster and more inclusive of all that is occurring in the multidimensional universe.

Our own inner experiences of the higher-dimensional, non-physical worlds have convinced us that this is so. During four decades of our own spiritual journeys and thirty years of assisting others to awaken to these inner realms, the reality of an omnipotent, omnipresent, omniscient Presence~Beingness has been validated beyond question for us. This is our reality context, and the rest of the book will be written from that place in consciousness.

This universe is so vast, complex, and exquisitely organized that many of us find our intuition telling us it is improbable that it all came about through happenstance. For anything to exist, something or someone had to "image"ine it, and that inner image is the seed-thought that eventually brings it into existence. What else but a supreme intelligence is capable of creating, sustaining, dissolving and re-creating everything in Creation unceasingly and eternally? We find it impossible to believe that all that we see around us — and our very selves — could be the product of random events.

How does all of this relate to what is transpiring during the first decades of the 21st century on planet Earth? If all that is occurring in the universe, right down to the globe we call home at this very moment, is somehow orchestrated by this supreme intelligence, then the "why" and "what" that motivate this beingness must be at the apex of causality to everything that is going on.

A hint of this is given by the supreme, eternal questions humans have asked throughout history. The Big Questions have always been, *What is God? And what is Its central purpose and motivation, related to our ourselves and our world?* Since many of us do not believe we can ask such questions of God and get answers directly, there must be another way to glean some understanding.

Have you ever considered that the universe is both holographic and fractal? This is important to grasp as we contemplate these big questions. If we accept that each of us is a holographic fractal of the One Great Being (be sure to read the links just above if we're losing you here), then what we are made of must be identical in every respect to the composition of the Divine, even though we exist as a much smaller subset of the fractal matrix of the One. In other words, we need go no further than to deeply examine what motivates us to determine what also motivates the Source Creator.

Now we can loop back to the big questions we've all been asking forever and ever. *Who am I? Why am I here? What is this all about?* If **we** are asking these questions, then God — the one infinite, eternal being with no "other" to consult — must have these same core considerations, since we are made of the exact same stuff as the Divine. And God must possess the same deep desire to answer them that we all feel within ourselves.

Imagine for a moment that you are the only being that is. There is no "other" — nothing external to yourself. At some moment beyond time, you would become aware of the fundamental fact that you exist. Your first realization would be *I AM*. The question that would naturally arise next is *What am I?* And then, *Why am I here? What is this existence all about?*

Seeking answers to these questions is the impetus that began the great play of Creation, the unending dance of Life. The One began to explore itself to come to know its nature and what its existence is all about. This is expressed in various ways in the world's great spiritual traditions. For instance, in Hindu Vedic iconography, the aspects of God called Brahma or Vishnu are often portrayed as lying on a dais, dreaming the dreams of creation into existence. The Christian Bible tells the story of God creating the world in six days, while on the seventh, he rested, contemplating his creation.

So, according to this view, the world as we know it is, in essence, a dream or mind-play of something vast and supreme — that "something" many of us refer to as God or Source. That One creates multidimensional universes, galaxies, solar systems, planets, and the many life-forms that inhabit them, all products of its divine play of self-discovery. Everything in creation is the One exploring itself through its experience in the many universes, from galaxies to planets, and all the species on them, even down to subatomic particles.

Let's take this a step further. As the One created myriad multidimensional universes to experience and explore its nature, it came up with a new possibility to vastly expand its potential for self-knowing. Being a fully-unified One, it could only experience itself from the perspective of that Oneness. What would happen if that unified nature were apparently individualized into innumerable sub-aspects of itself?

Perhaps the One dreamt the dream of countless individualized souls, each one a holographic aspect of God/One/All That Is. This enabled it to project itself through all those souls into its own creation. Instead of simply being the overlighting consciousness above it all, the Divine could now also experience itself from within.

This is the second aspect of the triune nature of God common to many spiritual traditions. The first aspect, the Source or Father aspect, is the overarching intelligence that dreams the myriad dreams of creation. The third aspect is the dark matrix or reflective facet of being, the fabric of creation itself, which is often called the Divine Mother aspect. The second aspect is the fruit of the divine marriage that occurs when Father/Source projects itself within its creation and becomes embodied in physical and subtle forms as individualized souls.

An answer to the primal question that is heard within many religious and spiritual traditions is that God is the great Ocean of Being that is the multiverse, and we are each drops in that Ocean of Being. At the same time, we are also the Ocean of God within the drop of our being. The great, endless exploration of the One to realize its true nature is really the journey of all of its souls to realize this simple truth.

This may sound like a New Age metaphysical idea, but it is not, nor is it recent. Variations of this theme have been recorded since the beginning of history. Its tenets are at the core of many traditional peoples' spirituality; they form the basis of all of the world's great spiritual/religious traditions. This way of looking at life has been called the Perennial Philosophy, which simply states that we are no other than drops in the Ocean of God, and the purpose of our existence is to realize this.

A Grand Experiment

Imagine for a moment the following possibility. A little more than four and a half billion years ago, the Source of all that is created a planet called Earth, a beautiful, watery world upon which its divine play of Self-realization could begin a new chapter. Out of the fabric of the planet, it began to sculpt life forms through which it could manifest and reflect its nature over time. It began by creating the simplest of these forms, the first single-celled, barely sentient organisms such as the prokaryotes.

Slowly the process of evolution unfolded. The single-celled organisms grew and proliferated until, as we learned in Part One, an evolutionary crisis occurred. Through that potential extinction event, Source was able to manifest a new possibility within the realms of life on Earth — the photosynthetic cyanobacteria. The result was a new, higher-order species with more intelligence, more complexity and more capacity than anything that had lived on Earth before.

This same story has been repeated again and again. Species emerge, grow and flourish until an evolutionary crisis is reached, an extinction event unfolds, and out of the ashes rise new, higher-order species. Thus the phylogenic tree unfolded with ever greater complexity and sentience, producing life-forms that were capable of expressing ever more of the life intelligence of Source Creator.

This divine play of Self-realization reached a critical threshold point a mere few million years ago, when a new species appeared that was radically different from all previous species, save possibly the cetaceans. From the great apes and early hominids, a new "homo" species group emerged, which ultimately evolved into Homo sapiens sapiens. This was a major evolutionary leap. The new species had a sufficiently complex subtle and physical anatomy to allow the pure holographic-fractal essence of the One, an individualized divine soul or atman, to be embodied within a third-dimensional form. This opened up the potential for this species to awaken to and realize that the very essence of Source Creator, in its totality, resided within itself as its essential nature.

What incarnated into the early hominids was invisible, immeasurable to biological examination. While a process of physical evolution would follow, the greatest new demonstration was on a psycho-spiritual level. This is the missing link in evolution which will never be discovered on the physical level. That missing link has its basis on the spiritual level, which cannot be measured by even the most diligent scientists. This invisible something that allowed hominids to embody an eternal soul began an entirely new phase of evolution, one that would bring us to the pivotal moment we are now rapidly approaching.

11

The Essential Evolution of Consciousness

Falling Asleep in Matter

When a divine soul or atman — an individualized spark of the One — incarnates into physical, animal form, its consciousness merges with the subhuman, programmed, reactive impulses of the animal nature. The totality of those unconscious reactions, together with survival instincts, need fulfillment, conditioning, and all the biological processes that maintain and sustain life, are the abode of the life intelligence and programming of the Divine Feminine matrix that evolved as the phylogenic tree unfolded. The first divine souls, even though they contained a spark of the infinite light, intelligence, and mind of the One, embedded themselves within the human form, fully merging and identifying with it. They went to sleep to their true nature, fully identifying with the third-dimensional physical body and sensory experience. The story of the "Fall" from the Garden of Eden could be considered an analogous mythology related to this process.

This falling asleep and becoming immersed in the human, animal nature was the necessary beginning of the journey of the divine soul or atman to ultimately realize its full divine nature. The human form became the vehicle through which the various higher qualities, characteristics, and capacities of divinity could slowly be remembered by the soul and realized in daily life, resulting in the psycho-spiritual evolution of the species.

Thus begins the cycle of Self-realization, which starts with the involution of spirit into matter, experiencing itself as a separate, finite beingness. In a way, it is the journey away from the soul's ultimate, undifferentiated unity with God, as it becomes more immersed in matter and individualized existence. This, again, harkens back to the story of the "Fall" in the Garden Of Eden. The soul then explores its beingness until it has manifested a psychic nature that is so highly individualized that it has the capacity to fully incarnate and express the Ocean of God through the drop of its being.

Becoming the Wise Ape

In his classic *Up from Eden*, consciousness researcher and philosopher Ken Wilber lays out the stages of this journey as an evolution of consciousness. The story begins with the first humans, functioning on an almost completely physical level, deeply embedded and identified with the physical body and animal nature. They were hunters and gatherers with minimal impact on nature and a very simple sociocultural world.

As evolution proceeded, human consciousness gradually advanced, gaining increasing understanding of itself and its world. Humans discovered their innate creativity, making basic tools, discovering fire, learning how to elevate their life experience above that of animals. The hunter-gatherer stage of human evolution eventually progressed from its primitive, tribal origins as the mind evolved, becoming increasingly capable of understanding itself and the natural world. Along the way, humanity's capacities to create and transform its world steadily grew more sophisticated.

One of the species' most significant achievements was learning how to grow food. Cultivating the land, rather than relying exclusively on hunting for food, meant that tribes no longer needed to keep moving in search of new sources of sustenance. As tribes settled down and made more permanent homes, they grew into larger communities and then towns. Within these settlements, greater differentiation of responsibilities now occurred, and culture began to unfold. No longer was everyone involved in the rudimentary aspects of survival. The higher, divine nature of the soul had time and energy to manifest in new ways, leading to art, music, architecture, science and all the other predecessors of the complex, technological world we live in today.

With each stage of evolution, the soul expresses more creatively through the human form, bringing forth more of the intelligence, will, power, and love that are central aspects of its nature into the physical, human world. This brings us to the present, the point at which we have reached the final stage of individualizing and embodying in matter, which Wilber calls the mental-egoic stage. Our mental capacities and individualized, egoic abilities allow us to manifest our wills to a very high level, as our sophisticated, techno-industrial world attests.

The Critical Passage In Our Journey

Wilber points to the mental-egoic stage as the most critical — and possibly dangerous — chapter in the long, gradual evolutionary cycle. Why would this be the case? We only need to look around us to see the results of overemphasizing individuality at the expense of remaining aware not only of the needs of all other forms of life but also, most importantly, of one's true nature as an aspect of God/One/Source. As souls focus on highly individualized self-expression, it can be easy for them to lose contact with the larger Whole. The access to higher-dimensional levels of mind can be lost, leaving a limited and fragmented perception of reality. Said another way, the arc souls travel as they develop egoic individuality takes them furthest away from their innate unity with the One. While these highly individualized souls are now capable of great mastery over their environment, they are also veiled in the illusion that they are separate drops of being, physically identified human beings.

On the absolute level, nothing ever truly changes. We are always and forever a drop in the Ocean of God, and the Ocean of God is likewise fully present in the drop of our being. But in our mental-egoic trance, we have gone to sleep to the ocean, thinking we are only the drop. We see ourselves as individual entities, separate from one other, all of nature, and the Source of All That Is. We perceive ourselves to be limited and defined by what we see in the mirror — a physical, third-dimensional being whose existence is exclusively related to and defined by the body. In this state of amnesia, we have lost touch with the infinite will/power, wisdom, and love of the Ocean of Being within which we are but a drop. All the divine qualities, characteristics and capacities that are inherent in our true, eternal nature are diminished, if not forgotten altogether.

Now, we are effectively disconnected from the unified field of organizing life intelligence that orchestrates all of creation, which is mirrored to us by living beings and ecosystems. The ancients used many names to describe this eternal life intelligence, including the "Sanatana Dharma," "the Tao," and "the Way." Life flourishes when our thoughts and actions honor this underlying, interwoven unity. Disconnected from it, we can only damage and destroy life. Perceiving that we are solely physical and temporal, we are quietly haunted by the specter of the end of our existence when the body dies.

Our resultant false sense of self exists in a nearly constant state of fear, most of it subconscious, of what might happen to the body. We can pretend all we want that it/we will not someday die, but deep down inside we all know the truth. Faced with our apparent — yet illusory — vulnerability, impermanence and imperfection, we attempt to sculpt a false self that will serve the role that our soul-awakened state once had. Each soul in forgetting is self-hypnotized into believing *I'm it. I'm in charge. It's up to me.*

An empty, hollow arrogance thinly veils our fear and terror. Spawned by ignorance, it grows like a fatal disease eating away at our insides, threatening all of life. Our conception of ourselves as purely physical beings results in our believing that the boundary of our being ends at the surface of our skin. Thus we see ourselves as separate from all other humans and, for that matter, all forms of life on planet Earth. Conflict, war, and destruction of the biosphere are the inevitable results of this primal, tragic illusion.

Can anyone argue that this is anything other than exactly where we find ourselves now as a species? We view our highest potential as the full expression of the linear, concrete mind and intellect. At this stage of soul evolution, that is the ceiling of our perception and creative interaction. The mental-egoic aspects of our being have taken over so fully that we can travel no further on this vector.

Transcend or Die?

It is becoming ever more obvious that we must go beyond these evolutionary limitations. We must awaken from our sleep of believing we are separate, mortal, limited physical beings. The health and well-being of not only ourselves but all other forms of life may depend on it. Somehow, we must move on to the next stage in the evolution of the soul. But what **is** that phase of the cycle?

Well, if we have moved as far as it is possible to travel away from our inherent unity with God/One/Source, the next step must be to begin the long journey back. It's time for the collective soul of humanity to wake up from its identity with physical matter and form -- time to go beyond seeing our entire context of being as limited to the human, third-dimensional, physical world. As we release our identity with 3-D, physical existence, we automatically awaken to the transcendent and superconscious levels of being. These are the realms of consciousness that lie beyond what the human body~mind perceives and experiences through the senses and intellect. At these levels of consciousness, we again realize that we are souls — multidimensional, divine beings. As we awaken to who and what we really are, we begin to rediscover our innate divine qualities, characteristics and capacities.

The entire first part of this book is a testament to the precipice upon which we find ourselves at this juncture. The single crisis that is causal to all the myriad predicaments we've discussed is a spiritual one. The root of our destruction of the planet through overconsumption and wanton disregard and abuse of life is the dis-ease of soul forgetting. No longer feeling and knowing our fundamental unity with all of life and our Source, the Divine, is the core wound and unfillable emptiness that drives most of our outer actions. We are mired in a deep sense of fear, separation, limitation, lack and doubt. On a conscious level, most of us are not aware of this, but deep within we may feel it as a hole in the center of our being where communion with our true, divine nature is easily and naturally experienced when we are awake to that. Until we reawaken, deep in the unconscious lives a gnawing sense that something is missing; something is wrong about us. However much we try to ignore or suppress this lack of ease, it never fully goes away. But deep within our souls lives the faint, almost totally subconscious memory that we are so much more, and that another experience of being is possible.

This is what causes us to seek. But because we are asleep to our larger, multidimensional nature, our awareness can only turn to the things of the physical world and the senses in its quest to fill the hole in the core of our being. While we can satisfy our basic human needs and enjoy pleasurable experiences within the physical world, the core needs of the soul can never be fulfilled at this level. Thus we find ourselves in an existential dilemma. We seek and seek, and we may find some temporary enjoyment on the material plane, but none of that even begins to touch, much less fill, the void created by our loss of communion with our true, eternal, divine nature.

> Ken Wilber eloquently describes this in *Up From Eden:*
>
> *An individual will create or latch on to a host of external or objective wants, desires, properties and possessions, goods and materials — he searches for wealth, fame, power, and knowledge, all of which he tends to imbue with either infinite worth or infinite desirability. But since it is precisely infinity that men and women truly want, all these external, objective, and finite objects are, again, merely substitute gratifications. They are substitute objects, just as the separate self is a substitute subject.*

There is no greater loss, no greater pain, no greater need than to fill this hole with the vastness and depth of our true, divine nature. But we seek for our soul in all the wrong places, and are unable to release our false identity as the solely physical human ego-personality. This sets up the ultimate double bind. While we deeply yearn for our transcendent, divine nature — our true, eternal Self — we are attached to and identified with our physical, human self sense. We desperately cling to this limiting, false identity, because we are sure this is who we are. To let go of this illusory, egoic self sense is perceived as an existential threat — no less than the death of one's self. If anything destroys us as a species it may be this double bind. Will we be able to drop our separate ego self sense in time to prevent this illusion from destroying the planet?

> Ken Wilber articulates this fundamental double bind in *Up From Eden*:
>
> *Now according to the perennial philosophy, the rediscovery of this infinite and eternal Wholeness (oneness) is man's single greatest need and want. For not only is Atman (God/One) the basic nature of all souls, each person knows or intuits that this is so. Yet notice immediately*

that men and women are faced with a truly fundamental dilemma: above all else, each person wants transcendence, Atman consciousness, and the ultimate Whole; but, above all else, each person fears the loss of the separate self, the "death" of the isolated ego. All a person wants is his wholeness, but all he does is fear and resist (since that would entail the "death" of a separate self). And there is a dilemma, the double bind in the face of eternity.

Anyone who has walked any significant distance on the spiritual path has come to realize the truth in what Wilber is saying, through their own inner journey. The thirst for Self and God propels us to seek, and at the same time we find ourselves distracted and obstructed by the separated ego self sense that does not want to die. The ego has most human beings so entranced in the dance of the senses and the body-mind that there is little to no possibility of finding what it truly seeks in the transcendent levels of being.

This, however, is changing rapidly. The physical and metaphysical dynamics of our little locus in the universe are going through a great shift. The extinction crises we face are but a small manifestation of its symptoms. We will discuss many more later. Together, they will catalyze the shift of the ages that has long been prophesied by many spiritual traditions.

The journey of the collective human soul is about to make the biggest shift in its entire exploration of embodiment. Our core divine nature is beginning to stir, for it is time for this to happen in this great evolutionary drama. The inner light of divine presence in the soul's core is awakening — moving, expanding, radiating more powerfully.

As Wilber states, we fervently seek an existence that is so much more than we have known, but we think we will fill that need by becoming more beautiful, powerful, wealthy, or famous as a human being. Our egoic self sense causes us to compulsively look for whatever is more, better, and different in the material world. The growth we seek materially is a false substitute for the spiritual awareness for which we truly thirst. We are called to transcend our limited, human, egoic identification and re-awaken to ourselves as souls. Only this will assuage the desperate, gnawing pain of the void in the core of our being.

Eco-death or Ego-death?

Al Gore once said, "We are addicted to consuming the planet." His statement points to a basic truth. We will never stop seeking false, unsatisfying substitutes for what is real and true if we do not wake up to our spiritual dilemma. There will never be enough more, better, or different fascinations in the physical world to fill the hole in the center of our being. Our dis-ease is one of the soul. Until we realize this we will never solve our problems "out there."

The hallowed paradigm of continual economic and material growth is but another misplaced yearning. It expresses the need to expand into some new experience of being, but the next generation iPhone, a smart car, or even a smart home isn't the real "it." The growth we seek is at a spiritual level. We can grow there infinitely, while the planet is strongly telling us we cannot keep doing so at a finite, material level.

Because we are identified with the mental-egoic level of evolution, we humans keep telling ourselves that we are intelligent and creative enough to solve all our crises using our ingenuity. We attempt to convince ourselves that our minds can produce the technology that will not only save us, but create an Edenic existence on this planet. This is the cul-de-sac of being stuck at the mental-egoic level. It's the highest level of soul consciousness we have realized, but it is now a consciousness ceiling that we must, and ultimately will, transcend.

As we saw in Part One, the fact that our mental, creative capacities are untethered to our souls constitutes the source of the myriad crises we face. Our human, egoic minds created this vast, complex, techno-industrial culture, and it has now brought us into the event horizon of extinction. Yes, we've gone to the moon, extended life expectancy, and provided more material comfort for many, but are we, as souls, any more happy, content and loving? Have we transcended the hatred and separation that foment countless wars, genocides, and eco-annihilations? Are we able to live in balance and sustainability with the rest of life? Everything we've delineated in Part One would indicate that this is not the case. We are at a pivotal moment. It is either Ego Death or Eco Death. Will our species wake up in time?

12

The Gift of Facing Death

"Our Crisis is a Birth"

I love this statement from Barbara Marx Hubbard because it expresses a truth that transcends all sense of doom and gloom. Remember our little friends the prokaryotes? Our species currently finds itself in a similar predicament. They, like us, faced possible extinction when they reproduced beyond the sustaining capacities of their environment. Although the prokaryotes had no idea what was going on around them, their imminent death was a definite possibility, as is ours. But way back then, just as is true today, there was a larger picture unfolding — one that went far beyond the tiny lives of the prokaryotes, a context that encompasses the planet, solar system, and so much more.

And we humans differ in one core respect from the prokaryotes: the essence of our evolutionary impulse is spiritual, not material. We are asked as a species to wake up and remember that we are eternal, divine, multidimensional souls, temporarily incarnate in human, physical forms. That awakening requires us to die to the illusion that we are separate, human ego-personalities. And what better evolutionary matrix to catalyze awakening than facing extinction?

The Grace of Facing Death

The false, human self sense is based in body-identification. When we believe we are our physical forms, which are sure to die, our deepest, most fundamental fear becomes the fear of death. This is the Achilles heel of our egos, for ego is synonymous with body-identification. The death of the body equals the death of the ego, and our false self sense will do whatever it takes to remain alive and in control. Anything that presents the possibility of death, even in our minds, results in a variety of ego-defenses including aggression, denial, overwhelm, and hopelessness.

All of this explains why we live in such a death-denying culture, infatuated with perpetual youth. We desperately evade the reality that physical death will happen to us — yes, our very own selves — although that denial is obviously ludicrous. Even when a terminal diagnosis arrives, most of us mindlessly pursue any treatment option that offers even a slight chance of prolonging life, no matter how degraded its quality may become. Those closest to the person dying collude in looking at the bright side, keeping conversations upbeat, touting the latest miraculous treatment or drug, and above all, never mentioning the greatest taboo — the D word. In our death-denying culture, vast resources are allocated to extending the lifespans of those who are dying, even while that added time is often imbued with far more suffering than a peaceful, natural passing would have been.

Thus, death denial is at the very bottom of all our egoic defenses. What lies beneath all other, more superficial fears? The fear of death. Facing this fear offers the greatest opportunity for popping the bubble of denial, which results in ego death. When we truly face death, we can no longer avoid facing the loss of all the outer, material props, as well as the inner, psychological ones, that hold our human identity together. We come into this world with nothing and we leave the same way. No matter how beautiful, wealthy, famous, intelligent, educated, and talented we may be....all is meaningless in the end. The deepest anchor of our self sense, the body, is going to turn to dust. As we face and embrace this stark truth, the ego finds itself dissolving into the nothingness it always was.

As the ego is shredded, more consciousness becomes available to investigate the questions that really matter. *What becomes of "me" after death? Is there anything beyond this material realm?* As our minds and hearts consider these pressing issues, our consciousness expands beyond our egoic identification and all that we have ever known. Many on the threshold of leaving this world find this happening right before the death of the body. The veils between the dimensions thin, allowing us to see loved ones, angels, and divine beings whose homes are in the higher worlds.

But we do not need to wait until we are on the verge of leaving this world to receive reassurance that life goes on after the death of the body. One of the most compelling collective testaments that not only assuages our fear of death but also reminds us of what lies beyond physical embodiment comes from those who have died and, against all odds, have come back to earthly life. The experiences they share are often called NDEs, or near-death experiences — a label that, like so much that surrounds the subject of death, reflects our collective unwillingness to accurately name what has happened. In truth, these people have literally and actually died — and lived to tell the tale.

The experiences of those who have died and been "reborn" contain an astounding number of commonalities, independent of age, religion, gender or cultural differences. The vast majority report that, at the moment the heart stopped and breathing ceased, they entered a state of peace, bliss, and love unlike anything they had ever experienced on Earth. As they looked down at their physical forms, they became aware that they were the soul that had left the body and was now independent of it. Seeing the body as a separate object, they knew they were not that inert form. More, they nearly universally report experiencing a detachment from and indifference to what was going on with the body, even if it had been seriously damaged through trauma or illness. Instead, they were drawn toward the transcendent worlds, where many encountered loved ones who had previously died, and/or met divine beings. All were given the understanding that it was not their time to remain in the exalted realms they were visiting; their purposes on Earth had not yet been fulfilled, and they were encouraged to return. No one ever wants to do that. Many grieved over the necessity of leaving the heaven-realms, even while they accepted their "assignment" on Earth was not yet complete.

Most of those who have died and returned find that their awareness is greatly expanded; they now experience earthly life from a much more illumined state of consciousness. They are more loving and compassionate, less materialistic and more generous with their time and resources. Many state that they now know for sure that love is all that matters here. In effect, they have been sprung free from their former egoic context, and their fear of death is gone. Nearly all look forward to the time that this life will be over and they can return to the heavenly domains, where they know pain and suffering do not exist and life goes on forever.

The good news about these "death" experiences is that we do not need to physically die to experience this sort of transformation. What people experience when their consciousness lifts out of the physical form is a level of communion with their true, eternal Self or soul. This is available to each one of us while we are still on Earth. In fact, we've been facilitating such experiences for thirty years. We know that when the time is right, nothing can stop any of us from reconnecting with who and what we truly are.

This experience is not "out there" somewhere in a nebulous future. It is available right here and now. Is it time for you to wake up and directly experience the love, joy, happiness, peace, and fulfillment you long for? The first step is to admit that you truly want this more than anything else. Then, realize you won't find it "out there" — you can only find it by turning within, where the Self that you are always, already resides.

As we watch the tangible, outer world disintegrating before our eyes, something very different is happening on the inner, invisible levels: the spiritual energy on Earth is rising. A potent influx of higher-dimensional energies is already stirring our souls to come to the surface of our consciousness. Every day, more human-identified souls know it is time to awaken and return to their true nature. And just before our world looks likely to hit a Seneca Cliff, a massive spiritual awakening is taking place all across the globe. Suddenly, people who have never before explored the spiritual realms find themselves mysteriously drawn to things like mind-expanding hallucinogenic substances, meditation, past life regression, and traditional and new age spiritual paths. These and a myriad of other spiritual avenues serve to propel them beyond their previously held mental limits. There has never been an easier time to awaken than now.

But for those who are not yet prompted toward spiritual investigation, or those who are ignoring such inner impulses, life goes on as it has, with little impetus to change. When we are living as human beings, identified with the egoic self, we can read all day about what is unfolding all around us, yet remain in denial. It's as though we are wearing blinders that block out what is actually happening, and no amount of evidence will sway our conviction that those who talk about the approaching Seneca Cliff are deluded, want to control us, or any of a host of other rationales for turning a deaf ear to anything that has the potential to shake us out of our complacency. Never mind that we are facing the possibility of planetary extinction. *What can I do today to make more money, buy the latest item I'm craving, or improve my status?*

This rampant denial explains why world leaders endlessly put off any concerted action on climate change; why we sit back and do nothing as our oceans warm and acidify, killing the coral reefs, the rain forests of the ocean. Denial is why even the direst reports of accelerating species extinction do nothing to snap us to our senses. Subconsciously, it's simply too terrifying to look at where things really are.

These looming events will certainly continue to make their presence known, even while we collectively go on consuming more. It sometimes seems we humans will do anything to avoid facing the ultimate fact of earthly life: impermanence. No matter how affluent some of us might be, "the skull always grins in at the banquet," as Ken Wilber so starkly puts it. The specter of our impermanence is grinning at us every day as the weather becomes ever more erratic and intense, as financial woes threaten the false affluence of the stock markets, and as exotic species like elephants, chimpanzees, lions, and tigers disappear, along with the bees and butterflies in our own backyards. As the web of life collapses, with extinction rates 1,000 to 10,000 times higher than normal, we may no longer be able to avoid the one thing that all human-identified souls dread facing: death, in any and all of its forms, especially our own.

All of this is more than an inconvenient reality to be escaped at all costs. If Barbara Marx Hubbard is correct that our crisis is a birth, we can reframe everything that is unfolding. These crises are not accidental, coincidental or even solely the result of our own collective ignorance; instead, they are meant to serve as evolutionary drivers — mirroring our state of consciousness, perhaps even providing a karmic rebalancing of massive proportions. The hidden gift of facing extinction is that the very act of releasing our denial has the capacity to stimulate awakening, individually and collectively.

At some point in the not too distant future, it is quite possible that we will reach a critical mass of collective awareness that our species is in overshoot and collapse. We may realize that we will not be able to fix it, stop it, or avoid it. We may even wake up to the fact that it is we, ourselves, who largely caused the situation. Then, instead of continuing to look out there for the way through, we will collectively turn inward to inquire what **in us** is the cause of our malaise. This kind of introspection reveals our false, egoic self, and is the path to awakening. We are made aware that the source of our suffering is never "out there" — the roots lie within ourselves.

The question is, will we reach the bottom of our materialistic ego-addictions in time to recover and discover a new way of being? Until enough of us realize that our own inner soul disease is the real problem, we don't have much of a chance. Think of alcoholics or drug addicts who are in denial, unwilling to admit they have a problem. Nothing can change until they confess they are helpless in the face of their substance of choice. In 12-step programs, the first step is to realize you have an overwhelming problem. The second step is to admit you're powerless to save yourself. The next steps are to realize that you need help from a Higher Power, and to turn to the Divine and your Higher Self for that assistance.

For millennia, spiritual teachers, gurus and adepts have been teaching the same basic philosophy that 12-step programs put forth. As the Buddha said, believing we are the body is the prime ignorance that causes all delusion and suffering. There is one sure ticket beyond the evolutionary crisis we face: to know that we are eternal, divine souls, not human, ego-identified beings. The purification that is just beginning has an infinite, loving intelligence behind it that will employ a new form of natural selection — only those who have awakened to their true nature as souls will advance into the incoming New Age.

13

Prophesies of a Great Evolutionary Leap

The Ancients Knew

When we witness the polluting, life-annihilating way of being that has become epidemic on our planet, and mourn the resultant destruction of the biosphere and loss of species, we may conclude that our current crises have nothing to do with what has come before. Yet those with eyes to see and hearts to listen with have known for some time that this era was coming, although what they inwardly saw and felt was shocking and antithetical to their own ways of living in harmony with all of life. For centuries, even millennia, prophets within many traditions and cultures have foretold a time when humanity would go through a major death and rebirth process.

One of the most famous is the Hopi prophecy, which foretells the end of the Fourth World and the birth of a new cycle of human existence, the Fifth World. The Hopi call this an "Emergence," a spiritual rebirth. According to their tradition, the world has experienced cataclysm on three other occasions, the last being a great flood. They say that we are already in the beginning of the next cataclysm, which will come by fire.

The essence of the journey into the Fifth World is inscribed on a boulder called Prophecy Rock near Old Oraibi, at the sacred heart of Hopi land in northern Arizona. The picture depicts two paths, one that leads to the New World and the other, to destruction. Hopi prophecy states that only the single-hearted humans will make it to the New World, while the two-hearted will perish. What might this mean?

One interpretation is that the two-hearted are those who worship themselves and their material possessions over the great Creator. Their focus is literally split between the Divine and worldly concerns. They may pay lip service to what is holy and sacred, but what they do and how they live reflect what really matters to them — earthly, materialistic values. In contrast, the single-hearted exist in a state of oneness with the Divine, living God's will and not their own. They surrender egoic preoccupations as they arise and do their best to live according to the higher will of the One.

Here's an example of how it looks to be single-hearted in daily life. The Hopi people have long practiced traditional, hands-on farming in harsh, arid conditions. This requires them to be deeply in touch with the promptings of Spirit on when and how to plant, raise, and harvest their crops. Modern methods of irrigation and chemical fertilizing would make their job easier and possibly provide a more abundant harvest, but they stick to the old ways. Their connection with the great Creator is more important than crop yields or other parameters. Using the traditional farming methods inspired by the Divine is central to the Hopi way of life.

Most of us have heard about the end of the Mayan calendar in 2012, but may not be aware that the lesser-known Cherokee rattlesnake prophecy and Aztec prophecies also focalized around the same date. All of these predictions pointed to a date when the transition in the Ages would begin, but this window in time was not necessarily when, as has been commonly believed, the great cataclysmic changes would occur. Nonetheless, these messages all pointed to the end of an age, a time of great crisis and the birth of a new human era.

Some prophecies specifically discuss the nature of the new human that will emerge out of the destruction. The Dogon tribes of Africa believe we will soon be uniting with our space brothers, who will help us go to a new level of consciousness. Incan prophecies indicate we will pass through a "Crack in Time" into a new dimension of reality. In recent times, Q'ero shamans have descended from seclusion high in the Andes to tell us that our materialistic ways are destroying the planet. They also state humanity is in the process of birthing a new, higher-dimensional species they call Homo Luminous.

Many of the world's great spiritual traditions look to this as a time of great crisis, but also the time of great awakening. The Bible contains more prophetic passages predicting upheaval at the end of the age than any other major religious text. Hindus point to these times as the end of the cycle of ages, including the final age in the cycle, the Kali Yuga. The last age in the cycle is a time when humanity is most asleep. During the Age of Iron, humanity has completely forgotten its true nature and faces self-destruction as a result. At the end of the Kali Yuga, there is always a time of great destruction called the Mahakranta, or great crisis, in which the planet is cleared of the distortions of the previous age, including those humans who are of "evil" heart.

Recent calculations on the end of Kali Yuga by Bibhu Dev Misra point to 2025 as the time the great purification will culminate, with the birth of the new age of the Dwapara Yuga. Misra correlated the beginning of the current great cycle of the Mayan Long Count Calendar with the most agreed-upon date of the beginning of Kali Yuga, then determined the length of Kali Yuga through correlating many age-duration calculations from various cultures and religions to arrive at this date. He also shows evidence of previous cycles of destruction at the ends of bygone ages to further justify his calculations. If Misra is right, we are within a decade of the shift of the ages.

The Hindu tradition also points to this as the time when the tenth and last incarnation of Vishnu, their Christ-like figure, is to appear on Earth as the Kalki Avatar. After millions of years of Vishnu avatars, the appearance of the final one marks the time of the collective human awakening to its true nature.

The Jews await their Messiah, while Muslims anticipate their personal savior, the Imam Mehdi. Buddhists expect the Maitreya Buddha to descend to Earth within the next few hundred years, and, as we know, Christians are preparing for the second coming of Christ.

Biblical Prophesies

Hidden within the final book of the Bible, the Book of Revelations, are the proclamations of the seventh angel, which reveal not only the "end times," but a new era in which the Earth will shift into a higher dimension in which humanity is awakened and all exist within a Christ-conscious world.

In Revelations 10, verses 5 and 6, the seventh angel reveals this time of a dimensional shift:

> *and the angel I saw standing on the sea and on the land LIFTED UP HIS RIGHT HAND TO HEAVEN, AND SWORE BY HIM WHO LIVES FOREVER AND EVER, WHO CREATED HEAVEN AND THE THINGS IN IT, AND THE EARTH AND THE THINGS IN IT, AND THE SEA AND THE THINGS IN IT, that time shall be no more.*

The classic interpretation of this verse is that God is declaring the end of time and the onset of the great cataclysms, which is certainly one of the chief messages of Revelations. But deeper meanings reveal themselves when we consider this passage in a different light. The Lamsa version of the Bible, which was derived from the language Christ spoke, Aramaic, replaces "time shall be no more" with "there shall be no more **reckoning** [our emphasis] of time."

Meditating upon the Lamsa version of this passage, it became clear to me that that there is great significance in the idea that we will no longer be able to reckon or perceive time. At present, we live in a world defined by three dimensions of space. The fourth dimension is time, which delineates the next dimension beyond us. We might call 4-D **space–time**. Beings operating at a fourth-dimensional or higher level of consciousness do not perceive time as a linear phenomenon. They live in the eternal Now, a characteristic of the awakened state. Highly awakened beings transcend time altogether, and can not only access what happened in the past, but also see into the future. Some play with slowing or stopping the aging process, or time itself, while others confound the expectations of those living within 3-D by appearing in two or more locations simultaneously.

While such abilities have been rare for millennia, they may become commonplace during the era of awakening to come. Further testimony to the idea that humanity will be living in an awakened state arrives in the next verse of Revelations 10:

> ... but in the days of the voice of the seventh angel, when he is about to sound, then the mystery of God shall be finished/fulfilled (depending on the translation).

The seventh angel seems to be intimating that, as we shift into a higher-dimensional existence, there will be no more mystery as to our relationship with God. It will be "finished" — the promise "fulfilled." The search for God will at last come to an end as we penetrate the veils of separation that have surrounded Earth and humanity for so long. At last we will realize our inherent oneness — often called the **atonement** — with God.

The prophecies delivered by the seventh angel imply an end to the illusion of separation, the fundamental source of all dis-ease, suffering, conflict and pain on Earth. When we live in conscious unity with All That Is, we become incapable of harming anything or anyone. We act in accordance with the unified intelligence that pervades all of Creation. Conscious of our innate, divine nature, we rediscover capacities heretofore dormant, such as the ability to experience truly unconditional love, and to create with the limitless intelligence that is in complete alignment with the will and power of the One. This is a definition of Self-realization or Christ consciousness: the ability to see beyond the veils that perpetuate the illusion that we are separate from our true Self, one another, all of Creation and our divine Source. In that all-knowing state, the mystery of God is finished, over and done, for what seemed an inscrutable puzzle is now crystal clear. Now we know beyond all doubt that we are one with the One Great Being, an inextricable, eternal aspect of God.

This awakening implies the death of the separated ego, the source of all suffering and the origin of the existential crisis our species now faces. The Bible assures us that the very issue that has brought about all that now threatens the Earth and all forms of life is going to be resolved. It will be transcended through a great awakening into a higher-dimensional state of existence in which there is **only** conscious union with God/One/ All That Is. In this world to come, everyone is awakened to their true nature. Doesn't this sound like an Edenic existence, a true heaven on Earth?

      This is the luminous possibility that awaits us beyond the apparent impending crises and cataclysms at the end of time. Beyond the veil of third-dimensional, physical existence lies a higher-dimensional world that awaits our discovery. Are we ready to, as the Incas foretold, pass through the crack in time?

14

Signs of an Evolutionary Leap

If, as prophecies have promised, a new, luminous human species will be emerging within the next few decades, surely there must be signs that would validate this possibility. In this chapter, I will present strong evidence that we are already in the process of making this evolutionary leap. Recent physical events on our planet and beyond point to the fact that this evolutionary shift is underway, and that it will probably culminate during the handful of decades to come. What are these changes, and what might they portend for humanity and our world?

Magnetic Reversal

Most of us know that the Earth is surrounded by a magnetic field with magnetic poles that are near, but not on, the north and south rotational poles of the planet. The geomagnetic field acts like a womb or protective envelope around the Earth that prevents most potentially harmful solar and cosmic radiation from penetrating down to the planet's surface, where we live. Radiation from space would cause many illnesses and even genetic mutations if we weren't shielded by the Earth's magnetic field. We take this cocoon of protection for granted because it is almost always there. Our magnetic field is a *nearly* constant presence around the globe, but at specific times it diminishes and even briefly disappears.

When does that occur, you might wonder? It happens during something called geomagnetic reversals. This information gains relevance in light of recent changes in the Earth's geomagnetic poles and magnetic field. Some researchers estimate the strength of the field has been declining for somewhere between 500 and 1200 years. Actual measurements were taken beginning in the mid-1800s. From then until around 2000, the strength of the field dropped by 10%, which means we were at less than 90% of our normal magnetic field strength at the turn of the new millennium, adding in the presumed loss over a 500-year period.

The really important point to grasp here is that the *rate* at which the field declined has *increased* during the 150 years between 1850 and 2000, which indicates the speed of the decline is something to pay attention to. From 2000 to 2010, the magnetic field north declined another 5%, which is nearly ten times faster than the previous rate. The speed at which the magnetic field is weakening is accelerating rapidly, on an exponential curve. This may well signal that something bigger is underway: a geomagnetic reversal.

Until recently, the possibility of a magnetic pole flip wasn't discussed much, even in scientific literature. This changed when Rune Floberghagen, the ESA Swarm mission manager, noted the rapid decline and admitted that a magnetic reversal was likely to occur. The ESA Swarm project utilizes three spacecraft to study the Earth's magnetic field and is the most advanced and accurate attempt at analysis to date. The rapid changes are now being noted by those whose mission it is to monitor the Earth's geomagnetic field. Although the above evidence seems compelling, virtually no published scientific sources even discuss the possibility that a geomagnetic pole reversal could happen any time soon. Many researchers say the field is weakening, and some predict a magnetic pole shift, but not for hundreds or thousands of years.

The most widely accepted theories insist magnetic reversals take a very long time. There is, however, a lot of evidence to indicate that these theories may not be correct, and that, in fact, magnetic reversals can happen within the span of a human life. A 2014 study "by a team of scientists from Italy, France, Columbia University and the University of California, Berkeley, demonstrates that the last magnetic reversal 786,000 years ago actually happened very quickly, in less than 100 years – roughly a human lifetime."

We are already within those parameters, since we know the field began to decline 150 years ago. As you will read later, other geological evidence indicates the rate at which reversal can occur accelerates rapidly as time progresses toward the moment of the reversal. This seems to be happening right now on planet Earth.

Projecting the acceleration of the rate of change, it is possible that the reversal could occur in the not too distant future. To see what the exponential rate of magnetic field decline looks like in animated graphic form, I suggest you visit Magnetic-Reversal.org, and activate the video link at the very top of the page. You will observe the rapidly accelerating decline in the field, and with a little mental projection of the direction of that curve, you will see for yourself that the zero point is most likely to occur prior to 2030. I've done the math myself and come up with the same result. The graph is contained in a blog post I wrote entitled "The Magnetic Reversal and the Birth of Homo Luminous." This piece also contains in-depth information on how magnetic reversal affects the birth of the new species.

While the magnetic field intensity is declining at a rapid rate, the magnetic poles are zooming away from where they had been for thousands of years, confirming that we are in a magnetic reversal or at least a magnetic excursion. In an excursion, the process does not go to completion, but eventually reverts to the previous field strength and pole positions.

The north magnetic pole is moving more rapidly than the south pole, and its rate of change is of the same order of magnitude as the loss of magnetic field strength. North magnetic pole had been over northern Canada for a long time, and is now rushing toward Siberia. The rate at which all of this is occurring has led many scientists to realize that the Earth's magnetic poles are most likely in the process of reversing. When that occurs, the Earth's magnetic field drops to nearly zero.

From the standpoint of our third-dimensional, human experience this can be a very big issue. As mentioned above, the magnetosphere protects us from incoming solar and cosmic radiation. If the magnetic field continues to weaken, a lot of that radiation is going to cascade down upon all living things on the surface of the planet. Ionizing radiation will have ramifications for human health and for much of the rest of life on this planet. We know radiation causes cancer, impacts the immune system, causes neurological disorders, and eventually creates genetic mutations. That last factor may turn out to be the potential gift and ultimate role of the inpouring cosmic energy in what lies ahead. If a new species is to be born, the genetics will need to mutate to create it. More on that later.

Ample geological evidence indicates previous magnetic reversals have resulted in extreme weather events, rapid global warming or cooling, earthquakes, and vulcanism. We'll dive further into this below. For more info, you might want to watch the video entitled, "<u>5 Truths About Earth's Magnetic Reversal</u>." You will find many links to other videos about magnetic reversal on the same page.

As we prepare this book for printing, some important information has just surfaced. First, here's a bit of background. Since magnetic fields aren't expected to rapidly change, the World Magnetic Model is normally updated every five years. The next update on the geomagnetic field condition is scheduled for 2019. During the interim periods, the models that project future trends are assumed to be adequate. However, <u>a notice was just released indicating the model projections are no longer valid</u>, as the rate of change has exceeded model projections. This confirms that the loss of field strength and shifting of the poles is speeding up. For a concise explanation of what is transpiring, watch this <u>Suspicious Observers video beginning at 2:03</u>.

Solar Events

Yet another evolution-catalyzing situation is now unfolding. It centers on the Sun and the energy it releases into our solar system. From time to time, solar flares and CMEs (coronal mass ejections) spew forth huge amounts of ionizing radiation, which streams into our magnetosphere, usually around the poles. This radiation creates the aurora borealis, with its beautiful displays of light and color, in the upper atmosphere of the higher latitudes.

As the magnetosphere declines, more of that radiation will be pouring into the Earth's atmosphere. It will immediately impact all satellites orbiting the globe, affecting communication and the other monitoring functions they perform. As the field continues to weaken, that radiation is going to penetrate to the planet's surface, where all of our electronics are. As the Earth is rapidly unshielded, a large solar flare or CME could easily damage or destroy the microprocessor-based technology we humans count on. That could mean goodbye to computers, cell phones, and the Internet, along with virtually all transportation, food distribution, and manufacturing. If the solar event were strong enough, or the magnetic field were very weak, it could take down the power grids themselves.

This may sound like wild speculation, but it's actually happened before. The so-called **Carrington event** occurred in 1859, before humans had developed such a sophisticated global network of electronics. Massive releases of energy from large Sunspots cascaded down to the Earth's surface, despite the fact that the magnetic field was 15 to 20% stronger than it is today. The only major electrical devices in use at the time were telegraphs. As the sky took on a crimson hue over parts of the planet, telegraph communications went down in many places, and in some instances, transmission lines caught on fire.

If a similar event were to occur today, the results would be catastrophic. A Carrington-type event, on top of everything else humanity is facing, has the potential to push us toward a point of no return. A lot depends on how widespread the damage is. If it were localized, the chances are far greater that we'd be able to repair the grid in those areas and carry on as usual. But if the solar event affected a huge swath of the globe, would our financial, energy, and raw material resources be sufficient to reestablish what had been decimated?

A larger question is *would that return to "normal" even be in the highest for humanity?* As we consider the larger context of our species' evolution toward a whole new level of being, we have to ask ourselves what might need to happen to expedite that. Could the destruction of the grid, and all that goes with that, act as a major — if not essential — catalyst in the process of breaking down the old reality matrix so a new one can unfold?

The changes in the Earth's magnetosphere are only the first level of a series of larger-scale changes that extend beyond our small blue planet. The Sun is also experiencing significant changes that have a great bearing on our planet.

Changes in the Sun

Let's telescope back out into space and consider a few more facts about the star we call our Sun. That fiery ball may be 93 million miles away from every one of us, but it has the most significant influence on everything that occurs on our planet and in our lives. While Earth's magnetic field is declining and its poles are shifting, the Sun is also going through some changes. Our star is becoming quiet. The number of Sunspots has declined significantly over the last decade or so, causing some scientists to suspect that we may be entering something akin to a new Maunder Minimum, the period between 1645-1715 when Sunspots and CMEs declined to nearly zero. But while flaring is decreasing, the coronal holes which have typically opened up near the Sun's poles are now becoming larger and more widespread. Coronal holes are breaches of the heliosphere through which the inner realms of the Sun are made visible. They appear on photos as dark spots, letting us know that contrary to our imaginings, the Sun is not fiery-hot all the way through, but rather just on its surface. As coronal holes open, high-energy particles and other forms of radiation are emitted into the solar system.

We might think that a solar minimum offers a certain amount of reassurance that we are in a safer time, with less possibility of a solar event causing havoc on Earth. But as it turns out, solar minima do not necessarily mean that large, X class solar flares or CMEs will not happen. In fact, the solar burst that caused the Carrington event occurred during such a time.

Yet another solar phenomenon is not being discussed anywhere in scientific circles or the media, but many of us who have been on the planet for a few decades are well aware of it. In the 1950s and 60s, when I was growing up, the Sun had a distinctly golden yellow color. As teenagers, we thought nothing of lying out in the Sun; we didn't know we were being exposed to x-rays for hours on end. We may have gotten Sunburns, but we did not feel uncomfortable in any other way. During the past couple of decades, the color of the Sun is becoming almost pure white, and its radiation literally *feels* stronger. We no longer find ourselves happily basking in its rays; in fact, we take cover whenever possible. This intensifying experience of the Sun's rays could at least partially be caused by the declining magnetic field. But we wonder if other factors are involved. In case you're wondering, I'm not the only one who has noticed this. Google

"Sun is white no longer yellow" or something similar and you will find numerous articles and videos that discuss this. Is this yet another sign that is related to the evolutionary shift on Earth?

Changes on Other Planets and Beyond

The Earth's weakening magnetic field and wandering magnetic poles, along with the Sun's changes, are significant enough, but the story doesn't stop there. The forces driving the next stage of our species' evolution may originate even further out — from the solar system and beyond. Russian scientist Alexei Dmetriev has published numerous papers that confirm important changes are occurring on many of the other planets in our solar system. For instance, dark spots on the surface of furthest-out Pluto have unexpectedly increased. Neptune's magnetic field has experienced a 50° shift. On Uranus, there has been a similar magnetic axis shift, as well as a large uptick in the intensity of its magnetic field. The rings around Saturn have become more numerous and more brightly colored. Jupiter's magnetic field has nearly doubled in less than twenty years, and a tube of glowing plasma energy is flowing between the giant planet and one of its moons, Io. The density of the atmosphere of Mars has increased 200% in the last ten years, and a cloudy area has been observed near the equatorial zone. Observations of Venus indicate a substantial decrease in sulfur-containing gases, a reversal in the areas of light and dark spots, and an increase in the planet's overall brightness.

All of this would seem to indicate forces bigger than those affecting the planet and the Sun are at work. This expands our context once again, but we're not done yet. The heliosphere, the magnetic field that surrounds the entire solar system, is also going through changes. Think of the heliosphere as similar to the magnetosphere around Earth, on a far larger scale. It is the solar system's shield, protecting everything within it from radiation streaming in from deep space. Its leading edge, called the heliopause, has grown significantly in the last fifty years or so.

As the solar system moves through space, it creates something termed a bowshock. To visualize this, envision what happens when a boat moves through water; a buildup of water occurs at the bow. The increase in the intensity of the heliopause's bowshock seems to indicate the solar system is moving into a part of the galaxy with a higher energetic potential —

or a wave of increased energy is moving into the solar system. Now we are adding another layer of potential causation to what is occurring in the solar system, on the Sun, and on Earth. Where would this higher-intensity energy be coming from? For this answer, we need to look further out to the next organizational level we exist within — the Milky Way galaxy.

Galactic Superwaves

If something is happening at a galactic level that is creating effects on the Sun, the planets in our solar system, and the heliopause, what might that be? Some researchers are fascinated by such big-picture phenomena, and Paul LaViolette is one of them. In particular, LaViolette is known for his writings about periodic "Galactic Superwave events" that have the potential to greatly affect life on our planet.

The theories he has introduced are considered by mainstream scientists to be fairly radical, but some are being increasingly validated by other research. And LaViolette's own track record is impressive. Paul LaViolette was the first to assert that high-intensity volleys of cosmic ray particles strike our planet from distant parts of the galaxies. He also pioneered in discovering high concentrations of cosmic dust in Ice Age polar ice samples, indicating the occurrence of a global cosmic catastrophe in ancient times. Based on this work, he predicted the entry of interstellar dust into our solar system ten years before its confirmation in 1993 by data from the Ulysses spacecraft and by radar observations from New Zealand. Clearly, LaViolette has generated some proven insights into the dynamics of our galaxy. In *Earth Under Fire*, he presents his theory of Galactic Superwaves in depth.

So what are Galactic Superwaves? Imagine immense waves of energy, charged particles, and cosmic dust and debris that are thrust from the galactic center during a galactic core explosion. It has been known for some time that a certain class of galaxies, called Seyfert galaxies, undergoes periodic galactic core explosions, resulting in vast waves of energy, charged particles, and cosmic dust being ejected radially from the galactic core. It is now understood that spiral galaxies like ours also undergo the same phenomenon. They tend to be quiet about 85% of the time, and are active in some form during the other 15%.

That such galactic core explosions have occurred in our galaxy seems almost certain. Evidence of previous superwaves exists in the form of radial waves of cosmic dust and charged particles moving from the galactic center towards the edge of the galaxy. The arc-shaped pattern of these waves matches what would be expected from a galactic core explosion and subsequent superwave.

Traditional peoples hand down stories of periodic cataclysmic disasters that could easily be attributed to what occurs during a superwave. Some relate these catastrophes to events originating in the center of the galaxy; the Hopi, for example, believe the cataclysms that ended the previous worlds came from the galactic core. Their prophecy for the imminent ending of the current cycle involves the Blue Star Kachina, an enormous, bright, blue-white star which will appear just as the cataclysm begins. Interestingly, distant exploding galaxies are observed to emit a bright blue light. Our galactic core would probably also appear as a vivid, blue star a thousand times more brilliant than the brightest star in the night sky. About 80% of the light would come from a region less than a third of an arc minute in diameter – in other words, from a region smaller than the apparent diameter of the planet Mars. The blue light would appear suddenly without warning, and would likely be visible even during the day. According to Hopi prophecy, the appearance of the Blue Star Kachina would mean the quantum moment is upon us.

Other traditional peoples knew that the galactic core was centered between constellations Sagittarius and Scorpio. The iconography of Scorpio has the tail with its stinger pointing in this direction, as does the arrow in the bow of the Archer Sagittarius. They knew that the galactic core was of major significance to longterm evolutionary cycles on Earth. The Maya called the Galactic Center the Hunab Ku, which meant "The Only God."

Could an incoming Galactic Superwave be related to the changes in the solar system, Sun, and the Earth's magnetic field? It might seem unlikely, since it was previously thought that core explosions occurred on the frequency of tens of millions of years, but Paul LaViolette discovered otherwise. He attempted to determine when superwaves have occurred in the past by studying deposits of beryllium 10, an isotope produced by cosmic rays striking the atmosphere. His research showed that cosmic ray beryllium 10 peaks occur approximately every 25-26,000 years, with occasionally spikes at the midpoint, or 12-13,000 years. The last beryllium 10 peak was around 12,600 years ago, which would support the possibility that another superwave is on the way. The Hopi have been expecting their Blue Star Kachina to dance any time now. And while the Blue Star has not yet appeared, cosmic waves could be entering the solar system from a still-invisible galactic core explosion.

Galactic Superwaves would necessarily bring significantly increased cosmic radiation into the solar system, and ultimately to planet Earth. Biological extinctions tend to occur at times when the planet is exposed to high cosmic ray influxes. Studies have also shown that these influxes are also related to magnetic reversals. LaViolette believes the majority of the genetically mutating radiation would come from the Sun, which would be activated to emit increased radiation by the Galactic Superwave. Considerable evidence indicates the Sun could become so active that it would release massive solar flares and CMEs that could literally scorch the Earth.

Archaeologist Robert Schoch (author of Forgotten Civilization) discovered that a major plasma event that was catastrophic on a global level occurred around 9700 BCE, which reinforces LaViolette's timelines for the last superwave. Plasma events are catastrophic excursions of superheated gas plasma and ionizing radiation coming from a CME or large solar flare. Schoch was the first to re-date the Sphinx to 9,000-10,000 BC, using rings of erosion caused by floods that occurred at that time. Schoch also discovered an ancient ruin called Gobekli Tepe in Turkey, which radiocarbon analysis dated to 10,000 to 12,000 years ago, far earlier than we thought such civilizations could have existed. Schoch's numerous papers offer compelling evidence that advanced civilizations flourished prior to the catastrophic end of the last Ice Age.

Schoch believes a major solar plasma event occurred, based on his studies of ancient pictographs that accurately portray the way such an influx of light would be experienced. Recent study of high-altitude atmospheric discharges called sprites, caused by solar radiation, reveals configurations that look like stick men, donut-shaped objects, intertwining serpents, and stacks of discs, all found in pictographs. Schoch also cites fused and melted rock materials found around the planet, which would occur under the extreme heat of a superheated wave of gas plasma from the Sun. The theory of a plasma event is also supported by geologic records of greatly accelerated melting of polar ice masses, resulting in massive floods such as those that occurred at the close of the last Ice Age.

A commonality in these disparate theories is that major catastrophic events that appear to have been caused by extraterrestrial phenomena occur according to a 25-26,000-year cycle, with occasional events at the midpoint of that cycle. Asteroids and other celestial objects have traditionally been cited as causal to these events; however, the beryllium deposits, the mutations that occurred during these events, and the fused rocks and vitrified materials all point to a cause that includes radiation and extreme heat. A solar plasma event fits these criteria better than all other possibilities.

As discussed above, magnetic reversals result in more radiation affecting life on Earth, causing illness and death but also genetic mutation. If a new species is about to be born, we might expect some causal mechanism to stimulate the process. We've examined a number of possibilities, some of which may already be underway, if the evidence presented above is any indication. For instance, hard data point to the fact that either a magnetic reversal or excursion is currently in process. Whichever it is, more radiation will continue to reach the Earth, causing genetic mutation. We've also seen that a source of extra-solar system energy, most likely the galactic core, is causing transformations throughout the solar system, and that the Sun is also going through changes. We cannot be sure it is a Galactic Superwave, but we do know that some energetic dynamic is occurring, and that it is probably already affecting life on Earth.

More puzzle pieces came together when I came upon the work of Robert Felix, whose book title, *Magnetic Reversals and Evolutionary Leaps*, aptly describes his area of focus. Felix insists the widely held idea that evolution is a long, slow process is simply not correct. Yes, in some cases evolution occurs slowly, but most of the time it takes place in sudden, big leaps, as whole new species emerge.

Felix cites the work of paleontologists Dr. Robert Bakker and Dr. Eugenia Gold. *"The idea of slow, gradual, imperceptible evolution is wrong,"* says Bakker. *"The population is immediately replaced with an entirely different species with no forerunners."*

Gold elaborates on the theme:

Most new species appear with a bang, not a protracted crescendo. Gradualism is not a fact of nature. Species seems to remain unchanged in the fossil record for millions of years, before abruptly disappearing, only to be replaced just as rapidly by a species that is, though clearly related, substantially different. Nature takes leaps.

Numerous examples of this include the jawless fish with no known predecessors that appeared during the Ordovician period, the time during the Devonian when conifers suddenly came on the scene, and the mid-Triassic moment when crocodiles and turtles appeared out of nowhere.

Some scientists have observed that gradual evolution simply doesn't make sense from the standpoint of Darwin's theory of survival of the fittest, which is based on the premise that those species survive which are best adapted to do so by their physiology. "What good is having a wing?" asks geneticist Richard Goldschmidt in *The Material Basis for Evolution*. If the appearance of wings was a slow process, that would mean some creatures would exist for periods of time with less than a full wing. He points out the intermediate stages never appear in fossil records. Like many others, Goldschmidt believes radiation-caused rapid mutation is the almost certain cause of the sudden emergence of so many species.

At these major extinction~evolutionary leap junctures, the planet often experiences intense, rapid warming that is typically followed by an ice age. LaViolette, Schoch and others have confirmed this. At the end of the Cretaceous and the beginning of the Tertiary periods, approximately 65.5 million years ago, dinosaurs disappeared. It is commonly believed they became extinct due to cataclysmic events caused by volcanoes going off. Something like 70% of all ocean creatures also died as ocean temps shot up 10-12°C in a very short time. Sub-sea vulcanism on a very massive scale could possibly cause this, but there is another piece of data related to the extinction event that vulcanism can't explain. High levels of Iridium — an element very rare on Earth but plentiful in space — were found in the clays at the boundary between the Cretaceous and Tertiary periods (the K-T boundary). LaViolette demonstrated that high levels of Beryllium

10, another element related only to cosmic energy sources, also occur on Earth during Galactic Superwave events and magnetic reversals.

Robert Felix cites a number of scientists who confirm the relationship between reversals and evolutionary shifts. "New kinds of animals appear in the geologic record virtually simultaneously with magnetic reversals," said Kennett and Watkins of the University of Rhode Island. "Reversals strongly influence population trends," said C. J. Waddington of the University of Minnesota. "Faunal (animal) changes occur near several reversals," said Alan Cox of Stanford University.

According to Felix, there appears to be a direct relationship between the emergence of new human species and magnetic reversals. Apes and humans branched apart about 5 million years ago at the end of the Miocene, during a magnetic reversal event. Homo habilis appeared about 2 million years ago at a magnetic reversal, and Australopithecus went extinct about 1 million years ago, also at a magnetic reversal period. Homo erectus (speaking man or job man) appeared about 780,000 years ago at the Brunhes magnetic reversal. Homo sapiens neanderthalis suddenly appeared about 115,000 years ago at the Blake magnetic reversal. Neanderthal vanished about 34,000 years ago at the Lake Mungo magnetic reversal. Once again we see the synergistic combination of magnetic reversals, radiation, and the emergence of new species.

It was once thought that geomagnetic field reversals and excursions were rare events. More recent research reveals numerous geomagnetic excursions and reversals, with specific names and dates, that have occurred much more frequently than anyone expected. For instance, the Gothenberg magnetic excursion occurred 12,350 BP (years before the present), Mono Lake 23,000 BP, Lake Mungo 33,500 BP and Laschamps 47,000 BP. Note that excursions are more frequent and less intense in their impact.

The traditional view on magnetic reversals is that they take place over hundreds or thousands of years. Another gradualism idea has also recently bitten the dust. The previously mentioned study by scientists at <u>Cal Berkeley says that reversals can occur in less than 100 years</u>. Felix presents evidence that studies of lava flows at Steens Mountain, south-central Oregon (which erupted during a reversal, by the way), by scientists Prevot, Mankinen, Coe and Gromme, show that magnetic intensity had fallen from full strength to less than 10% of today's intensity in under one year — perhaps in just a few months. During a followup study in 1989, Coe and Prevot found that the poles had reversed at the rate of 3° per day. Not content with earlier findings, Coe and his colleagues took another look. The magnetic field had reversed at "an astonishingly rapid rate," their study found, moving 6-8° per day.

The pieces appear to be fitting together, joining superwaves, magnetic reversals, radiation, extinction, mutation and then new species. It seems highly significant that this pattern occurred with the other "homo" species that were our ancestors. It's been almost 12,000 years since the Gothenberg event. The magnetic field is rapidly declining, the magnetic poles are migrating, and they may shift within the next decade or two. A larger energetic source, possibly the galactic core, is causing major changes throughout the solar system and on the Sun. We face a possible extinction and new species emergence event — not only of our own making, but also catalyzed by forces far beyond our control.

Maybe the prophecies were accurate in pointing to this as a time of planetary death and rebirth. Are we entering a global chrysalis of transformation? Will we die to our physical, human "caterpillar" identity in order to birth our higher-dimensional, divine human "butterfly" selves?

15

Galactic Re-Seeding

Transmissions From The Galactic core

By now it probably seems apparent that some larger force is causing changes in the heliosphere, the other planets, the Sun and our Earth. Based upon prophecies and the research of Paul LaViolette, the galactic center seems to be the source of periodic upheavals and evolutionary leaps. This idea is further supported by the important December 31, 2012 date that marked the end of the Mayan calendar. This calendric system was more advanced than anything of its kind, even to this day, and demonstrates a sophisticated understanding of cosmic cycles. Specifically, the end of the Mayan calendar corresponded with a very important event within the long, slow precession of the equinoxes.

The ancients knew there was a larger cycle that governed entire ages of evolution and consciousness unfoldment on Earth. Long ago, they observed that the axis of the Earth precesses through the entire 360° of the celestial background of stars approximately every 26,000 years. Something very important happens during a particular 30 to 40 year period during that long cycle. John Major Jenkins, who has thoroughly researched the Mayan Calendar, focused on this Galactic Alignment that occurs only once in the cycle, when the moment of Sunrise on the winter solstice is conjunct with the Galactic center. This creates a direct energetic connection between the Earth, the Sun, and the galactic core. Jenkins calculated that the current Galactic Alignment is occurring between approximately 1980 and

2016, give or take a decade. Thus, humanity is now, and has been for some time, within the window of this major alignment.

The ancients understood the importance of the astrological basis and significance of this moment in time. Only recently is modern science beginning to grasp this. It has been discovered that the <u>sun is connected to the Earth directly through a magnetic portal</u> that causes a continuous interchange between our planet and the Sun. When the portal is fully open, charged particles and other electromagnetic phenomena flow directly without dissipation from the Sun to the Earth. It would stand to reason that, like any circuit, the connection is a two-way street, and energy from the Earth would also flow back to the Sun. All of this points to the interconnectedness of the universe, which is holographic, in an absolute state of unity. It would seem likely that magnetic portals join the Sun to all the other planets, and possibly interconnect planets with one another.

While we are aware of the physical phenomena, such as charged particles and electromagnetic pulses, that move through these portals, there is almost certainly something of a higher-dimensional, non-physical nature that is also streaming through these pathways, as the universe is multidimensional. Just as telephone lines contain electromagnetic flows that carry information, some types of higher-order data might be encoded in the energy flows between celestial bodies. These energetic connections might also provide a basis for the efficacy of astrology.

Downloading A New Blueprint

A purely physical model is insufficient to explain all that takes place within this universe. Think of the many phenomena such as telepathy and other psychic abilities, superluminal or faster than speed of light interconnections, emerging theories of a holographic universe, and mathematical models that require ten or more dimensions to explain why their components function as they do. The old Newtonian, physical paradigm is a thing of the past.

The same is true when we try to understand the evolution of plants and animals. Attempting to limit it all to physical DNA just does not suffice, according to many researchers. Among them is Rupert Sheldrake, who concluded a more comprehensive model was needed after fifteen years of studying the development of plants. Genes enable protein-creation synthesis, he admitted, but switching genes on or off does not determine how cells ultimately arrange themselves into larger forms. The DNA of various organisms is almost identical, yet their fully developed forms are radically different from one another. How can we explain that? Sheldrake hypothesizes that morphic fields, which are informational pattern fields, holographic in nature, form the underlying blueprint matrix of all earthly forms. These fields, according to Sheldrake and others who align with his ideas, comprise the subtle, non-physical levels of causation and organization infusing all living organisms.

The reality of this has been demonstrated through Kirlian photography, which visually captures the nonphysical dimensions of physical objects. These energetic fields have been recorded using Kirlian photography around all sorts of living organisms, confirming their existence and validating the myriad branches of energy medicine, such as homeopathy and acupuncture. The Phantom leaf effect displays the organizing, or morphic, field that Sheldrake's research posits. If a section of a leaf is cut away, a Kirlian photograph nonetheless reveals the image of the entire leaf.

Sheldrake's theories introduced the concept of morphic resonance, the interconnectedness of all forms of life within energy fields that unite all beings within one larger whole. Through these energy fields, subtle energies and morphic information are continuously shared on higher-dimensional levels. The concept of morphic resonance explains much that has puzzled scientific observers for centuries. For example, how do cells and tissues in the human body work together so precisely and efficiently? Somehow, they synergize astoundingly well within some sort of exceedingly complex, organizing entity — one that may well exist on a higher, more enveloping dimension. It is hard to believe that the information traveling through the brain and nervous system alone is adequate to keep all bodily systems organized and fully functioning.

The sudden appearance of new species concurrent with magnetic reversals may also be explained by morphic fields and resonance as the causal mechanism. Consider once again the development of photosynthesis in those long-ago cyanobacteria. It seems plausible that some nonphysical, nonlocal field of intelligence somehow encoded those single-celled organisms with the capacity to internally reorganize so they could create their own food through photosynthesis. Similarly, we humans are not capable of waking ourselves up or independently and volitionally evolving into a new, higher-dimensional species, no matter how much we want that to happen. We need some sort of infusion of vaster, more inclusive levels of information~energy~consciousness to catalyze this evolution. This is why spiritual seekers have traditionally sat at the feet of those who have realized levels of consciousness they aspire to embody. But not everyone can travel to be with awakened beings. Fortunately, as the morphic field on Earth becomes saturated with higher frequencies, realization of the spiritual dimensions of being grows far easier for every one of us. We no longer need to be in proximity to those who are awake — the morphic field of freedom is a nonlocal phenomenon that will intensify exponentially as more and more of us awaken and embody our luminous, divine nature.

It has long been conjectured that one possible way lifeforms have been seeded on this planet is through microbes, bacteria, and other substances that hitchhiked a ride to Earth on debris from space. That is definitely possible, but what if morphic fields for whole new species are projected through magnetic tunnels or wormholes from the galactic center through our Sun and into our planetary matrix? This may seem like wild conjecture, but it might turn out to make more sense than 3-D theories of evolutionary causation. Maybe the Maya also knew this, which would explain why they called the Galactic core the Hunab Ku, The Only God.

Many observers of life are convinced that an intelligent Source creates the complex informational patterns, or morphogenic fields, by which physical matter organizes itself into infinitely intricate structures. To them, this makes more sense than Darwin's theory of random selection. Is anything truly random within the universe? As we have seen, missing evolutionary links simply do not exist. How would the early amphibians have survived with half fins, half legs? Such strange protuberances wouldn't have been functional for swimming or walking, much less evading predators and finding food on a regular basis. New species emerge, fully formed and perfectly suited to their newfound conditions.

Not A Game Of Chance

On a purely statistical basis, the theory of evolution appears to be an improbability. The Institute for Creation Research did some mathematical calculations to determine the likelihood of complex life forms emerging by random selection. The model calculated the probability that a simple organism with only one functioning part would successfully mutate, based on random selection, into a creature with 200 whole, unified, functional parts. Here is their conclusion:

> ... the chance that a 200-component organism could be formed by mutation and natural selection is less than one chance out of a trillion, trillion, trillion, trillion, trillion! Lest anyone think that a 200-part system is unreasonably complex, it should be noted that even a one-celled plant or animal may have millions of molecular parts.

Considering how many life forms there are on this planet, and how they all function within an integrated, larger system we call Gaia — the living Earth — the statistical probability of this happening through the process of evolution and natural selection, much less by chance, is close to nil.

Could the seeding of new life-forms during Galactic Superwaves and magnetic reversals be less likely than natural selection? Maybe not, especially when we may not be that far away from discovering a literal extraterrestrial life seed. Scientists at the University of Buckingham in England have actually found a microscopic metal globe spewing out biological material. They believe it could contain genetic material – the precursor to all life. Consider the ancient theory called Panspermia that posits life is seeded throughout the universe by asteroids, meteorites, comets, and other space material. The Greeks first came up with the idea, but many credentialed scientists explored this theory during the 1800s. During the last century, scientists including Francis Crick — who, with Watson, discovered the structure of DNA — believed the origin of the genetic codes lies somewhere out there in the universe.

If Galactic Superwaves are composed of vast amounts of cosmic debris, which could contain microbes with DNA and morphogenetic fields of organisms encoded in them, why couldn't these cascade to Earth during a superwave and/or magnetic reversal? Could DNA be the physical level of encoding that carries with it morphogenetic fields imbued with the informational intelligence of other life-forms? Is there a more logical theory to explain how life arose from a fiery, molten orb, devoid of anything living, to become the amazingly abundant Earth with its 8.7 million species?

Even more baffling is how rapidly species come and go; more than 99% of all species that have ever lived on our globe are now extinct. At least five billion species have come and gone during Earth's existence — each a unique, complex system of living intelligence. Considering the unlikelihood of natural selection alone producing so many highly-adapted species, the idea of an extraterrestrial origin for Earth-life makes more and more sense.

16

The Birth of Homo Luminous

As we have seen, it looks increasingly possible that Earth-life has its origins in deep space. Many factors — magnetic reversal and Galactic Superwave chief among them — may indeed be converging to bring about a reseeding of our planet with new life-forms suited to the emerging conditions on the globe. What makes this galactic reseeding so important is that the wave of light entering our solar system carries a vibrational frequency that is much higher than we have experienced so far. Whereas the Earth and its organisms have been operating within a third-dimensional context, the new frequencies pouring into the planet vibrate at fifth-dimensional and vaster levels.

Not only is a new species of humanity about to be born, as traditional peoples have known for some time. This new species will exist within a much more expansive and spacious energetic context. Its bodies will no longer be of a third-dimensional, physical nature, but instead will be imbued with a more etheric, light-filled quality. Beings will still have perceptible forms, but those forms will not feel as solid, dense, and unchangeable as our bodies often seem now. These more rarefied forms will have to deal with far less of the distortion and chaos that is common within third-dimensional life.

It's important to remind ourselves that all of this does not lie "out there" somewhere in a nebulous, faraway future. Here and now, we are in the process of a dimensional shift, an ascension into a "new heaven and a new earth." Ancient prophecies of this time have been joined by more recent spiritual presences who have come to Earth to shepherd humanity through this turning-point. Let's meet some of these extraordinary beings.

Harbingers of Homo Luminous

During the twentieth century, Indian sage Sri Aurobindo and his consort, who chose to be called "the Mother," predicted that a new superhuman was about to be born. They established a prototype community in south India called Auroville, designed to support the cultivation of spiritual awareness and the eventual flowering of the new species. Sir Aurobindo and the Mother believed it was their task to incarnate the new, supramental light frequencies within the planetary mindfields. After Sri Aurobindo made his transition in 1950, the Mother spent many more years in deep inner work, focusing on shifting the cellular intelligence of the body from a programmed, biological level to the illumined consciousness of a light body.

Throughout human history, other great beings have served as prototypes for the new species, and they are way-showers we can turn to for unfailing inspiration and encouragement. Such beings have already done what many of us know we are here to experience and embody; their presence here has blazed a trail they assured us we can follow. Christ Jesus is deservedly the most widely known way-shower because he offers us the greatest demonstration of what is possible. He transcended the laws of the physical plane, and even the apparent limitation of physical death — the illusion that seems the most final and unavoidable to human beings — through the crucifixion and the resurrection. This being not only performed any number of miracles that defied what anyone believed possible, he also showed us what it is to **know oneself** as a divine, multidimensional soul when he ascended into the higher realms.

The mother of this unparalleled being whom millions consider to be their Lord and Savior is another extraordinary presence who came to Earth in a feminine form. Miracles surrounded her, from her Immaculate Conception and the virgin birth of her son, Yeshua (widely known as Jesus), to her eventual Assumption, making Mother Mary another evolutionary prototype. We can all look to this being for Her all-loving compassion and comfort, which flow unceasingly from Her radiant heart. But She also models unfailing strength and courage in the face of being deeply misunderstood by the prevailing culture, just as many of us often feel.

The Asian spiritual traditions offer many examples of beings who reached the heights of superhuman accomplishment. In the Taoist tradition, stories abound of immortals who ascended. Before they left Earth, these beings were known for flying like birds and performing other magical acts, enabled by their long, deep meditation practices to surpass human limitations. Many spiritual traditions describe those who succeeded in creating light bodies as demonstrations of their spiritual achievements. For instance, eyewitnesses insist a Tibetan monk created a "rainbow" light body and ascended in 1998, and many other traditions contain similar records of such phenomena.

South Indian spiritual tradition reveres the twelve siddha yogis who not only escaped the wheel of rebirth but turned their bodies to light. Ramalinga Swami was the most recent and famous of these. His life, which spanned the years between 1823 and 1874, bore many resemblances to that of Christ Jesus. Although he followed a different religious path, Ramalinga Swami was a Christlike being who embodied love and prophesied a profound transformation for humanity. He invited all to join in it, just as Jesus did.

Eastern religions traditionally viewed mukti, or liberation, as the culmination of the spiritual path. Ramalinga Swami proclaimed that liberation was not, in fact, the end of the journey, but an interim goal. Thus, he and other siddha yogis forged a new path within the context of the rich, ancient Hindu tradition. Ramalinga Swami described the progressive transformation of his body through three stages, resulting in a deathless, universal, golden body.

This Indian way-shower experienced the total transformation of all levels of his being, including his physical body, into a manifestation of the Source or "Father" presence. As a full incarnation of God, he gained all the yogic siddhi powers, including bilocation and not casting shadows or leaving footprints. During his final days on Earth, he stated that he had gained the power to resurrect the dead. His final act was asking to be locked into his room. A short time later, a blinding flash of light was seen to emanate from the room, after which no visible sign of the great swami could be found. He had dematerialized.

Before he left, Ramalinga Swami proclaimed the advent of a new manifestation of the Divine on Earth, in which everything and everyone would be transformed. Like Christ Jesus, he told his disciples that he would be going on, but would return again in bodily form when the God of Vast Grace-Light, as he described the Universal Christ presence, arrived. When he returned, he said, he would bring the Resurrection Body, forever beyond death, to all who were ready to receive it.

Could all these beings be evolutionary harbingers, seed crystals of a nascent new human species that is about to be born? Could the intense volleys of cosmic light and energy be the very catalyst for seeding and raising a certain portion of humanity into a whole new level of being and potential? Like the prokaryotes that became cyanobacteria capable of avoiding extinction through the evolutionary grace of photosynthesis, perhaps this new species will be, like many great masters who have gone before, capable of things that we now consider superhuman. This would explain how they would not only survive but flourish under conditions that would kill off most species.

17

Visions of a Wave of Light

It has been an indescribable blessing to be taken on this decades-long journey of revelations on the end of the age and the shift into a new, higher-dimensional Earth. Nearly four decades of inner and outer experiences have brought me to the conclusion that the capstone of it all involves a wave of light and a solar event that are one and the same. This wave of light has been building for decades and will crest sometime within the next decade, shifting the Earth and humanity into a fourth- and fifth-dimensional level. In this chapter, I'll share the essence of what this event is about, and what it might be like. I will relate my personal experiences and visions, as well as the supporting, confirming, and corroborating evidence and experiences that have combined to form a coherent picture of what lies ahead as we transit the death and rebirth of the human species.

The personal experiences I share here are among the most potent of all that I have gone through in my journey of awakening. They are visions and inner experiences that I felt would provide you with very important information during these years of accelerating change prior to the shift.

As mentioned earlier, I became aware of the changes in the Sun sometime in the early 1990s, while living in Hawaii. Karen and I noticed that the Sun was becoming whiter and brighter, no longer the golden-white orb of our youth. Exposing ourselves to the Sun had taken on a new quality -- a burning, stinging sensation in place of the pleasant feeling of warmth we remembered from our earlier lives. Simply put, the Sun felt a lot more intense.

This intensity continues to gather momentum. For two decades, we have both worked each summer at fire lookouts on mountaintops, where we are exposed to the Sun's rays all day. During the early years on our mountains, we felt comfortable sitting outside on our catwalks to catch some rays. Then we began to notice that we donned hats and Sunglasses whenever we ventured out onto our catwalks. Now, we find ourselves spending little to no time outside in the direct Sun.

Many inner experiences over the past decades, coupled with the prophecies we have mentioned and the revelations of many spiritual adepts and seekers have reinforced the knowing that the Sun, transducing energy from the galactic center, is a key source of the spiritual illumination that is catalyzing planetary awakening. Our Sun functions as a step-down mechanism for the incoming light and evolutionary codings from the Great Central Sun in the galactic core. The transformational impulse of the wave of light has been gathering momentum for decades now. Two of the key events in that progression, leading up to the end of the Mayan calendar in 2012, were the Harmonic Convergence in 1987 and the Timeshift event in 1992. Each of these critical junctures provided a potent experience of the upleveling in the ever-increasing spiritual light frequencies from the galactic core, as a result of the Galactic Alignment discussed earlier. Over the years, I have received numerous visions of future times in which very unusual light phenomena will take place in the upper atmosphere, along with strong infusions of pure white light.

2102 Wave Of Light Crystals Visions

In 2008, Karen and I were attracted to a display of crystals in a shop in Boise, Idaho. A small group of very clear quartz crystals on a glass shelf was labeled "2012 crystals." When we asked the store owner about them, she replied that they transported people into the future to the 2012 (or later) dimensional shift-point. When we left the store, two of these unusual crystals were among the many treasures we purchased that day.

Back home, we sat together, holding the new crystals. As we merged with them, we were propelled out into a brilliant field of pure, white light, so strong and clear that nothing else existed within it. Although we often receive information and insights during such experiences, nothing came through but the presence of the absolutely brilliant, boundless luminosity. The same thing happened whenever we again held the crystals during the next few months.

Our experiences led us to conclude that an immensely luminous wave of light is somehow related to the shift-point. But what does the wave of light mean for the human experience? Since that time, we have asked on a number of occasions to be taken out to the moment of the big shift. Each time, we find ourselves in the same field of brilliant white light. Whenever we've asked for clarification on what this means to everyday, physical reality, all we see is the same field of white light. The inner experience of this infinite light is very similar to the empty-yet-full space of pure enlightenment. All is dissolved away except the absolute, boundless emptiness of pure being. Nothing but the light of absolute truth exists.

While these experiences made it clear that the wave of light was a potent spiritual manifestation, one that would bring the potential for illumination for many, we still never saw anything about how this might manifest on a physical level. I held that inquiry for a number of years until I was given another experience that answered this question.

2015 Solar Event/Wave of Light Vision

I was sitting in our meditation room on the farm we live on in northern California when I began to experience a very bright light in my brow chakra. At first I thought it was simply another experience of my third eye opening. But then I began to experience a bright light coming through the window directly in front of me. It was so sharp, vivid, and encompassing that at first I wasn't sure if my eyes were open or closed.

I quickly realized that my eyes were closed, and that what I was seeing was more than an inner light experience. It was a real-time experience of a future event. In other words, I was "there" experiencing the event, not "here" witnessing some future event. In the "experience" I got up and peered through the venetian blinds to make sure it wasn't a vision. I felt a need to see things as they were by looking out into the world.

As I gazed through the slats in the blinds, I noticed that the white light was not just in my inner vision, or simply filling the room — it suffused everything. It took my eyes a while to adjust so that I could see the objects outside the house. Everything looked as it always did, except that the normal levels of Sunlight were superseded by this intense, bright-white light.

Once my eyes were accustomed to the brilliant white light and I could see and maneuver in the outer world, I decided to walk outside. All of this felt so real to me, it was hard to remember that I was experiencing these things in a future time, while my body remained sitting in our little meditation room. As I walked toward the woodshed, all around me was this bright, white light. In every direction, the same light suffused everything.

Looking out across the fields, I realized it must've been sometime in the early afternoon that day, for the Sun or the source of this brilliant white light was slightly to the west of the midheaven,. I attempted to move my gaze toward the Sun, but the light was so much more brilliant than anything I had ever seen coming from the Sun. It was also immediately apparent that the Sun itself has expanded to 4-5 times larger than its normal size. There was no appearance of a yellowish tint, just pure white light. It seemed to me that the Sun had gone into some sort of mini-nova.

As I continued to look around, attempting to get a grasp on what was transpiring, I noticed that everything looked the same physically, but in the luminosity that permeated the entire scene, everything was also somehow very different. I knew inside that the long-awaited shift was happening.

I decided to get into my truck and drive out from beneath the trees into the open fields so I could see more clearly. When I turned the key, the starter didn't engage. All the electronics were dead, leading me to believe the truck had a dead battery. When I walked over to our car and got in, the very same thing happened.

This propelled me back into the house to find Karen and tell her what I was experiencing and realizing. Looking around, I realized that the clocks, lights, DVD player, and computer were off. There was no electrical power. Karen was walking around, obviously aware that something of immense significance was transpiring, and we found ourselves going back into the meditation room, the most sacred space in our house.

I was mentally taken back to September of 1992, as Hurricane Iniki was gathering force on the North Shore of the island of Kauai. We lived there then, and as we heard and felt the winds increase, we got ourselves situated in a small bedroom, where we soon were launched into one of the most intense earthly experiences we had ever had. (The full story is in our first book, *Soul Awakening*.)

Now, as we sat in our little meditation room on the Farm, surrounded by the intensely white light, we felt the energy continuing to rise, while an equally strong inner illumination was occurring. All our energy bodies and chakras were speeding up their vibration, expanding and opening. We knew this was IT! This was the moment of translation.

We let go, just as we had when we faced physical death during Hurricane Iniki. We were instantly carried into a timeless, samadhi-like state, feeling ourselves expanding, opening, and rising in vibration. The bright white luminosity without and within continued to build. All sense of human focus went on melting away. Our minds dissolved into pure white light, bliss, and love. No fear or anything like it was present in the field of consciousness.

As we expanded, the veils and doorways between the dimensions began to open. All that might keep us physically identified was dissolving. Our crown chakras opened and we realized we were free. We naturally began to ascend, rising up out of the physical form, lifting out of the house. Looking down, we saw our physical forms and our little home becoming smaller as our panorama expanded. There was no longer a sense of connection with any of it. Vaster and vaster expanses of the surface of the planet lay below, all bathed in the white light. At one point, our vision shifted to the expanded Sun. It seemed as though that white light from the expansion had been projected even beyond the Earth, further out into the solar system. It was brighter, looking directly at the Sun, but it was also bright looking away from it.

Our focus shifted again, and now we looked out into deep space. Beyond were the planets, stars, and other galaxies. We knew we were free, and going home. The feeling was beyond any bliss or ecstasy ever experienced during our most exalted spiritual illuminations. We were being drawn by a loving intelligence to our new home in the galaxies. Our physical forms gone, we were beings of light with form being but an expression of our consciousness as needed.

I was drawn to look back at the Earth and the Sun, and saw a wave-front of superheated gas plasma coming from the Sun toward the Earth. Then I remembered something that had occurred while we were still in the meditation room, prior to lifting up out of our physical forms. As we were dissolving into bliss and light, I had heard sounds that reminded me of a night many years earlier, when we were sleeping on the ground in our backyard in Ashland, OR. As dawn came we heard low, groaning sounds coming from deep inside the Earth. Later that morning, we heard the news and realized we had heard the sounds of an earthquake in Klamath Falls, an hour or so away by car. This memory helped me understand that I was now hearing earthquakes that were occurring on Earth. Before we lifted up and heard the sounds from the planet below us, we also began to feel it move under us. As time went by, the sounds and shaking intensified. This continued as we sat in samadhi until we began to be lifted up.

Drawn back into the present and the perspective of being out in deep space, I again felt my awareness pulled to the area between the Sun and the Earth. I saw the wave of superheated gas plasma pushing debris with it, slowly expanding outward in a great ring from the Sun, and soon to reach the Earth. It seemed that it might hit the Earth. (Remember the scene at the end of the movie "Knowing"?) I felt a sense of deep peace, even in the awareness that untold destruction would soon occur on the Earth. There was a deep sense that all was in perfect, divine order and that whatever came next, this, too, was part of the birth of a new age and a new, higher-dimensional planet and species.

Aftermath Of The Vision

For days after this experience, I was shaken, almost in a trance-like state. The blast of energy and higher-dimensional light had been so great that I couldn't do much except sit in my meditation room and let everything settle in. A few months later, this process was still going on, as I integrated all that I had seen.

It became clear to me that what I was shown was a sort of mini-nova of the Sun. Its gas shells had expanded considerably, causing it to become larger and extremely bright. The light was full-spectrum, both visible with the physical eyes and **felt** right up into the highest spiritual levels. The wave of light and mini-nova were one, integrated event.

In this future vision, the electromagnetic impact was very clear. All the electronics in our vehicles and house were destroyed. The incoming wave of superheated gas plasma invoked a strong sense that major destruction was about to unfold. This was the end of the human experience, as we had known it, and probably for a very long time. All electricity, devices, computers, internet, and communications would be gone, and some portion of the planet might literally be torched. What an immense juxtapose of this intense devastation with the corresponding experience of ascending with Karen in our light bodies, in an absolute state of ecstasy and enlightenment.

What was I to do with all of this? What was my responsibility with regard to this vision? Should I tell it to anyone, and if so, whom? How could I be sure that some of my own issues and projections weren't part of it? Questions arose: *If I tell people what I see, is it going to be shocking, even overwhelming, for them? Will it be helpful, or will it cause them to live in fear of the future?* These and many more questions went on percolating through my consciousness. I felt a deep sense of responsibility to let Spirit guide whatever was to happen as a result of this experience, and not to let my ego get involved in any way.

The first person I felt I could talk to about it was Karen. I found it most difficult to convey the immense spiritual impact of this experience, and the potent sense that something of major significance had been revealed to me. There was no doubt in my mind that this was a divine revelation. Nothing that had ever happened before approached this level of magnitude. When I talked to Yeshua/Christ Jesus about it, he helped me see that it was true and clear as given, and part of the long-term soul destiny and purpose of receiving information about the personal and planetary awakening and ascension process.

A few days after the vision, Karen and I went into deep meditation together, connected with Source, and asked some further questions that arose from our discussion of the vision. Karen asked whether other souls were lifting out with us. I was immediately brought back to something I'd experienced during one of our teleconferences a few days earlier. As Karen began the group by inviting everyone to join together on the inner, I saw us all as luminous presences high above the Earth in the various locations in which our physical forms currently resided. These souls and many others were there again in my inner vision, and all these beings of light were still connected to the Earth by a cord, human-shaped but of light and translucent.

I realized I was seeing our ongoing connection with other souls in the process of translating. This group of souls is already in the process of being "raptured" or lifting out of their human embodiment and incarnation; they are already partially beyond the human world. I was shown that if and when the Sun goes into its mini-nova and releases the hot plasma gas shell, these beings will have completed their service on Earth and will drop the silver cord that connects the soul into the body. They will soar out into higher-dimensional space, just as we had in the vision I experienced. A group ascension of a portion of humanity would occur at the time of the mini-nova~wave of light.

Karen remembered that she had experienced something like this before, during the sinking of Atlantis. In that lifetime, her soul occupied the form of a spiritual elder in a male body. Standing on the rocky hillside near the small temple he watched over, he looked down to the cities below and felt a great sadness for what had happened there. He knew the scientific experiments and technologies had gotten much too far out of balance with Life and the Divine, and all the distorted creations would have to be cleared away. Soon, the earth started to rumble and the island began to subside into the sea. He could see the land breaking up far below, along the coastline. His heart was heavy, but he knew there was nothing he could do to mitigate what was unfolding. He had tried to warn people, to remind them of what really mattered, but no one wanted to listen. Now, as the human-created world was annihilated, he turned away from the destruction and slowly trod up the hill toward the small, simple temple. Continuing uphill, step by step, he simply and easily lifted out of that form and left the planet.

Karen's past life experience completely correlated with what I've been told for some time, which is that the two of us would not experience "death" as death has been known on Earth. Many of us will lift out of our bodies, like the Atlantean elder, as we ascend into light. Most humans, though, will go through the normal process of physical death. After leaving Earth life, we vibrate our way into one of a variety of future scenarios. Some of us will be reborn on a fourth- or fifth-dimensional Earth, while others will go on to explore higher-dimensional realms. Those who are not yet complete with third-dimensional experience will return on another planet that is focalized within 3-D, where they can continue to explore the material plane awhile longer.

    The vision/experience of the wave of light~solar event described above was, and still is, another pivotal chapter in this long journey of being shown much about the process of personal and planetary awakening, the dimensional shift, and ascension. It was a major catalyst that I continued to chew on mentally and spiritually during the following years. It didn't feel like time to share it with anyone other than Karen, and I wasn't at all sure what kind of impact it would have on others. I only knew that further illumination and corroboration would follow, and sure enough, that is what unfolded next.

18

Understandings and Confirmations of the Visions

My concerns about sharing the vision/experience described in the previous chapter eased as I received inner and outer confirmations of everything the vision had revealed. One of the first of these arrived through re-examining the works of Jay Weidner. I remembered that his book, <u>The Mysteries of the Great Cross at Hendaye: Alchemy and the End of Time</u>, had something to do with a solar event. Weidner had become interested in the works of an enigmatic alchemist named Fulcanelli whose writings mentioned an unusual cross in a churchyard in the small coast town of Hendaye, in southwestern France. Erected 350 years ago, the cross contains a number of symbols including a starburst, a grid of letters, and an angry-looking Sun.

After decoding some of the letters and symbols, Weidner concluded the cross portends some kind of disaster involving the Sun. One of the symbols, a circle divided into four quadrants, each containing the letter A, seemed to indicate the four cardinal points of the astrological zodiac as they relate to the nearly 26,000-year cycle of the precession of the equinoxes. This was known to the ancients as the Great Year, which includes four major ages. Jay Weidner's research into cataclysms that ended previous ages revealed the angry Sun to be a solar event or CME, which occurs every 13,000 or 26,000 years.

Then Weidner discovered the works of Paul LaViolette, and suddenly realized the starburst symbolized a galactic core explosion, which created a superwave that pushed cosmic debris, dust, and waves of energy into the Sun, triggering a massive solar event. So many pieces tied together again — the end of the age, a galactic core explosion, and a superwave, precipitating a solar event.

I then found myself looping back to Ken Carey, one of the major spiritual icons of the 1980s and 90s. During that time, he brought through some of the most illumined books about the shift into the new age, among them *The Starseed Transmissions*, *Return of the Bird Tribes*, and *The Third Millennium: Living in the Posthistoric World*. When we read these books decades ago, we felt they carried a clear transmission of the energy~consciousness of humanity's next steps.

Ken fell off my radar for many years, but surfaced again through one of those synchronous encounters that provided another important piece of the puzzle. A blogpost by Lisa Gawlas contained an account of a pivotal experience by none other than Ken Carey, entitled "The Awakening Solar Intelligence." Note that in the blogpost, the first writing is by Lisa and below it is Ken's account, written in September of 2012.

Ken wrote of a "life changing experience" that occurred in early 2012 and lasted for two days. He stated, "It was so far beyond anything I had ever before imagined possible, so far beyond the ability of words to convey, it will never all be shared in print." This struck me, since I felt exactly the same way after my experience of the solar event and ascension.

Ken Carey was contemplating writing a blog post about the possible ways a solar event could play into the collective awakening, when he was taken into a higher state of consciousness and lifted up out into space, where he saw the Earth and Sun from a distance. He felt and knew that the presence of the "Starmaker/Creator" was "incarnated" in the Sun, something that he sensed periodically occurred; he also had a knowing that he was seeing through the Creator's mind.

Suddenly the Sun began to "slosh around," with a bulge appearing on the side toward the Earth. The bulge then erupted out into space in a "huge tongue of solar fire" headed toward the South Pole of the Earth, where it stopped just short of hitting the surface. Still, the South Pole exploded outward into the ocean, creating 200-foot tSunamis heading north. Carey was amazed that what he was seeing didn't cause a geographic pole reversal or burn humanity off the planet. He knew that what he had seen was a worst-case scenario that would only occur if the human experiment failed.

When the experience ended, he was stunned and needed time to integrate. He often watched CNN while writing, so he turned it on and immediately saw, in an astounding synchronicity, a news report showing a huge flare erupting from the Sun, which was supposed to hit the planet in the next few hours. The report warned that it could cause disruptions in cell phones, iPads, laptops, local radio stations, hand-held gaming devices, and wireless computer communications.

This propelled Carey back into the vision, where he saw the Creator playing with other scenarios for the solar flare/CME, wanting to create one that would only be strong enough to trigger the Earth's dormant cleansing mechanisms. There's much more to Carey's vision experience for those who care to read about it, but the essence is that a solar event is a planned possibility by the Creator to not only catalyze planetary cleansing but also to re-seed a new evolutionary cycle.

Extraterrestrials may also be telling us a solar event is coming, through crop circles that confirm the possibility of a mini-nova of the Sun. This information arrived via a presentation by David Wilcock at the Project Camelot Awake and Aware Conference in Los Angeles in September, 2009. One crop circle in particular caught my eye and caused me to stop the video. It portrayed the Sun and the planets of the solar system. What galvanized my attention was that the Sun appeared to have expanded out beyond Venus. I later traced these images back to a website where I found two crop circle photos that explicated what the ETs were communicating. The crop circle depicts the position of the Sun and the planets on December 21st, 2012, the end of the Mayan Calendar date. The Sun is much larger than normal, having expanded considerably, and now encompasses Mercury and Venus. The crop circle is clearly illustrating something like a mini-nova of the Sun, with the potential date of December 2012. As we all know, that did not happen. Time is slippery when it comes to information from beings who live beyond time. Dates are usually unreliable, since higher-dimensional beings perceive the flow of events and possibilities in ways that are unrelated to the linear, human concept of time.

While my vision of the Sun in an expanded state didn't appear big enough to match the crop circles' scale, they offered

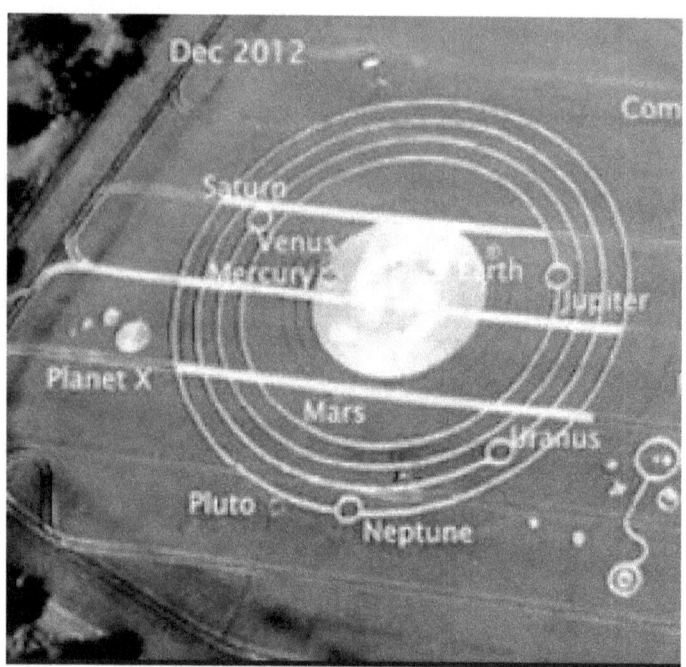

another confirmation that beings with far greater intelligence and perspective are attempting to communicate something of importance to us. I believe this to be a solar event coming at the end of the age, which is what the end of the Mayan calendar signifies.

    Recent years have brought abundant inner and outer validations of the coming shifts and changes on the Earth and Sun and in the solar system, all of which indicate that a major event is already unfolding and is likely to reach a crescendo not far in the future. As the December, 2012 end of the Mayan calendar date approached, my inner knowing was that the big event so many of us intuited lay out in the future would not occur then. Alignments of cosmic and celestial influences simply create the conditions for the shifts to occur — they don't at all guarantee that outer events will happen at those moments. So, when that window came and went, I wasn't surprised. Yet I still had the sense that the event I had come to this planet to be a part of in this lifetime awaited us all in the not-too-distant future. The question that I, and many of you, still hold is *When?* Are we talking about a timeline of decades, or years, or an even shorter interval of time? One of the factors that precipitated writing this book is that I feel I have been given information on the potential "when."

You might recall the projections I shared earlier, stating that the shift of the magnetic poles looks likely to occur sometime between 2020 and 2030. Another piece of data arrived recently in the form of an article entitled <u>1 in 8 Chance of Catastrophic Solar Megastorm by 2020</u> by space physicist <u>Pete Riley</u>, senior scientist at Predictive Science in San Diego. He came to his conclusions by analyzing historical information on the connection between the occurrence intervals of solar flares and their sizes. While 1 in 8 isn't a large percentage, it tells us we may be getting closer to a big solar event of some kind. Coincidentally, the year 2020 also shows up in the projections about the time of a potential magnetic reversal. And it aligns with the prophecy of a well-known incarnation of the Divine Mother from India, Mata Amritanandamayi, who is simply known to her followers as Ammachi.

Confirmation from Ammachi

I first met Ammachi in a small meeting room in Taos in 1987. Since then, Karen and I have been in her presence together and came away feeling that she is indeed a fully-realized incarnation of Divine Mother. Amma's greatest wish in this life is to "hug her children." To that end, she travels the world with a coterie of followers, offering spiritual gatherings and staying until every last one of her "children" is hugged, even if that means she goes without food, water, and rest for an entire day, through the night and into the next day, as sometimes occurs. For Amma, every one of us is her child, and her vast, nurturing presence exudes a kind of love few of us have ever experienced.

So we really paid attention when we heard that Ammachi was warning her followers about a coming catastrophe. In July of 2016, a Midwestern friend visited Ammachi's Chicago Center during her annual US summer tour. He told us Amma warned her devotees about a solar event that will be hitting the planet sometime around 2020. She strongly suggested that everyone begin to grow food and work diligently to set up communities in preparation for this life-changing event.

When I heard this news, I felt shaken to my foundation. The Universe had given me the final corroboration I needed to know that the solar event vision was definitely for real — and was probably going to happen soon.

But there was more. A friend in the Bay Area mentioned that she knew a devotee of Ammachi who had heard something similar during Amma's visit to her San Ramon, CA center. During the retreat, someone asked Amma about the future of the planet. She answered vaguely with some personal advice on how to maintain spiritual integrity. The questioner wasn't satisfied, and asked more pointedly what was going to happen.

Ammachi rarely gives any sorts of predictions, instead turning people back to God and their own spiritual practice. But in this case, she quoted Vedic scripture of an Old Testament sort, full of violent, bloody imagery. I was once again taken aback.

If twice wasn't enough for me to get the point, some months later our friend in the Bay Area forwarded another communication from Ammachi. It arrived as I was compiling the research presented in the first section of this book. The deeper I went down the rabbit hole of how large the planet's crises were and how little time we probably had left, the more assurance I needed to make sure that what I was being guided to say in this book was accurate, and, most importantly, spiritually correct to communicate. When I read the information below, I felt that Ammachi was once again communicating with me to let me know that I must present these things.

During another darshan, an exchange between Amma and one of her devotees was recorded.

> *She [Ammachi] was initially asked by a devotee about the tough times the Earth is facing, knowing that a time of expansion and love and light was beyond the darkness and could Amma speak to that time of light that is coming.*
>
> *Her response was lengthy and unequivocal. She began by saying:*
>
> *"We are a little too late. We created this mess. We wanted cars, more cars, more factories, poison in the water, to get more food we added poison to the plants, and even the water. We did this. Being sad about it won't change anything. We acted against the laws of nature. Digging for oil in the ocean. Drilling and destroying the mountains. GMO culture of making things more*

productive or larger. We have exploited nature. She's upset. Our mental balance is lost. Earth's equilibrium is lost. There's no point in worrying.

We did this because we were selfish. We are destroying everything. We have lost compassion, we are selfish and cruel. Our minds are out of balance, the Earth has lost her equilibrium due to our selfishness. Even our birthmother lets us sit on her lap for only so many years and then we must sit on our own. Mother Earth lets us spit on her, pee on her. Mother Earth has stage four cancer. We humans have become like termites — God gave us a beautiful garden and we destroyed it. Looking into the future is dark, deep darkness.

But we have the candle of faith to light the darkness and we must carry that candle of faith.

Time will pass whether we laugh or cry. Happiness is a choice. It will not make a difference to the Earth if we are sad. Let us do what we can to create inner balance and try to do our part to protect and preserve nature. Plant trees. Pray. Sincerely pray for the betterment of the world."

Ammachi's words confirm what most of us intuitively know. They also verify the information presented in the first part of this book. We are probably approaching the end of the human experience as we have known it. Lost in the sleep of human egoism, our species has brought itself and this planet to the brink.

But even this is still held within the overall divine plan, for apparently we had to take our exploration of separation and egoism to this degree in order to be ready to birth the new species. There is a larger plan, one that I have consistently been shown, that will not allow us to destroy this planet. It's a plan that involves an incoming wave of energy, light, and higher-dimensional consciousness, which will cleanse and purify this planet and seed a new cycle, eventuating in a soul-awakened human species living on the higher-dimensional Earth.

19

Approaching the Quantum Moment

Infusions Of Coherent Light

A number of times in meditation, I have been shown that the current quieting of the Sun has to do with the influx of higher-dimensional light into the solar system. The wave nature of fourth- and higher-dimensional light frequencies is extremely coherent. The quieting of the Sun, which means the lessening of solar flares and CMEs, is a sign of the dimensional shift process. Yes, immense quantities of higher energy are pouring in from the galactic center, but the majority of this influx is coming in beyond the third-dimensional level. Thus, while we are experiencing any number of significant shifts within 3-D, the real story is taking place on the superluminal levels.

The Sun is emanating higher-dimensional light frequencies, which are in turn raising the frequency of the Earth and the other planets in the solar system. Our planet and all the souls who live upon its surface are experiencing the increase in vibration as the "soul-ar" center at the core of our being, just above the heart and heart chakra, is being activated. This is where the luminous presence of our I AM or God nature is focalized. The activation occurs through a step-down process, beginning with the incoming higher-dimensional light frequencies of the galactic core as a result of the Galactic Alignment, which is transducing these frequencies into the solar system and specifically the Sun, which is in turn inducting these frequencies into all the planets, including Earth, and down into each human being. Magnetic portals connect all levels of the process, creating one giant, complex circuit from the galactic center to us. This higher-dimensional light is also carrying the evolutionary genetic codes which will birth the new species. This transformation is occurring on all levels — mental, emotional, spiritual and physical.

The coherent light cascading into the solar system and ultimately the Earth most closely resembles laser light. Through laser light, we have discovered holography and the true nature of the universe. Laser light is akin to the coherency of the light in the core of our being. This innermost radiance is expanding and intensifying, bringing forth its inherent divine nature, its higher consciousness, its essential qualities of love, wisdom, will and power. Because that higher light is so coherent and pours in from beyond third-dimensional reality, it is innately dissolving to all 3-D matter~energy matrices.

Consider the way laser beams are used to cut steel. They do not act on the steel destructively by burning through it, which is what our senses and mind might seem to perceive. What actually happens is that the coherency of the light rapidly releases the chaos in the molecular structure of the steel, so quickly that it disintegrates. In essence, all third-dimensional entropy and chaos is released, which is what is now happening on Earth. We will see an ever-quickening release of all 3-D energy~consciousness and form into a fourth- and higher-dimensional level of vibration.

We are essentially making a leap from one octave of creation to the next levels. Just as a rainbow has seven levels of color, which represent seven different frequencies of light, the universe contains many different bands of dimensional frequency. The Earth is simply in the process of shifting from the "red" third-dimensional frequency to the "orange" and "yellow" fourth- and fifth-dimensional frequencies.

Our planetary crises are the byproducts of the release of the distortion and chaos as a result of the incoming light. Everything we see will be translated to the next level, and that which cannot transform its 3-D energy~consciousness matrix will begin to disintegrate. Witness what is happening to our financial system, which is completely materialistic, based in fear and separation; it cannot translate to a fourth-dimensional Earth without a fundamental redo. The same is true of our energy system, based on fossil fuels. We can't live in a fourth-dimensional world while burning the remnants of plants and animals from millions of years ago. All we need to do to see what is not part of the new system is to look around us and notice what is breaking down. From my perspective, there is quite a bit that will not be able to make it as the planet leaps into higher-dimensional frequency realms.

The incoming wave of light is building more rapidly every day. Imagine watching a foam-tipped wave arise out of the ocean and head to the shore. In an inexorable movement, each wave can only continue on toward the shore — there is nowhere else for it to go. In the same way, this wave of light will crest and then crash upon the shores of planetary reality. It has a very steep wavefront, rising exponentially faster and faster as we near the point at which it crests. Sometime in the not-too-distant future, linear time and third-dimensional reality will fade away.

Just as a Tibetan Buddhist prepares for death every night before bed, we, too, can begin to prepare for the death of our third-dimensional, human identities as we awaken to and embrace our multidimensional, true Selves. The information age is over and the transformation age is in high gear. We are shifting the locus of our identity from the mind to the soul.

It is time to begin to turn away from our infatuation with and attachment to the things of the outer, material realms. It's time to unplug a bit more from the Internet and plug into the "inner net." Those of us who are to be part of the new, higher-dimensional Earth are like caterpillars entering into the chrysalis to allow our limited, 3-D nature to dissolve. Many of you who are reading this are probably feeling the need to go deeper within. You may be finding that the things of the outer world have less and less appeal. You're probably experiencing more of the "entropy and chaos" of your unfinished mental and emotional issues and personality distortions coming to the surface in the coherent light of your true nature. This is the journey of awakening to our vastness and magnificence. The final section of this book will delve into this process of awakening more fully.

As the wave of light crests, the very subatomic structure of matter~energy is going to make a quantum leap in vibration. What will occur is akin to what happens in an atom when any new energetic input is added. As energy is gradually absorbed by an atom, its vibrational rate increases. Everything speeds up in the atomic structure and things become more chaotic as the system attempts to cope with the increased energy. Then, in the blink of an eye, something magical happens. A quantum leap occurs within the atomic structure, as an electron disappears from a lower level of energetic potential and simultaneously reappears at a higher one. In this instantaneous migration, the atom leaves no track or trail as it translates.

This is exactly what is happening on planet Earth. We are approaching that quantum moment. When it arrives, the most important shift will be the shift in consciousness, which is causal to what occurs at the level of energy and ultimately matter. This is the moment we have waited for, since the time millions of years ago when souls first incarnated in the most primitive human forms. It is the moment when God's quest for Self-realization through human souls bears its fruit, falling off the tree into the new Garden of Eden that will surely unfold thereafter.

The Quantum Moment Through Other Eyes

The late Ken Carey expressed his sense of what lies ahead in <u>Starseed: The Third Millennium</u>:

> ....A moment of quantum awakening. A nanosecond will be stretched into infinity and become non-time, during which we will all experience full consciousness of who we are and why we have incarnated. If we choose to return to human form, we will do so in an awakened state, as "reflective cells of the starmaker."

Terence McKenna, who has also migrated beyond third-dimensional reality and no longer inhabits a physical form, realized through his studies of the I Ching and his exploration of mind-altering substances that we face a moment of radical discontinuity. He expressed this in his inimitable style in his article, <u>New Maps from Hyperspace</u>:

> What is happening to our world is ingression of novelty toward what Whitehead called "concrescence," a tightening gyre. Everything is flowing together.... the alchemical stone at the end of time...When the laws of physics are obviated, the universe disappears, and what is left is the tightly bound plenum, the monad, able to express itself for itself.

From the way the gyre is tightening, I predict that the concrescence will occur soon -- around 2012 AD. It will be the entry of our species into hyperspace, but it will appear to be the end of physical laws...The transition from earth to space will be a staggeringly tight genetic filter... The object at the end of and beyond history is the human species fused into eternal tantric union with the superconducting Overmind/UFO.

In his wonderfully eccentric way, McKenna is expressing the realization that we, as a species, are transcending laws of time and space as we have known them. We are translating into an entirely new vector in consciousness, reflecting what others, including Ken Carey, have predicted. Passing through a quantum moment, we are leaping beyond everything we have previously known, as a new human species unfolds.

In a piece called Light, Consciousness, and the White Hole in Time, Peter Russell contemplates what the quantum shift might be like:

How can a caterpillar guess what it's going to be like as a butterfly? I think we can get some sense for saying what it might be like if we look at the lives of the great saints and the enlightened people throughout history, with their sense of freedom and all that love in their hearts. What would it be like if the whole of human culture was founded on that? Or it could be something even far more strange than that. For example, we might move into something equivalent to a collective near-death experience. This might have similar stages to what individuals report from near-death experiences, such as stepping outside the physical body, moving into an experience of light, along with feelings of infinite peace, love, and light where there is no longer any fear of death.

It could be that at the white hole in time, this might happen on a collective level, where we all somehow simultaneously transcend our physical bodies and come together in a collective experi-

ence of awakening or transcendence.

Pierre Teilhard de Chardin, a Jesuit priest trained as a paleontologist and geologist, developed a profound cosmo-conception of the evolution of humanity and the Earth. His major work, *The Phenomenon of Man*, is an account of human nature and destiny developed through a fusion of his academic training and mystical experiences. He, like Carey, McKenna, and Russell, saw the Earth and humanity passing through a doorway into another dimension of reality. He called this "a translation or dematerialization to another sphere of the Universe."

De Chardin followed the unfoldment of creation, or cosmogenesis, to its ultimate conclusion, which he viewed as <u>the development of a new, Christed species</u>.

> *Cosmogenesis reveals itself, along the line of its main axis, first as Biogenesis (biological) and then Noogenesis (mind), and finally culminates in the Christogenesis (God/Self Realization).*
>
> *What, on the other hand, do we find if our minds can embrace simultaneously both contemporary neo-Christianity and contemporary neo-Humanism, and so first suspect and then accept as proved that the Christ of Revelation is none other than the Omega of Evolution?*

De Chardin understood that what we are about to experience in the birthing of a Christ-conscious species is the culmination of this long history of evolution. It began with the biological evolution of the species and continued into the unfoldment of its psyche, resulting in a species capable of realizing its true, eternal nature as an aspect of the One Great Being. Our evolutionary prototype was Jesus, who demonstrated the Omega of the soul's human experience through his resurrection and ascension.

20

Beyond the Quantum Moment

Every ending is a beginning, and it is good to remember this as we approach the ending of this entire cycle of evolution on planet Earth. The fullest expression of Source so far, Homo sapiens sapiens, is about to exit the evolutionary stage. Beyond the quantum moment, a whole new reality awaits us. What will the journey be like as we transit the end of time? How might the evolutionary journey of the Earth and humanity unfold, and what can we expect the new reality on the other side of the shift-point to be like?

On the most intriguing windows into what may lie beyond the shift of the ages came through the work of Helen Wambach, a transpersonal therapist in the San Francisco Bay Area. She reasoned that if subjects could be regressed to previous lives, they could also be progressed into the future. She wondered what people would report if they were hypnotized and taken to a time that has not yet arrived. The initial results of her future progression work were astounding, causing Wambach to seek assistance in gathering more data. She trained Chet Snow, who took over her work after Wambach died in the mid-1980s. The conclusions they drew from thousands of future-life progressions were published in _Mass Dreams of the Future_.

What Wambach and Snow discovered initially shocked them. By the middle of the twenty-first century, more than 90% of the hypnotic subjects experienced themselves as floating in a quiet, peaceful void, which the hypnotists interpreted to mean they were no longer in a physical body. This surmise was corroborated as they progressed subjects further into the future, and they found themselves back in embodiment on a radically different Earth.

During the period between 2100 and 2300, subjects found themselves inhabiting one of four basic scenarios. Three of them involved a planet that had been decimated to varying degrees by human impact and Earth changes. The first storyline portrayed a future that was very bleak indeed. The planet had become nearly uninhabitable, and human life had been reduced to foraging in the ruins for useful things from the past and securing food through hunting and gathering. The second group of subjects found themselves living in contained environments on an Earth that barely supported human existence. These biosphere communities used advanced technology to create completely enclosed habitations in which a relatively high level of culture could continue while the planet healed from the catastrophes. The third group lived outside the planet's biosphere in an advanced technological environment on space stations orbiting the Earth.

The final scenario is the most intriguing, in that it cannot be placed in the same reality framework as the first three. These subjects found themselves living on an Earth that was a paradise, a lush and beautiful planet existing within a very refined octave of creation. This realm suffered no devastating climatic events or Earth changes; to the contrary, in this Edenic environment, all species lived as one in a state of harmony and peace.

More than two decades ago, prophecies of the future were a hot topic. I had read Chet Snow's book and had received the visions of the new Earth that are included in the next chapter. I devoted a lot of time to pondering what the path to the new Earth might present, and what it might be like when we got there. Gradually, an understanding emerged that integrated all the pieces that were floating around.

The *Mass Dreams of the Future* research was pivotal in this process, for it did not indicate there would be one, uniformly experienced future for us all. As the hypnotic subjects described their surroundings, their accounts revealed multiple, seemingly mutually exclusive realities. These very different scenarios seemed to corroborate the possibility that multiple timelines or reality paths lie ahead for humanity. The quantum moment appears to be an interdimensional doorway on the other side of which a number of different possible futures lie. Quantum theory has shown that multiple realities are possible at a subatomic level and that what is experienced directly reflects the consciousness of the observer. Spiritually awakened beings have long said the same is true on a macroscopic basis — we are continually co-creating our future realities with Source Creator, of which we are each a part.

After considering this for decades, I have come to believe that many future timelines are possible. As shared above, the subjects in Wambach's and Snow's future progression sessions described four possible or probable futures. We could consider those four possibilities as four timelines, and as we know, timelines can change at every point along them, as new decisions are made and new paths of action are pursued. Possible or even probable futures can still change at any moment, because we have free will. It is crucial to remember that no predictions are absolute. We humans tend to give our power to such prognostications, forgetting that we are key players in all that unfolds, not only in our personal lives but also within the larger contexts of soul groups and species evolution.

Given the plethora of crises we face, it seems unlikely that humanity will somehow escape living on a diminished, if not decimated planet before too long. Many of the crises discussed in Part One could bring this about, and global warfare could do it even more quickly. Therefore it does seem likely that at least one timeline in which humans live on an Earth that is recovering from the effects of climate change, pollution, and destruction to the biosphere — or worse — is probable at this writing. And, that can all change in the next moment depending on the collective consciousness.

The Wambach/Snow scenario that was hard to integrate within the future possibilities was the fourth one. A new Garden of Eden didn't easily fit into the picture, considering what we know of the planet at present and the fact that the other three timelines involve a devastated planet. But we need to remind ourselves that when Earth and humanity go through the dimensional quantum leap process, we will leave the constraints of third-dimensional reality behind. And one of the biggest of these is time.

Within 3-D, we experience the event-flow of our lives like beads on a string of time. One experience leads to the next and the next, sequentially, in a linear fashion. That is not true from the fourth-dimensional level on up. Free of the limitations of time, other possible futures could be experienced on parallel realities and timelines.

As I contemplated this, it became clear that the fourth group in the future progression study, living in an earthly paradise, had vibrated into another timeline entirely, one in which the Earth had been healed and resurrected into an Edenic, fifth-dimensional planet. It seemed possible that these subjects were seeing a future Earth, existing in a different timeline, or perhaps in the far future after it had time to heal. Many sensitive souls around the planet have seen this Earth. It could very easily already exist in the Eternal Now, as my personal experiences and those of others indicate is true.

It is also quite possible that the other three groups in the study were on different timelines from one another. The souls foraging in the ruins might inhabit a space~time locus that closely follows major Earth changes or human-caused catastrophes, while those living in biospheres and on space stations may exist on timelines much later in the future. The new EarthHeaven, the fourth scenario the progression subjects described, represents a planet that has evolved and ascended. As many have directly experienced, this Earth already exists in a parallel reality on a different timeline, at a higher octave than that experienced by the first three groups. This is where the part of humanity that remains with the Earth and rises in consciousness with her are probably going to wind up, sooner or later.

The two of us experienced parallel realities during Hurricane Iniki on the island of Kaua'i in 1992. Iniki was a Category 5 hurricane with sustained winds of 160 mph and gusts over 200. Over half of the structures on the island were destroyed, but amazingly no one's body died as a direct result of the storm. The hand of the Divine was clearly guiding those ferocious winds with an amazing precision. Later, we walked down many streets to see one house leveled, with nothing but drainpipes protruding out of its concrete slab, while the next house was virtually untouched. Many people commented on this mysterious phenomenon. What a demonstration of parallel realities existing side by side! You can read more about this amazing story of grace in the first book in the Birthing the Luminous Self Trilogy, <u>Soul Awakening: The Journey From Ego to Essence</u>.

21

Many Futures

One thing we learned during and after Hurricane Iniki was that, in the end, it is our state of awakening and realization of our true, eternal nature that will almost certainly determine what timeline we find ourselves on, and which future reality we inhabit beyond the shift point. Although many humans prefer to see themselves as helpless victims of outer events, external reality is not a collection of random, meaningless circumstances. What goes on "out there" can be nothing more or less than a holographic projection of our internal state. Quantum physics has validated this in showing that the mere presence of an observer affects the outcome of an experiment at subatomic levels. Soon it will become common knowledge that this is true on all levels. Our consciousness literally forms the template from which external reality is constructed. To the degree that we are full of fear and asleep in the illusion of separation, we will experience a world that mirrors this. Crises, war, destruction, disease, and death are magnetized to us via the Law of Attraction. If, however, we have realized the divinity at the core of our being, this, too, will be beautifully reflected in the harmony and grace in our outer life.

Consciousness is always causal to manifestation. And we always get exactly what we need to awaken. All experiences come as gifts of grace, when we have eyes to see them as such. We may need some intense mirrors of our unconsciousness in order to snap us out of that trance and into a more aware state. Whatever comes into our lives originates in the endless love of the One, no matter how it appears or how much it triggers our egoic resistance and rebellion. Thus, some might experience a very difficult future existence, foraging amidst the ruins of a defunct city, while others may have acquired the technological means to exist on the decimated planet or to escape and live beyond it. Those who are complete with living in any sort of limited reality may "graduate" to the new, Edenic Earth.

What is different about this time is this: it is the Will of the One that this planet evolve into its next state of divine expression. Many, including ourselves, have received repeated revelations that we humans will not be allowed to destroy ourselves or the planet. Much destruction may be allowed to occur, but it will be in service to the awakening and collective evolutionary leap. There is a joker in the deck that could change everything. Grace is descending upon us through it all, bringing both the necessary purification and the higher frequencies of energy~consciousness necessary to catalyze planetary awakening. While Grace does not skip any steps in the evolutionary process, it operates beyond linear time, thus making great leaps possible. This is why locking one's mind into immutable, catastrophic scenarios, even though based on solid scientific evidence of where trends will take us, is invalid.

The Earth's vibration has been upleveling during the decades since the Wambach/Snow work, and as the global awakening continues to unfold, the possibilities are expanding with each passing day. As the wave of light flows into our solar system, the field effect is pulling everyone's consciousness up to meet it. The base frequency of the Earth and humanity is already ascending toward a fourth-dimensional vibratory range. As this gathers momentum, the entropy and chaos of 3-D will lessen, along with the subsequent destruction needed to purify and raise the Earth.

The vibratory frequency of Earth has already contributed to an upleveling of human consciousness, as evidenced by the work of consciousness researcher David Hawkins. Through extensive, planet-wide studies, Hawkins developed a scale of human consciousness spanning levels 0 to 1000. Level zero signifies those human beings who are asleep, lost in shame and guilt, while 1000 equals the fully enlightened state. As we become more conscious and awake, we rise on the Hawkins scale. Each new level signifies the transcendence of particular emotional states and the transition into greater inner freedom and peace.

Level 200 is an important demarcation point in Hawkins' system; above 200, human beings are leaving behind anger and violence, and are no longer self-destructive. Hawkins claims that humanity passed this major turning-point in collective evolution a few decades ago. This may seem questionable when we view the apparent disintegrating state of human relationships, and the state of the planet. We need to understand that Hawkins is measuring the *collective* consciousness, which is greatly elevated by a small number of awake and awakening beings who have dedicated themselves wholly to the spiritual path. These beings function at elevated levels that balance out the lower vibrational levels of literally millions, possibly billions, of souls. Such beings include not only the few Great Souls like Gandhi and other spiritual titans, but also lightworkers, adepts, sadhus, monks and seekers of all races, religions, ages and paths.

Hawkins found that the scale of consciousness is logarithmic. The higher we ascend, the greater our effect on the overall field of human consciousness. Higher states are always superior in effect over lower ones, exerting a powerful, inexorable lifting of consciousness. Neither individual nor collective egoic will can resist this raising effect, as it works on the consciousness substrate out of which everything arises. Hawkins concluded that one individual at the 300 level could raise and counterbalance the effects of 90,000 people under the 200 fulcrum point. At 500, the frequency of love, an individual offsets 750,000 others, and at the 700 level of enlightenment, 70 million people are raised. Twelve individuals who calibrate at 700 or above have the effect of one great being such as Buddha or Christ or Krishna, who functioned at 1000, lifting all of humanity.

This information offers a potent reminder of exactly how humanity has the potential to transcend apocalypse, or at least mitigate the destruction. Imagine what would happen if not just twelve individuals reached these higher states, but a hundred, or a thousand. It only takes a few who have fully committed their lives to soul awakening to lift many others. What would be the effect of having dozens of consciousness avatars, or thousands living in a state of love, in embodiment simultaneously? The research of David Hawkins indicates that a rapid collective awakening is not just a pipe dream.

Are New, Brighter Timelines Emerging?

We may feel discouraged when we contemplate how much ignorance, hatred, greed, and other ego manifestations still erupt on a daily basis across the planet. We may not know where or how to begin to address all the specters of planetary extinction described in Part One of this book. At times, the pace of human evolution can seem glacial indeed. Yet evidence is building that increasing human consciousness has caused future timelines to shift in a positive direction. Consider the following.

Many of the direst prophesies have failed to materialize. Think of all the Earth changes that were predicted to happen by the end of the 20th century. For example, Edgar Cayce foresaw a cataclysmic shifting of the Earth's rotational axis in the late 1990s. Ancient seers such as Nostradamus saw a totally decimated Earth as a result of cataclysms such as those presented in the biblical book of Revelations. The many predictions of catastrophes associated with the end of the Mayan Calendar at winter solstice in 2012 also didn't happen. How many of us believed we would make it to the year 2018 without major earthquakes, global wars, worldwide economic crises, and who knows what else?

This doesn't mean that many of these will still not occur. As we have seen, some climate and ecological crises seem likely to play out, along with the possibility of a solar event and magnetic reversal. But there is one major mitigating factor: with each new day, more and more of us are awakening, lifting the frequencies of the planet and making it easier for more sleeping souls to wake up.

We recently discovered a current version of Helen Wambach and Chet Snow in <u>Allison Coe of Portland, Oregon, who also does future progression work</u> with clients. Allison regularly shares what her clients are experiencing through YouTube videos. During their sessions, some of her clients began to spontaneously experience translating or ascending to a new, Edenic Earth. They describe diverging timelines and possibility paths branching out from what they call "the Event" — a global wave of light~consciousness shift phenomenon.

"The Event" appears to function as a cosmic sorting mechanism that sends souls into various new pathways, depending on their level of soul-evolution. Many will immediately go to a pre-existing fifth-dimensional Earth. Others who are prepared for the upleveled frequencies of the wave of light and are destined to help anchor them will stay on the Earth. They will immediately become higher-dimensional beings, as will the entire planet. From her clients' descriptions, it will be a fourth-dimensional world. People will realize the state of oneness with all of life and discover they now possess abilities such as telepathy. The aging process will slow, and they will not become ill with the same frequency and to the same degree as on the 3-D Earth. All life-forms will be more vibrant, shimmering with a radiance that is fourth-dimensional.

Many of Coe's clients relate their understanding that the wave of light~dimensional shift could happen at any moment. They seem to experience no fear whatsoever around the future scenarios they were shown, at peace in the knowing that all will be held within a larger cocoon of safety and rightness.

During the times when I have become depressed or fearful about what might lie ahead, I have always been brought back to the deep knowing that something new and wonderful is going to happen on the other side of whatever destruction is needed, and that the very highest possibility we can open to will unfold. Working with people for so many years, together with my own journey of awakening, have taught me that the Universe is based in love. Nothing happens that is not founded in love, even those things that are destructive to physical life. Whatever transpires during the times to come, I know in my heart and soul that the least amount of destruction and loss of life possible will occur, and the highest possibilities will unfold — for each one of us, and for humanity as a whole.

22

Visions of the New Earth

During the early years of my spiritual journey, one of my biggest questions was *What will Earth be like after the dimensional shift?* It took nearly a decade to get an answer, which came to me in the form of two visions. The first arrived shortly after Harmonic Convergence in 1987, and the second came nearly two decades later, confirming the first. In both visions, I was lifted out of this dimension to a "new Earth" that already pre-existed on a higher dimension.

These experiences were so tangible and visceral, with all senses involved, that I knew without a doubt a new Earth-Heaven exists beyond the current hologram we collectively agree on as reality. When I have shared these visions over the years, others have spontaneously mentioned that they, too, have had similar experiences. The uncanniness with which these visions match the fourth scenario in the Wambach/Snow future progressions further corroborates that a higher-dimensional Earth already exists.

The visions I was shown resulted in a potent inner reorientation. A lot of free-floating anxiety about the future disappeared. Any thoughts that the planet and humanity might not make it were erased. Concerns about how difficult the times might become were eased, knowing the magnificent future that surely would come.

The First Vision: 1988

This vision occurred just after the Harmonic Convergence in 1987, when so much information on the dimensional shift was pouring through to awakening humanity. Interestingly, the vision came in before reading the future progressions in *Mass Dreams of the Future*.

During a morning meditation, I found myself being taken up through the dimensions and "landing" in a very bright place. At first I could not see much of anything, as the frequency was so much higher that the light was very bright to my Earth eyes. Slowly I found myself to be standing in brilliantly green grass that was waving in the wind as quickly as a hummingbird's wings flutter. This made it apparent that this reality was operating at much different frequency than my senses were accustomed to.

As I adjusted to the heightened vibration, everything slowed. All my senses were much more refined, and at a level well beyond "normal." The best word to describe it would be super-sensory, as the experience had so many more facets and dimensions that third-dimensional sensory experience seemed "flat" in comparison.

I found myself looking down at a small community of beings who were living in a futuristic setting. What lay before me was an outpicturing of a highly advanced level of consciousness. A collage of subtle, multicolored structures, including pyramidal and geodesic dome-like buildings and others exhibiting sacred geometric principles, formed a tapestry woven in deep harmony.

Everything flowed together seamlessly, and the life-imbued aesthetics pleased the soul on a level we have no concept for on the present Earth. The walkways were lined with colorful flowers in brilliant pastels unlike anything we know. The colors were much more vivid, yet at the same time softer than what we experience with third-dimensional eyes. Edible plants were everywhere, providing the minimal material sustenance that these more refined, higher-frequency beings needed. Nowhere did I see any presence of animals, which precluded them as a food source.

The layout of the community was based on the golden mean spiral, and everything flowed in perfect harmony, with winding walkways between structures laid out in integrated patterns that formed mandalas nestled in lush, semitropical landscapes. The experience of moving through it flowed in a way that was deeply nurturing to the soul. Life energy was enhanced by the harmony that evokes our deepest nature. Everywhere was a deep, pervading peace, and great joy and happiness.

Work was unknown, even conceptually, as it was understood that life was a joyful, creative exploration, just for the sake of being. Everyone seemed engaged in a life of "play." The idea of something not being joyful simply didn't exist.

It was also clear that the genetic anomalies we experience in third-dimensional, physical bodies weren't present here. Everyone possessed forms we would call nearly perfect, which, while still solid and tangible, were much less dense than ours. People did not have accidents or diseases; their advanced consciousness became aware of and resolved any distortions that would precipitate such occurrences well before they manifested. There was no need for governments, police or other emergency services. No one needed to be governed; crimes and what we call "accidents" never occurred. Truth, love and wisdom pervaded everything. A oneness that unified all minds insured harmony, cooperation and co-creation.

Mechanical conveyances were not needed to move from one place to another. These beings either enjoyed a leisurely stroll or simply shifted their locus in consciousness, emerging bodily wherever they chose. Although they exhibited higher capacities, the bodies these beings inhabited were not vaporous or of light; they had a solidity, although it was much less dense than our three-dimensional bodies. There was no sense that we would be sacrificing anything we love and enjoy in these new forms -- quite the opposite. These bodies were far more sentient, experiencing a level of subtlety unknown to the human senses. As I felt the gentle winds, it was as though I was being caressed, and through their touch I could feel and know all the movements of the air for many miles. Everything was vividly alive and communicating its essential nature.

There was no harshness in any sensory experience. The soft gentleness was accompanied by a profound increase in the magnitude of each sensation that was magnificent and satisfying to the soul beyond anything we can now comprehend.

The natural world that surrounded the community, while having trees and other plants similar to those on the third-dimensional Earth, exhibited a symmetry and perfection that gave the impression a cosmic gardener had arranged it all. The "wild" areas did not include the chaos that is found in our current forests. Nowhere was there tangled vegetation or even one stunted, distorted tree or weed. Instead, the countryside looked as sculpted as a park. Everywhere -- in the people, the buildings, and the natural environment -- the perfect symmetry and geometry of the divine image was manifest. Truly, this dimension, free of entropy and distortion, was a heaven on Earth. The closest images I have ever seen on this level are paintings by Maxfield Parrish, and as magnificent as they are, they do not accurately express the beautiful paradise of the new EarthHeaven, for it truly is heavenly.

After this experience, a lot more of the subconscious clinging and attachment to this world dissolved away, replaced by an experiential knowing that the new Earth was already in existence on another dimension, one that I would gladly -- no, excitedly -- embrace going to when the time comes.

The Second Vision: 2005

Not quite two decades later, Karen and I found ourselves in a small hotel in Alturas, California, near the Warner Mountains. This part of northeastern California is a place we love to visit because it is very quiet and wide-open, energetically. As I lay in bed that morning, I found myself being taken out of my body and toward the Warner range, which has always been a magical place for us. We often stop to meditate there when we are passing through, and always feel exalted energies pouring onto the Earth.

As I approached the lower Warners, I became aware of a dissolving of the veils between the worlds, and soon I was landing in a community on the New Earth. It was very similar to the one I experienced in 1988, but smaller and somewhat less sophisticated in its development. The same feeling of harmony and beauty prevailed, and I was particularly struck by the loving emanation from the luminous, advanced human beings I communed with.

The message they gave me is that the veils are already beginning to thin between this higher octave of Earth and the present, consensus-reality version. The apparent barrier will continue to dissolve during the years ahead, especially in particularly pure, pristine, higher-vibrational areas such as this one. The veils between the dimensions are already very thin there. There was a sense that the time would come when movement back and forth between the worlds would occur, with the possibility that some of us would step through the veil and then come back, albeit briefly and with purpose.

This resonated with numerous previous visions of encountering what I had come to call the "wall of water" at some time in the future. In these visions, I would be walking in a natural setting when just ahead an ovoid shimmering would appear in the air. The quality of the visual experience resembled a mirage caused by hot air rising off a blacktop highway, but was more iridescent and faster-moving, vibrationally. I always found myself instinctively walking up to the shimmering portal and stepping right through, to find myself on the other side in a higher-dimensional body similar to the ones I had seen in the two New Earth visions. Once through, all the distortion and imperfection of the human form would be completely gone. One would also be able to walk back through the veil with the new bodily form to assist others, but only for a limited period of time. When I've shared this experience with others, a number of people have responded that they, too, have seen the "wall of water" portals.

23

The End That Is The Beginning

To recapitulate our journey through what it might mean to awaken at the end of time, let's consider what we've looked at so far. The first section of this book focused on a physical plane perspective on what is happening on Earth nearly two decades into the 21st century. A wealth of scientific reports fueled projections about where things might go if our current third-dimensional reality system continues in the direction it's going.

We can see where we have been, and how the situation looks now, but we cannot know precisely where we are headed, because consciousness and the vibratory level of the Earth are continuously rising and expanding. The wave of light is inundating our planet and its inhabitants with vastly expanded frequencies of energy~consciousness, which might mean those 3-D projections are probably not going to play out exactly as forecast. That does not mean we've escaped all destruction, though, especially if human beings are unwilling go through the requisite ego-dissolution and spiritual awakening that will further shift our future timelines.

In Part Two, we shifted to a larger perspective, and looked at what is transpiring from the vastest viewpoint that's been revealed to us so far. From this level of inclusiveness, what is going on in 3-D turns out to be the tangible level of a far greater process — a mega–evolutionary event which will result in the birth of a soul-awakened species. We have touched on what the journey through the dimensional shift process might be like, as well as what lies on the other side.

In the end, it comes back to each of us. What determines how this journey unfolds? Our state of consciousness deeply affects future timelines and reality scenarios. Possibilities we can't even imagine yet inhabit the unknown regions stretching out before us. Which of them will manifest? Which will fade away, no longer resonant with where we are in our awakening? Since consciousness inevitably outpictures in our outer surroundings, we can wisely conclude that the most important thing to focus on is our inner state. That is why it is so absolutely important at this pivotal time that all awakening souls commit themselves more fully than ever to their spiritual path.

A planetary awakening could occur quite quickly and unexpectedly, with the help of exponential functions. Remember the lily pond example? Our theoretical pond had only one water lily growing on its surface on day one of this monthlong experiment. The supposition of the experiment was that each day, the amount of pond surface covered by water lilies would double. On the 21st day, just .02% of the surface of the pond was covered by lilies. Even on the 25th day, the pond was only 3% covered. On day 29, the pond was still only half full of water lilies. But on the very last day, just as the month was about to end, the pond was completely covered by this beautiful life-form.

Could it be that this same process is unfolding in the human collective consciousness? Could breathtaking leaps of awakening occur in not just a few of us, but every one of us, in the not-too-distant future? When we consider the enormity and breadth of the crises we face, alongside the current spiritual state of humanity, it may seem there is no way our species will ever awaken in time to avoid catastrophe. But that may only be because we are unable to perceive the ever-accelerating upward curve in the level of collective consciousness.

Those who are not complete with experiencing separation, fear, conflict and other aspects of the egoic journey will be exiting in increasing numbers. Perhaps they will continue their exploration of 3-D on other worlds. Simultaneously, those who are to be part of the nascent New Earth-Heaven are experiencing an exponential expansion of consciousness. This could result in a mass awakening occurring at an unimaginable rate.

In the dualistic universe, everything is balanced by its opposite. If we are experiencing exponential rates of the breakdown of our third-dimensional world, would it not seem reasonable to postulate that the birth of a new, higher-dimensional world is occurring just as rapidly?

Awakened beings throughout history have demonstrated the capacity to perform miracles. Many people believe nuclear and other kinds of cataclysms have already been prevented by higher-dimensional beings working to assist humanity's evolution. As we shift into a fourth- and fifth-dimensional reality, such beings may well precipitate the grace necessary to transcend some portion of the unfolding catastrophes.

During the first coming, 2000 years ago, Christ Jesus used the parable of the Fig Tree to deliver a potent teaching.

> *32 Truly I tell you, this generation will not pass away until all these things have happened.*
> *33 Heaven and Earth will pass away, but My words will never pass away. 34 But watch yourselves, or your hearts will be weighed down by dissipation, drunkenness, and the worries of life — and that day will spring upon you suddenly like a snare....*

My heart and soul tell me we are in the time of that generation of souls in the human experience. Surely "heaven and earth" — the totality of the third-dimensional reality we have known — will pass away, but the ultimate truth that Christ, as well as many other great masters, demonstrated will never pass away, for that is our true, eternal nature. As Jesus warned, it is time to shift the focus of our lives away from the things of the world that distract us from our all-important spiritual unfoldment. Could His words have been any clearer? Remember, He also promised, *"Seek ye first the Kingdom of Heaven and all things will be added unto you."*

The time of the Great Shift is upon us. Our human minds may still not be able to refrain from wondering how this experience will end for us. In the Gospel of Thomas, Jesus responds to this question.

> *The disciples said to Jesus: Tell us how our end will be. Jesus said: Since you have discovered the beginning, why do you seek the end? For where the beginning is, there will the end be. Blessed is he who shall stand at the beginning*

(or in the beginning, depending on the translation), and he shall know the end, and shall not taste death.

The beginning of all things is the Source of All That Is. That One births all of Creation as an emanation of infinite, eternal light, love, and life. In the beginning, that One differentiated itself into an infinity of forms of being, be they universes, galaxies, solar systems, planets or human souls. The purpose? So that One could realize its nature through its creation.

We are that Source, that One, temporarily residing within myriad differentiated forms. We are still as we were in the Beginning. Our true, eternal, whole, divine nature remains the real truth of our existence. It is what always, already is — despite all appearances in this human drama — and will be, at the end and beyond.

As we come to the end of the journey, we will know that we are infinite, eternal beings, drops in the ocean of God, and the ocean of God in the drop of our being. In this realization, we will know and experience that death is but an illusion. What is eternal can know no end. Forms come and go in Creation, whether they be galaxies, solar systems, planets or human bodies. But the luminous, divine beings we truly are existed prior to all beginnings and will persist beyond all endings. Eternity is not a very long time. It is the truth that exists when all illusion of time is finally gone.

PART THREE

✧ ✧ ✧

Bringing it all Home

✧ ✧ ✧

24

Embrace and Transcend

We've come to the end of our journey of exploring the current state of our species and our world, as well as scenarios of future possibilities. In Part One, we viewed the state of humanity and its potential futures through the lens of third-dimensional, human perception. In Part Two, we expanded our viewpoint to include extra-planetary and higher-dimensional perspectives. I hope this journey has assisted you in expanding and deepening your own understanding.

Now it's time to integrate it all, at least in a preliminary sense. It is going to be a journey for all of us to process our way through the labyrinth of shifts and changes caused by the evolutionary drivers that our many crises represent. At the same time, we will also feel ourselves being raised in consciousness, in the awakening and quickening that the ever-building wave of light is catalyzing. You may find yourself shifting back and forth between these perspectives, at times looking through a dark lens — the third-dimensional perception of our dying caterpillar selves — and at others lifting above it all and seeing it from the transcendental viewpoint of our emerging butterfly Selves.

Both perspectives are integral parts of the journey. In this alchemical process, we are challenged to embrace and include our intensely challenging sojourns into 3-D caterpillar consciousness, even as the luminous experiences of our emergent divine, butterfly Selves raise us through and beyond it all. This synthesis of the imminent and transcendent is what catalyzes the birth of Homo Luminous. As Ken Wilber assures us, **include and transcend** is the way all evolution occurs. Every part of ourselves and our experience is to be embraced as integral to the journey of birthing our luminous Self. Even our seemingly distorted, shadowy aspects will transform into whole, divine expressions once they are embraced and transcended in the light of our vaster Self.

This book has presented a sort of "test-drive" in consciousness through the possible futures that may lay ahead. As such, it can serve as a mirror to show us where we are attached and identified with the illusory, human self sense. The path to transcending that is through facing and embracing the fear that hides in the shadow aspects of the false self.

The "test drive" period has really already ended. With each passing day, we will have more up close and personal opportunities to engage with the death and rebirth process that is upon us all. We live in the reality that the world as we have known it is ending. We don't have to read about it anymore — it is occurring right where we live.

The past year has brought many harbingers of immense change right here at our home near the California-Oregon border. They leave no doubt that the climate is changing rapidly in our part of the world. Winter was pretty much nonexistent for months — no major storms or snow accumulation, and temps much warmer than average. Most years, our first spring flowers appear in mid-March. This year, they poked up through the soil in late January, only to be frozen out when a sudden cold snap showed up in late February and lasted through most of March, a time when winter is usually releasing its icy grip. For the first time ever, we saw our first hummingbirds in mid-March, a full three months ahead of their normal return.

Seeing these kinds of things runs right up against the longing for stability that lives deep within our human selves. Registering such changes vibrates the survival programs in our bellies, bringing up feelings of vulnerability and fear. Watching the world change and watching ourselves react to that reflects back to us our tendencies to look for safety and security in the outer world. Most of us are not aware of how much fear we carry deep within, for our egos are masters at distracting us from what is really going on inside of us. Instead, our minds become caught in the ego's defense mechanisms — denial, blaming others, projection, magical thinking, and many more. All these forms of ego-resistance do their best to distract us from experiencing what is happening within.

If we are to experience the freedom of awakening, becoming aware of ego-resistance is key. But let's remember that this is not a once-and-done event — most of us will not suddenly see through the ego and be free of it forever. Instead, we will learn about it every step of the way Home to who we truly are.

And it is good to remember that the ego is not our enemy. **It is simply who we are not.** One way to describe the process of awakening is that it is the continual juxtaposition in consciousness of who we really are and who we are not. We temporarily identify with limited aspects of our humanness, then wake up and shift back into knowing we are the soul, the true Self. We suffer, and then we experience the peace and reasonless joy of the Divine in us. Back and forth we go, until we finally see through all the disguises and fully remember that our limitless, eternal nature is who we truly are.

We are all somewhere along that continuum of awakening. Seeing ego, remembering soul — this is the nature of the journey Home. Until we are fully reabsorbed into the infinite Oneness of the Divine, we will meet manifestations of ego all along the way. This is not a tragedy, nor is it something to be ashamed of. It is simply What Is — the landscape of awakening.

So let's dive in more deeply and learn how the ego tries to keep us asleep. The more we know about that, the less susceptible we will be to its machinations. In each moment, we can choose where to focus our awareness. Do we want to give power to the ego, and be lost in forgetting our true nature? Or do we want to see through the ego's games and wake up?

25

Dealing with Ego Resistance and Defenses

You may be experiencing ego-resistance to some of the thoughts and feelings this book has stimulated in you. It may help to learn how to spot, and then transcend, ego-resistance. It is safe to say that pretty much everyone on this planet is going to experience some ego-resistance in the days ahead. That's not a bad thing; we can drop any ideas that we should be beyond this and welcome whatever arises as a necessary aspect of our awakening process. When we shift from avoiding ego-stuff to facing it head-on, we stop resisting the resistance and invite it to join us at the table. Resistance is to be expected and even honored as an essential part of the journey of awakening.

Why does resistance so often arise? To understand that, it can be helpful to delve into how the ego works, and why it does what it does. The personal ego is designed to keep us feeling safe under all circumstances. It knows what our "comfort zone" is and does everything it can to keep us within it. That is how the psyche is built.

This serves a very important survival purpose. The ego subconsciously senses threats and does everything it can to protect us from experiencing the fear, overwhelm and panic that they can cause. When we are subject to psycho-emotional inputs that feel overwhelming, to the point that we may break down, the ego steps to the forefront and takes control. We are usually not aware that this has happened; it goes on subconsciously. And if this is true for each of us individually, imagine all that goes on in the larger body of humanity.

Every one of us is currently experiencing any number of informational inputs from our environment that could easily put us into psychic stress overload. This may be part of the reason we haven't collectively been able to face what is really going on with our disintegrating world culture and planetary ecosystem. Maybe it's why <u>one in six Americans is on psychiatric drugs</u>. It's a good bet that most of us are going to face numerous psycho-emotional meltdowns in the future, as we find ourselves propelled out of our comfort zones. That's not a disaster — it's how we evolve. Being catapulted beyond our safe zone is to be expected and even embraced as part of the process of awakening. Resisting What Is only amplifies our suffering.

The first step in moving through ego-resistance is to realize that it is occurring. Watching our thought processes and the words we hear ourselves saying is key. The ego employs a variety of disguises to convince us that its viewpoint is the only one that makes any sense. One of the principal ways the ego-mind deflects input that may trigger unconscious material is to de-legitimize the source of the information. You may, for example, find yourself rejecting outright some of the information presented in the earlier parts of this book.

Negative labeling is one way the ego does this. This enables us to discard something from real consideration, by putting into a mental box that denies the potential reality of what is being presented. When we hear the mind labeling information as "gloom and doom," for example, the label allows us to escape the feelings of anxiety and fear it brings up from the subconscious. The ego may also delegitimize the source of the information in any number of ways, which also allows us to dismiss what is being presented. When we believe the ego's judgments without questioning them, we feel free to discard the input without really considering it.

Outright **denial** is another strategy the ego-mind utilizes whenever possible. I've witnessed this in my summer job as a fire lookout. For years, I have pointed out the decreasing winter snowpack, the hotter summers, the dying of more trees due to disease caused by heat and drought, and the rapidly increasing incidence of catastrophic wildfires, as signs of climate change. Most of the people I work with dismissed this idea outright. Some cited these kinds of climate changes as normal: "It's just part of a cycle —nothing to worry about." Well, in the larger scheme of things, they were right in one way; there truly is nothing to worry about. But from my perspective, as shared in this book, they are denying the reality of human-caused climate change.

All of us are going to be receiving more unusual and alarming information as the changes continue to unfold across the globe. We'll also undoubtedly have our own direct experiences, like the one I shared above, that awaken us to what is going on. One way or another, whether the input comes from within and/or without, the Divine Delivery System will make sure we get the messages we are to receive in order to awaken. Ego defense strategies prevent us from examining whether there might be some truth to the information, something we can only know when our minds and hearts are open. In the days ahead, being aware of when we are closing down and when we are open to new input may be more important than ever.

The more open and available our consciousness is, the more easily we will find ourselves guided through whatever we face next. Life is always trying to present us with the information we need. If we dismiss it out of hand, we might miss an important piece that Life is doing its best to make us aware of for any number of reasons. The One is always attempting to guide us, and that will remain true through the many unpredictable and unprecedented passages that lie ahead. The Divine is also aware of exactly what we need to face in order to surface and release our unconscious shadow material, so our true nature can shine forth.

The **spiritual ego** is another, even more slippery aspect of the ego that we need to be aware of. The spiritual ego is masterful in helping us avoid conflict. Its core strategy is called "spiritual bypassing," a term coined by John Welwood. The essence of this strategy is to soar up into disembodied or spirit-polarized states of consciousness, which lets us avoid the unpleasant rumblings of the ego-stuff in our bellies. While a spiritual perspective is crucial, using it to disconnect from our embodied experience is another form of ego denial and escapism. Spiritual bypassing allows us, albeit only temporarily, to avoid actually experiencing what is really alive in us. Self-realization is about "realizing" or actualizing our transcendent spiritual aspects in the everyday, human experience. It's about living, expressing, and experiencing the love, peace, wisdom and all the other innate conditions and capacities of our divine soul, *in embodiment*. Our full magnificence can't be lived and expressed if whole parts of our subconscious mind are mired in darkness and illusion, and if we are prohibited by the spiritual ego from ever going near any of this unresolved material. Only through facing and accepting it can it be transcended.

Spiritual bypassing is almost always based on a couple of widely shared beliefs. One goes like this: *The mental-emotional "stuff" of the human realms is not part of my true nature, so it's better to ignore it*. Another says *If I face it and engage with it in any way, I will be giving power to it*.

As is nearly always the case, the truth lies exactly 180 degrees away from these beliefs. When we attempt to evade and avoid the uncomfortable emotions and harsh judgments bubbling up from our subconscious, we are actually giving power and reality to them. If we truly **knew** they were not part of who we really are, if we **knew** these thoughts and feelings have no reality and no power over us, we wouldn't work so hard to avoid being with them.

Spiritual bypassing can become a way of life — and an evolutionary cul de sac. To the degree that we are busy suppressing and denying the unfinished business in our lower chakras, we won't be able to fully **embody** our true, eternal nature. This is one of the fundamental goals of the human experience — to bring all of the light, love, and life that we are into this world of forgetting, so that we can shine as lamps of remembrance for other awakening souls. Those who practice spiritual bypassing often voice eternal spiritual truths, but while they are understood mentally, they have not yet been realized on all levels of their beings; the wisdom is not grounded in living reality.

Such people can seem ethereal, spaced-out, and out of touch with earth-plane concerns. Little wonder that they would prefer not to face hard realities such as what is happening to our beloved planet.

Another widely shared belief in spiritual circles is that we should be beyond it all, free from the arising of subconscious material. The ego's common traits of perfectionism, self-judgment and magical thinking all combine to create a spiritual double bind, which causes a lot of suffering. An internal voice may be saying something like, *I have all this mental-emotional* **stuff** *— if only I could get past it all, I could really get someplace spiritually.* But the truth is, we're not **supposed** to be beyond it all, because the path through and beyond it all **is** the path of awakening. Virtually all of us are still attached and identified with our human self sense. If were fully awake and liberated, we probably wouldn't be here at this time. In fact, we came to Earth precisely because of the potent opportunities for awakening presented by the many crises we face. As the waves of these crises crash upon the shores of our individual and collective realities, they will stimulate all the issues that lie hidden in the shadows of the subconscious. No soul is here "by accident." Each one of us chose to incarnate on Earth at this time to take part in the immense evolutionary opportunity these times present.

No matter what is unfolding, a fully illumined being experiences no loss of communion with the true Self. In such a being, even a wave of imminent physical death crashes against the imperturbable bulwark of lack of attachment and identification with this human experience, and deep communion with the true, eternal Self. Thoughts and emotions might arise, but there is no place for them to attach in the mind. They are seen for what they are, and with no place to stick, they flow right through an awakened being. When earthly life comes to a close, the form is released and the soul soars onward. That unflappable peace and surrender are where we are all heading, and the path there is right through everything that Life, in its infinitely loving wisdom, places before us as the Way.

There is a lot of spiritual talk about loving ourselves, and entire books have been written about that. Everyone agrees it is a worthy goal, but what do we really mean by it? What does loving ourselves look like on a daily basis? Could it be as simple as not judging ourselves when our "stuff" comes up? Maybe loving ourselves is as simple as realizing that the "stuff" erupting out of the subconscious is not a bad thing. Having unresolved issues come up is not a sign of spiritual inadequacy or failure. Loving ourselves may equal accepting the fact that being triggered, having "stuff" arising, is a necessary part of awakening, or it would not be happening.

The two of us like to say, "Our stuff is not IN the way, it IS the way!" Ultimately, we realize that every time our "stuff" arises, we are standing before yet another doorway to awakening. Opening to whatever presents itself, we develop the capacity to love ourselves through whatever arises, inside and out. Facing and embracing our "stuff" is suddenly no longer a nuisance. What we saw as an inconveniently rocky, littered path becomes the sacred Way Home.

26

The Essential Reframe

We humans like things to be normal. We tend to feel relieved when life goes on much as it always has, assuming we like what is happening. But as you have read, we are heading into a time when things will probably not continue to go on in the ways that are familiar. The essential reframe that is asked of us is to click out of any remaining <u>normalcy bias</u> and realize that our comfort zones are going to be shaken again and again as we head toward the dimensional shift. We are entering a time when there will be little that is "normal" as we have known it. Many of the ways we've framed ourselves and our lives are necessarily going to dissolve away. Each of us will go through countless small and large ego-deaths all along the way. This has to happen, so the 3-D caterpillar sense of self can dissolve and a soul-awakened, luminous Self can be born.

We don't know exactly what prompts it, but when a caterpillar somehow senses it is time to go through the Great Transformation, it crawls up into a bush or tree and builds a cocoon around itself. When it enters the chrysalis, life as the caterpillar has known it is over. It is not going back — it will never be a caterpillar again. It can only go forward into a mysterious *something* it has never experienced, something it can't even fathom. In this transformation, all that it knew as itself will, and must, completely dissolve. Its very body melts into a gelatinous mass. All that remains are a heart and rudimentary nervous and circulatory systems. The caterpillar essentially dies; that entire identity and way of being cease to exist.

Is this resonating anything within you? As you may have already realized, this is where we are, as individuals and as a species. We are entering the chrysalis. We can't become a luminous, soul-awakened species without dying to our human, earth-bound identities. This triggers the deepest survival mechanisms of our psycho-physical programming. That explains why we go into denial and resist — and why so much fear, anxiety and doubt arise as we contemplate what lies ahead. We can't escape the transformation ahead, nor would we even try, if we knew what it will be like to soar as radiant, magnificent butterflies on the other side of this great change.

As mysterious as this entire process can feel, we also receive tantalizing, enticing glimpses of our new Selves — usually, just when we need them most to bolster us through the challenging aspects of the metamorphosis. These experiences of our emerging butterfly nature will continue to increase, until we know ourselves to be more **that** than our former caterpillar identity.

The death of the caterpillar and the birth of the butterfly are not sequential events; they occur simultaneously. As the caterpillar's form literally dissolves, special structures called **imaginal cells** appear, and they contain the essential blueprint of the emerging butterfly. We, too, contain a blueprint for the "butterfly Self" that we truly are. The imaginal cells that birth our new nature lie within us, in the core of our being, as the qualities, characteristics and capacities of our true, eternal Self.

Just as the butterfly lies hidden, its potential quietly waiting within the caterpillar for that magic moment of emergence to arrive, the divinity of the soul is largely veiled in the majority of human beings until it can no longer wait to come forth in all its splendor. A spark of the Divine shines within each one of us as a flame at the center of our being, just above our heart, deep within our chest. This is where the essence of our luminous, butterfly nature patiently waits until it is time to be born. It resides within the soul lotus, which is beginning to rapidly open in those who are reframing what is happening on Earth as a great transformation into a far more desirable and glorious way of being.

A caterpillar does not know how to become a butterfly, nor does it "do" anything to make the process happen. Metamorphosis simply occurs as a magical, grace-filled transformation facilitated by the infinite, loving intelligence of God/One/Source. All the caterpillar has to do is surrender to the process. This isn't hard for caterpillars, because they do not have a complex mental-egoic structure like human souls do. Lucky them!

But even though we are far more complicated beings, we can emulate the caterpillar's ability to let go into the process of metamorphosis. We can remind ourselves that everything that is arising is a necessary part of the process, or it would not be happening. For instance, all kinds of unfinished mental-emotional "stuff" is bound to boil to the surface, for all of this caterpillar "stuff" is incompatible with our new, butterfly existence. We can expect to see our ego-selves doing all they can to deny, resist, fight, cling, and struggle in all sorts of ways. The temper tantrums may be formidable until the ego finally gives way to the soul, and the transformation has largely stabilized in the new butterfly identity. Our physical bodies will also go through changes as they purify, de-densify and embody the new evolutionary codes.

As we go through the metamorphosis process, we will all learn that letting the ego control our awareness is a sure formula for pain and suffering. We don't have to judge ourselves for letting this happen — again. And again. This is how we wake up and realize living as the ego-self is not an enjoyable ride. And it is certainly not what we want for ourselves in the future. As we withdraw our precious life energy from the ego, it dissolves away into the nothingness that was always its true nature.

Every time we bring awareness into what the ego is up to and make another choice, we surrender into and embrace the process of transformation more deeply. The ego thinks its job is to hold the existing pattern together, so naturally it fights and resists in the face of change. **But we are not our egos.** We are bigger than that, although we have temporarily forgotten that this is so. The key is to remember that we are holographic aspects of the Source that creates and sustains this entire multiverse and all things within it.

God/One/Source is governing this whole evolutionary experience, and knows exactly how to make it happen. In fact, the Divine is running this show with absolute perfection. Its infinite intelligence knows exactly how to assist each one of us to let go of our attachment and identification with who and what we thought we were. Its vast wisdom will help us to face, embrace, and release everything that is ready to drop away so we can soar free. The Divine is igniting the spark of Its nature in the core of our beings, and that sacred fire will eventually take full dominion over our dying, human 3-D nature as it disintegrates, making way for the full glory of our emerging butterfly Selves.

27

Faith and Surrender

Just as the caterpillar does not know how to become a butterfly, nor does it actually do anything to cause that to happen, we, too, are asked to trust that Something Larger is going to take us through what lies ahead. As we crash against the walls of our comfort zones again and again in the face of breakdown and chaos, we may feel overwhelmed and have no idea what to do next. It will help to remember that this is an evolutionary setup designed to catalyze ego-surrender. When we are overwhelmed and have no choice but to let go, surrender becomes our only option.

The more we desire liberation and freedom, the more we will perceive experiences through the lens of truth. Core to this is the reality that there is little we can do on our own. Awakened souls all through human history have attested to this truth. Remember the Great One who said, "I of my own self can do nothing. It is the Father in me who does all"? If that was true for Him, we might want to put our faith in the Divine, too.

The illusion of the separate human self is based in the fundamental misperception that we are not a drop in the Ocean of God, nor does the Ocean of God exist in the drop of our being. No wonder we humans so often feel separate and alone! Many of us have entirely forgotten about the Ocean of God, that which is the very source and fabric of our being. This is why surrendering to a higher power, our personal version of God/One/Source, is essential. Nothing has more power to bring us back into alignment with the larger reality, as the illusion of the ego's control and dominion dissolves.

In the days ahead the ego-self will be challenged repeatedly, and ever more of us will come into an attitude of humility and surrender when faced with the overwhelming circumstances that will appear on our paths. It will quickly become evident that we don't have the resources to make it on our own -- nor have we ever. These will be the "coming to the Lord" moments that many of us will face. We will find ourselves unable to do anything other than humbly submit to the infinitely loving, powerful and intelligent Source of All That Is. For we will know, as we've never known before, that this is our only chance. And, even more, this is what we want more than anything else.

As we realize that unfathomable resources are available to us through faith and surrender to the Divine, we will be guided impeccably into the freedom of Self-realization and the birth of our luminous Self. This overflowing fountain of grace has always been there, but we humans tend to get so caught up in the illusion of the control and dominion of our little, personal egos, we forget to turn to the Divine for help. Because we are loved so much, God/One/Source will not interfere in our lives. Our free will and our sovereignty as souls is always respected by the Divine and all who work with the One, because this is our inviolable, sacred inheritance. The Divine will never intercede unless asked. We must consciously surrender our free will, turning the power and direction of our lives over, before we can receive divine assistance. This only happens through a sincere, heartfelt request, a true willingness to let go of the steering wheel of our lives.

This kind of submission to Something Larger is something most of don't do easily; our earthly conditioning is to do just the opposite. We are taught to be "self-made" men and women, always in control of our lives. This is why it takes a fundamental thought reversal to open to surrender. It also usually takes time — and going through some challenging experiences that show us we are not the ones making our lives happen — to develop the faith and trust to do so. Now might be the time to start opening to this possibility. When we do, we find that asking for divine help works far better than anything we could come up with on our own. When we experience the truth and reality of this, it becomes the easy and unquestioned thing to do.

As surrender deepens, we are gradually lifted up beyond all the conflict, chaos, limitation and suffering of the human experience. As we approach the End of Time, the grace that is and will be descending is far beyond anything humanity has ever experienced. This will continue to grow stronger with each passing day. As souls turn toward the One with a sincere heart, they will experience awakening with the kind of ease and grace that has never been possible until now.

The two of us know this is true, based on the experiences of those who are guided to do soul-awakening work with us over time. The level of grace that is pouring in is beyond anything we could have imagined. Transformations that used to take years now happen in weeks or months. Lifelong patterns of suffering are dropping away with ease, leaving freedom and peace in their wake. Just as clinging and attachment will lead to more pain and suffering, there are ever-greater rewards for consecrating one's life to awakening and surrendering to the beneficent grace that is descending as never before.

28

Love and Acceptance

As we have seen, we can judge, resist and struggle with our life journey, or we can surrender. Letting go into the Divine shows us that everything in our lives is orchestrated by the loving intelligence of God/One/Source. An omnipotent, infinitely intelligent, and loving presence guides us with maximum ease, grace, and awakening through our challenges.

Surrendering reminds us that whatever arises, within and without, is there for a reason, and a good one. It is our pathway to awakening, our road Home. That's not to say it is necessarily easy. Facing the dark shadows of our fear and doubt, embracing our sadness and grief, accepting our guilt and shame — these are difficult passages on the path. When they occur, we can judge ourselves and what is occurring and suffer, or, embrace what is happening and surrender to it.

As the planetary metamorphosis unfolds, we are going to experience many small and large "deaths" and dissolutions. Can we remember that nothing that is falling away is the truth of who and what we are? Every bit of it has to be released, to make room for what is to come. Let us not cling to the caterpillar identity, but instead look forward to the flowering of our magnificent, butterfly nature, which will enable us to soar beyond anything we have ever known.

Embracing ourselves and our inner and outer experience with love and acceptance is the inner alignment that makes this journey as easy and free of suffering as the unfoldment of a rose. We can release the perfectionistic expectation that we should already be in a place of utter equanimity, and accept ourselves at every stage in this journey, wherever we find ourselves and whatever is arising. Holding our precious selves and our process of awakening in love is the key that unlocks the door to inner peace. Cultivating that loving acceptance of whatever is arising at every stage of this journey is a crucial and vital aspect of awakening. We can't awaken without love.

Despite appearances, which to our human eyes often appear to be inexplicable, if not tragic, everything that unfolds is the most loving thing that can occur. God is Love and Love is truly the underlying fabric of everything, including our very own beings. The myriad crises that are unfolding are simply the result of our losing touch with the reality that everything is held within God's and our true nature, which is love. When we are in communion with our true Selves, we are in communion with love. When we lose touch with our true Self, we lose touch with love and experience fear and separation. As we awaken, we become more aware of this fundamental divide in the mind...fear and separation, or love and oneness. One is true, and the way to heal and restore everything, while the other is illusion, and the path to more dis-ease and death.

The automatic feedback loop of karmic return is built into the loving fabric of creation to mirror back our inner state of being, which can only be projected through our actions. All that we experience is the necessary result, the outpicturing, of this loving aspect of creation. As we face personal and collective crises, it is crucial to remember that neither the problem — nor its solution — is "out there." It never was and never will be. The problem and the solution are "in here" within each one of us.

The outer world is but a holographic projection of our inner state of being. The holographic universe can only mirror us back to ourselves. If our consciousness is steeped in fear and separation, we will think, feel and perceive as such. We will continue to feel a great hole in the core of our being and consume more and more to attempt to fill it, without ever doing so. Perceiving we are a temporal, physical form, we will exist in fear of its demise and see nothing but threats wherever we look. Thus, we will continue to create neverending conflicts and wars. Perceiving that we are separate from the very life-giving earth with which we are inexorably one, we will continue to treat it as an object to satisfy our desires, and poison it without remorse.

When we are triggered by external events, it is crucial to remember that they come to reflect back to us our distorted inner state of being. What most needs to be dealt with is the fear- and separation-based consciousness within. Only when we lovingly face and embrace whatever is arising will it be allowed to surface into our consciousness, give us its messages and then pass on. As it dissolves into its primal, unqualified essence, another layer of veiling disappears and more of our eternal, divine essential nature can shine through.

Deep within us, the true, eternal Self has its seat in the Heart. This is where the individuated essence of God/One/All That Is focuses within the physical form. We must come back to the spiritual heart, leaving our mental-egoic identity, or our species will perish.

Love is the connecting, unifying essence of everything in creation. It is the core nature of our divinity. It heals and makes all whole. When we open our heart, we directly experience what lies therein, our true Self. In touch with the love that is our innermost essential nature, we naturally feel our caring, compassion, and unity with all other human souls and all of life.

The environmental, economic and climate crises that are already unfolding may be the only thing capable of cracking the hard shell of our egos and bringing us back to our hearts and souls. This is the hidden gift that lies within these disturbing outer events. Having experienced a Class 5 hurricane, I can attest that all the things we think are so important in our modern, techno-industrial culture can be swept away in a matter of moments. Then we discover they weren't so important after all. What remains are our basic human needs and our connections with one another. The walls that seem to isolate us fall away. We realize we need each other, on every level. It becomes clear that we are bound together by the essential unity that we lose in our everyday disconnected, fragmented mental-egoic states. With all of this gone, what is left is the heart.

Everything is set up to bring us back to the heart, back to the realization that Love is all that is really important. With love, we know our essential unity. With love, we tap into the wisdom that knows how to support life. With love we are transported beyond all the veils of separation to unity with God, ourselves, our brothers and sisters, and all of life. With love, we surrender to

God and Life. With love and surrender we open the door to grace. When this door opens, all is possible.

29

Finding Meaning and Purpose at the End of an Age

Each previous mass extinction has included the demise of entire species. Think about it — did any dinosaurs live on after the last cataclysmic cycle on Earth? The larger function of such mass die-offs is to usher in entirely new forms of life, with qualities and capacities never seen before. This is the way evolution progresses. Into the vacuum created by the exit of some species, Life pours in new ones.

So we need to face the probability that, for any number of reasons, much of humanity is likely to perish during the massive changes to come — changes that have already begun, as Part One of this book details. Will any of us survive? We can't know for sure.

How do we avoid falling into hopelessness and despair when it appears that so much death and destruction may lie ahead? How can we find a reason to live in the face of so much earthly loss? How can we contribute to the birth of the new age that we know we came here to be part of in the face of the possibility that most of us may not survive in these bodies to usher it in?

Considering these questions asks us to broaden the scope of our ultimate contribution to humanity's evolution. There is a distinct possibility that the Sixth Mass Extinction may differ from previous ones in one important way: the crucial vector of consciousness. As each of us experiences even the slightest shift, the tiniest opening, in consciousness, the collective vibrational field is heightened, enhanced and expanded. This is why focusing our life energies on awakening and making that the central aspect of our lives is so important. In our individual journeys of awakening, all that we each experience — whatever is faced, embraced, loved into wholeness, transcended, and resurrected within each of us — opens up pathways in consciousness that make it easier for awakenings to occur in all others. Thus, each incoming generation of awakening souls stands on the spiritual shoulders of all who have come before.

Just as we each benefit from all the inner work other awakening souls have done, this long chain of being and experiencing will eventually result in the birth of the new, soul-awakened species. As increasing numbers of homo sapiens commit ourselves to awakening above all else, our energies join to co-create an ever stronger evolutionary platform to support the emergence of homo luminous. Many of us have noticed new waves of advanced beings already among us. We know them by the light in their eyes and the glow radiating from their heart of hearts. These beings clearly embody and express more of the light of their true nature than previous generations. As we marvel at their luminosity, we can remind ourselves we are looking at some of the first manifestations of our collective future.

Not even the wisest among us can say how many lifetimes it will take until that future species manifests in its full glory and magnificence. It's safe to say that no one now on Earth will live long enough to see that happen. But a few of us will, through grace, survive the coming changes and give birth to the generation that is the next link in the great chain of being. Through their divine connection, they will develop the capacity to liveeven thrive in the conditions in which they find themselves. Those beings will in turn see their progeny radiating more brightly and living more consciously than those who came before. Highly developed souls, living as love, will take embodiment to continue re-populating the Earth, which herself is transitioning all the while into a more refined level of vibration.

Each of us plays a necessary part in this long process. That's why, now more than ever, putting our spiritual awakening before all else is so vital. That's true whether we leave this body tomorrow, next year, or sometime after that. Knowing we play a crucial role in the collective birthing of a soul-awakened species goes a long way toward mitigating the difficulties involved in facing our mortality. Douglas Vogt and Gary Sultan discuss this in their opus, *Reality Revealed: The Theory of Multidimensional Reality*. They refer to the fact that when a human sperm cell fertilizes an egg, it is one of about seven million who make that journey. "Do we mourn over the 6,999,999 sperm cells that died? No, we rejoice over the one who made it. This is not to say there was no reason for the others to have existed. They have to exist in order to give the one that makes it the necessary momentum and potential to reach its goal."

30

Beyond Hope and Hopelessness

We can't be reborn until we die. We can't ascend into a higher-dimensional world unless we let go of this one. Our human clinging and attachment to this third-dimensional life is deeper than most of us can comprehend. It operates far below the radar of our conscious awareness, and is anchored in the very soma of our body as the survival impulse. That is very helpful in emergencies, but it also restricts us when the unconscious fear it engenders causes us to cling to a limited, vulnerable sense of self.

Most of us are veiled by our attachment to this realm of existence, and that veiling dictates much of how we perceive reality. It causes fear, overwhelm, and hopelessness when whatever we thought defined ourselves and our world falls away. Subconsciously we all know that we live in an impermanent world, yet we still hope that it can continue forever. Our hope is based in the desire that Life maintain our world in the ways that support our deepest beliefs about ourselves and our lives. Thus, hope seems central to our being, and many of us believe it is an inherent, core aspect of the soul.

This results in considerable spiritual confusion about the concept of hope. Most spiritual traditions teach the idea that hope must never be surrendered. To give it up, they teach, is a failure of the soul that will result in ultimate despair and darkness. There is truth in this, if we put our hope in what is true and eternal. God and our true Self, which are one, will absolutely never fail us. But, as always, the human ego appropriates this concept and uses it to perpetuate its own illusory existence, which is based in attachment and identification with the physical body and the tangible world.

The obvious truth is that the physical body and all that is of our personal worlds will surely pass away. There is nothing here that endures. All is changing, and as you may recall, 95% of the species that have ever lived are no longer here. What does that imply for our future as a species, let alone for our short lives in these bodies?

Look around you and face the fact of impermanence. The home you know and enjoy will almost certainly not exist within a few hundred years at best. Walk outside and look at the earth around you. While we consciously rely on this as our ultimate foundation, the truth is the trees, the streams, flowers, plants and animals you see will one day pass away. Do the most challenging thing of all. Look in the mirror and reflect on the fact that your physical body is deteriorating with the passing years and will one day cease to function. It, too, will eventually disintegrate.

Yet we are conditioned to believe in the continuation of reality as we've known it, much as our younger selves believed the Easter Bunny was real. If things can't go on exactly as they have been — if there are going to be some changes in the mix — then could the changes at least happen gently, so they are easier for us to assimilate? History tells us that the story of this planet testifies otherwise, as you learned in Part Two. Sudden, cataclysmic changes have occurred again and again. Even the things we deeply hope are permanent — mountains, hills, valleys, oceans — were at one time not here. The deserts were oceans, and the oceans were deserts. The peaks that tower majestically over us once rose from the ocean floor. Everything that ever was and is will not be in the future. Even the physical form of the Earth will eventually disintegrate. Yes, the Second Law of Thermodynamics makes no exceptions on the physical plane.

Clinging to our hope for a gradual, linear process of change is central to the continuation of our human identities. It can also form a spiritual foundation that is misled and based in illusion. When reality steps in and pops the bubble, we hope and pray that our version of what life should be is maintained in a way that gives pleasure and comfort to our human sense of self. Daily prayers are often based on the hope that we will be given all the things we need to have our version of a good human life. We hope and pray that those we love will be well, happy and abundant, based on our personal perceptions of what this means. All of this seems, at some level, so understandable and even loving. Many of us never question it. Nor do we see that our own personal fantasies of what life should be and our own unconscious desire for ego dominion and control are really behind the clinging to false hope.

Nowhere is this more apparent than when we face the death of the body. Our healthcare profession supports this society's consensual reality that the death of the body must be avoided at all costs. Every day people whose bodies are dying, unconscious of the true nature of their soul journey, cling desperately to life, full of the fear of death. They demand that every attempt be employed to extend their mortal existence, no matter the cost financially, socially and spiritually. Their loved ones collude, praying for a miracle, hoping that somehow, death will be indefinitely postponed, even if it means they deny any deep inner knowing that the end is near.

This is what we face on a planetary level. The specter of death now overshadows our lives, whether we want to be aware of it or not. We continue to embrace the hope that somehow we will miraculously find a way to resolve the myriad crises we face. This tends to un-ground us from what is really going on. Hope becomes another ego defense that keeps us from being in touch with reality as it is. In her new book *Beyond Hope: Letting Go of a World in Collapse*, Deb Ozarko calls this "hopium," for it provides a buffer in our minds that keeps us from feeling and experiencing what is really going on deep within our heart and soul. It separates us from truth.

Because we cling to hopium, our species will no doubt struggle to continue our current, unsustainable and dying way of life, no matter the mental, emotional, physical and even spiritual cost. We will bet on every new technology that might miraculously allow us to keep living as we have lived. Anything, to avoid facing our attachment to a way of living that consumes resources at an ever-growing rate on a finite planet. The madness this is based on will continue to be bolstered by false hopes. Deep down inside, we all know life as we've known it cannot go on forever. But most of us are still too drugged-out on hopium to fully face this reality.

Hope is not a magical panacea, nor does it offer a sure way out of our malaise. Instead, hope is yet another doorway to awakening. Look around you once again and notice how attached you are to having all the things you like having as part of your life continue to be so. Think of all the other things you want to have and experience before you leave this planet. Then consider what it would be like if life asked you to give it all up. What would it be like to walk away from all the things you "love" that you believe you "possess"? How about all that you aspire to acquire and experience? Some of your unrealized desires will come to pass, and some won't. In the end, all of it goes. *All of this world shall pass away.* The confrontation with this truth is the source of our greatest crisis, one that will certainly track us down as an integral part of the path of awakening.

Most of the people who do sessions with us are in some sort of crisis, whether internal, external, or a combination. More than anything, they typically want that crisis resolved, so they can move on with their lives. They are rarely, if ever, initially aware they are standing before one of the most profound doorways to awakening — the death of hope and the embrace of hopelessness. The root of their crisis and its attendant suffering does not lie within what is actually occurring. Instead, their deeply attached and identified "pictures of reality" are crashing on the rocks of reality.

After employing every means we have to ensure that whatever we're most deeply attached to and identified with will continue to be part of our life pattern, we hit the moment when we run out of hope. We've hoped and hoped and hoped to the point of utter exhaustion of heart and soul. The hopium is no longer capable of anesthetizing us. As the false hopes that bolstered our illusions dissolve, we encounter the doorway of hopelessness, which is the dualistic mirror, the other side of the coin, of false hope.

At that moment of truth, we must face the fact that we are powerless to make things continue as they have been. We have exhausted every resource, and now the end has come. We find ourselves standing on the edge of a psychic cliff with nothing but darkness and emptiness beyond it, a certain plunge into death when we step off. Yet we know there is no turning back. We must jump off that cliff into the emptiness. Hopelessness arises and overwhelms us. An end is here.

As we face the hopelessness of the situation, something magic happens that is the opposite of what we had subconsciously feared. As our false sense of hope and illusory sense of control come to an end, we let go and fall off the cliff of what was. But surprise — we do not experience an end to our existence, but the doorway to our rebirth into a more honest and soulful experience of reality.

We have been blessed to walk through this doorway of hope and hopelessness many times in our own journeys and with those who have worked with us. These potent experiences reveal that beyond the dualistic illusions of hope and hopelessness is something that can lead us out of the fear, suffering, and limitation of our personal egos. When we let go and walk into the mysterious, terrifying void, something is always waiting to lift us up out of our suffering. Experience has proven that this is a concrete, absolute reality, as certain as gravity.

We have watched many people walk off that cliff of the secure, solid reality they had known, stepping into the dark void of the unknown. Although they felt certain they would fall to their death, each and every one found the opposite, as an invisible hand reached out and lifted them into a realm of greater peace, freedom, and joy than they had ever known. Never have we seen one soul walk through the doorway beyond hope and hopelessness and not have the ultimate truth of their invulnerable divinity revealed beyond all doubt. In every case, walking through this doorway brought them into a more soulful, authentic life.

We need not cling and struggle to survive in our personal version of reality as we have known it. Survival in these mortal forms is but another brief passage in our eternal soul's journey. Struggling against death is an optional path many humans choose to take, causing us to resist and suffer. This is not to be judged, though; it is yet another phase in the process of birthing the luminous, divine butterfly Self. Dying to our human, caterpillar identity involves letting go of deep levels of attachment and identification. These largely unconscious inner states cause us to want to continue this way of being, because it is all that we have known. Slowly we come to learn that our false hopes have no real benefit or reality. Our caterpillar world is passing away. Facing the utter hopelessness we feel as we release that identity is nothing to be feared; instead, we can embrace it as the final doorway to full surrender, which will carry us into the soaring, expansive way of being we want most of all.

While there are many false hopes, there is only one true hope — one that is not a hope of this world. It is a hope born of the knowing that no matter how dire things may seem in our human lives, there is something infinitely powerful, wise and loving that cares about us more deeply than we can fathom. The Divine is waiting for us to release all of our idealized pictures of reality, all our human "hopes," so it can lift us into the realization of the divine souls we really are.

This is what lies beyond both hope and hopelessness: the discovery that we are eternal, invulnerable beings, incapable of being harmed in any way. One way or another, our physical bodies will fall away, a fact that all of us must eventually face and accept. And when that occurs, our eternal souls will soar free to live forever.

31

The Path of Grace

Hopelessness is such a powerful doorway simply because it is the emotion that releases ego control and dominion. When hopelessness hits, we can go no further. All our attempts to control are revealed as futile. We find ourselves truly letting go, and meaning it to the core of our being. Our heart surrenders the struggle and says, "Thy will be done." We have passed through the doorway of surrender.

Most of us, at least in the beginning and again during those times when we hit deeper levels of attachment and identification, do not pass beyond the doorway of hope and hopelessness into surrender with ease and grace. Often it is when there is nothing left to cling to, or when we can't endure the suffering anymore, that we are finally forced to surrender. But letting go into surrender doesn't need to entail struggle; it can also happen naturally and easily. No great suffering is required to "earn" the grace of the Divine. It is always there waiting for the moment that we "let go and let God," for God/One/Source has always been there waiting for us to let go of the steering wheel.

Because we are aspects of God, our free will is inviolable. Even our Source Creator, of which we are inextricable aspects, cannot and will not impinge upon our free will, for the free will of the One is that we have the same free will. We are free will creators within our own subset of this vast creation. In a very real way, each of us co-creates our world with Source. We have chosen the path of seeking to explore ourselves as individual creators, in the illusion of being separate and apart from the one Source Creator.

We have tried to be individualized drops of God while renouncing and disavowing any association with the Ocean of God in which we exist. This can only be the height of illusion and folly, and has caused us to create a planet of limitation, disease and death. As the doorway beyond hope and hopelessness brings us to surrender, we are again in a position to release our sense of control and dominion as separate beings. Surrendering into the ocean of God, we return to our Source and true Self.

This is the path of grace. It unfolds as we finally, not in the mind, but in the depths of our heart and soul, let go and let God. We throw ourselves face-down on the ground and mean it as we say, "Thy will be done." The Divine doesn't care so much about our thoughts, but It cares everything about where we are in our hearts and souls. When we truly surrender ourselves and our control of our life, giving our will to God, then God will step in and take over. Otherwise, God/One/Source is simply unable to help us.

As we have said before, we have been taught to be self-made men and women. Since our culture is almost completely ego-based, it tells us we need to be in control all the time. We are conditioned to become powerful, dominant human beings who take charge and make reality be what we want it to be. This is such an obvious ego distortion, it is laughable. What a misinterpretation of the truth of our sovereignty and dominion as souls! Everything we have and are as the drops of God that we are has its source in the vast Ocean of God. It contains all the will, power, intelligence, life, love, and light of Creation. The distortion and confusion in our minds is caused by the ego's usurping of the role of the soul. When we embrace that illusory sense of self, we believe we are creators, separate and apart from the Source Creator that generates and perpetuates All That Is, including our very existence. This illusion persists until Reality confronts us with a situation in which we cannot deny our powerlessness.

Surrendering ourselves to a higher power is the way we plug back into the Source of all peace, freedom and healing. It has been proven time and again as the most effective path out of extreme psycho-spiritual pain, suffering and dis-ease. Twelve-step programs are just one example of the truth of this.

Surrender to a higher power is the doorway to accessing grace. When grace takes over, we experience transformations that transcend anything we could previously imagine. The magic of this can only be understood through experiencing it firsthand. We've all experienced it in small and large ways. We may have been teetering on the edge of some perceived disaster with no hope in sight, only to have a resolution appear out of nowhere to save us. We might call it luck, synchronicity, or coincidence, but what really occurred? The infinitely loving, powerful and wise One intercedes, simply because we are loved.

This is not something that happens only on rare occasions and under dire circumstances. Grace is always available to us, when we know that it is and know how to access it. When we do, Infinite Will, Power and Intelligence lovingly initiate the journey of extricating us from the inner and outer entanglements that are causing our suffering.

This loving Intelligence knows everything about us, and sees the most direct path to our freedom. It loves us beyond comprehension, far more than we could even conceive of loving ourselves. It only wants our best interests and knows exactly what they are. It sees and knows us as a divine being, while it supports us to be in our mortal, physical forms for as long as that serves our growth and evolution as souls. It maintains the pattern of our lives, despite our illusions that we are doing that. Everything we think we own is a gift from this loving, intelligent Source. Every breath we take, every beat of our heart is not something that we do, but a gift from God. When things are taken away, when the last breath goes in and back out and the last beat of the heart occurs, another doorway opens into a vaster universe. As St. Francis prayed, "it is in dying that we are born into eternal life." Perhaps he meant that it is not the death of the body that is our passage to eternal life, but the death of the false concept of our self. As that dies, we discover our true Self, which already **is** eternal Life. We need not wait until the death of our physical body to let go of this false, mortal identity.

In the days ahead each of us will be faced with one doorway to surrender after another. There is one before you now, in the next breath. We pass through the doorway in any moment that we realize we really do nothing. The enlightened and God-realized being Jesus testified to this when he said, "Truly, truly, I tell you, the Son can do nothing by Himself, unless He sees the Father doing it. For whatever the Father does, the Son also does." John 5:19.

Jesus was expressing what so many of the great God-realized beings have always told us. All power comes from the One. We are but empty reeds through which It blows Its breath to make the Music of the Spheres. The little power and will we have as drops in the Ocean of God are minuscule; all derives from the great Ocean. Awakened beings have forever counseled us to surrender all sense of ourselves as separate beings, all sense of any individual, independent will or power, to the One that is the only Source of all will and power, all truth and reality. Thus, we enter the heavenly fields of Grace in which we experience ourselves being lifted up beyond all the distortion and disease we have made in our limited, delusional state. There is nothing that cannot be healed or resurrected, as the great ones have shown us. This only occurs, though, when we have died completely to our false sense of self. The planetary death process now underway could be the doorway to the individual and collective renunciation and surrender of our false sense of ego dominion over our lives and this planet. Will we walk through?

Imagine the possibility of ever-increasing waves of surrender — the vision of billions of human beings turning back to the only One that can resurrect all the crises we face. There has never been a more auspicious time for miracles. What makes this time one of such possibilities for grace and the miraculous is that the Divine is now coming back towards us. At this time in the great cycle of Being, the Source of All That Is is descending onto Earth. In the great cycles of spiritual evolution, this is the time in which we ascend into the experience of a new EarthHeaven, the next stage in God's divine soul play for humanity and the Earth.

32

The Deep, Dark Descent of Ego-Death

Loss and Grief

Loss is a normal, unavoidable part of the human experience. Even as we feel inundated by waves of grief and despair, we may know that no one really dies, but we still experience loss, for we will not share this life with that person ever again. We arise in the morning and they are not there; there's an empty void their presence used to fill. A beautiful, meaningful part of our life is gone forever. Even if we know they continue to exist on a higher plane, the veil of separation that surrounds the planet causes us to temporarily lose our communion with them. We still feel despair at the thought of life without them. The soul must allow itself to grieve and mourn this human loss.

Because the Earth's vibrational field so strongly supports awakening now, even heart-wrenching loss and grief can become agents through which awakening occurs. Deep sadness cracks open the heart, breaking down walls and defenses of self-centeredness that the illusion of separation engenders. The sense of a separate, ego "i", with its closed mind and heart, is only interested in its own affairs. When it cares for others, it does so for its own selfish reasons. Love is confused with what it gets from them to fulfill its own needs and desires.

When the death of a loved one occurs, the loss can engender a deeper response of grief, which awakens us to the reality that we loved them because they were close to our heart. A crack had opened in our psychic armor, which allowed us to feel true love. We loved them — and continue to love them — simply because they existed. We love because love is the truth of all interconnectedness. The grieving that wounds the heart also rips it open, enabling us to discover the love that has been hiding behind the walls of fear and self-contraction. Things that we judged and rejected are seen to be of little import in the light of the now-opening heart. We see that the issues and grievances we might have held against that person are suddenly meaningless, and that they kept us from loving them as they were. All that is left is the love that is, in truth, all that ever was really there, hiding under our own judgments and separation.

Loss and grief are likely to become even more pronounced as the death and destruction increase across the planet. When we, as a species, face the demise of the ecosystem as a result of our selfishness, loss after loss will engender an outpouring of collective grief and sadness like we've never seen before. Ever more humans will awaken to the fact that they have been asleep, unable to see the many dying lifeforms as the beautiful and valuable parts of Creation they are.

I continue to feel immense grief at the mass beachings of the dolphins and whales. Through close personal contact, I have come to know them as sensitive, highly conscious beings, just like us. To see them perish engenders deep sadness that their lives have been cut short by human greed and selfishness. These encounters with the effects of our unconscious actions will be occurring again and again in more and more human souls. The loss will be ever-escalating, and closer to home. As each incident occurs, it will serve as a catalyst for awakening, a wake-up call to face what our species has done. Our hearts will cry out with the searing pain of grief. And this will open our collective heart to the truth of love and oneness. Thus do these deaths serve their purpose. Every day more of us pray that the insanity and madness stop. It is becoming more and more apparent that a planetary crucifixion is upon us. Already many species are on the cross, and soon many more of our own species are almost certain to join them.

When we witness such horrendous carnage, we may be tempted to view it as a dispensation of judgment and punishment from an angry God. The destruction and death is not a demonstration that the will, power and love of God are absent. It is of our own making, through our own God-given free will. We are sovereign beings, aspects of that One, and it would serve nothing for divine grace to stop these deaths until they have served their purpose. Each one has the capacity to tear away the hardened, heart and soul constrictions built of self-centered egoism. This is their purpose. They do not come from a God of anger and judgment, but from a God of Love. We are loved so much that we are allowed to experience the effects of our unconsciousness so that we may be shocked awake from our somnambulance, hopefully setting us upon the path back to truth and love. A planetary awakening cannot happen unless these hardened, encrusted veils of separation are removed.

It is and will be a painful process, but there is a great gift in pain. Pain brings us in touch with what we have been unwilling to face and embrace. Life is wholly loving and only brings us pain when there is no other choice. If we look back upon any process of coming into disease and pain, we will see there were many small notices that things were amiss before the situation reached the point of pain and the loss of well-being. Self-centered human consciousness tends to avoid these little signs; we dismiss and deny them. How many clues have we missed that all life-forms — not just our own — are ultimately in peril on our planet?

The time of Shiva's and Kali's dance is upon us. In the Hindu tradition, Kali is the most loving of all the goddesses, for she has the most power to destroy. This may seem to be a contradiction, but it is why, in the End Times, the Kalki avatar and the Christ come with a sword. The bonds and chains of human egoism must be cut — by force, if gentler measures do not suffice — for the awakening and soul evolution of humanity to continue. This is a supreme act of love, to free us all from that which is beyond our means to free ourselves from. We are asked to trust in the process and embrace the grief, sadness and loss we will experience, knowing that it is the way our hearts and souls will be opened. This is necessary to reawaken to our true, eternal natures, which always lie hidden under the veils and constrictions of the many layers of the separate self sense.

As we come to the end of the age and the clearing away of all that is not part of what shall ensue on the other side, which is likely a major part of what we have known, the dance of loss, despair and grief will almost certainly be a central aspect of our lives.

The Doorway of Fear

Since it comes into our awareness only occasionally, if asked, most of us would say we don't believe we harbor much fear. What we aren't aware of is that fear is always operating in our subconscious minds. The mind is like an iceberg, with only 10% of what goes on above the surface and in our conscious awareness. The other 90% lies below, in our subconscious. We are usually unaware of the fear that is held there until we are jolted out of our comfort zone, which causes it to rise out of the subconscious. Even then, we are not always aware that we are in fear, since most of us are cut off from what we are actually experiencing. We humans have developed a conditioned response to disconnect from the fear in our bodies, since it is uncomfortable to face and feel. Instead, we get locked in our heads, attempting to analyze and develop strategies to bring as many things as possible under control. This is a way of being we've been taught and deeply conditioned to resort to almost automatically, but it is often one that is least helpful and adaptive in challenging situations.

One of the reasons we carry so much unconscious fear is that we've been conditioned to fear our fear, causing us to deny and suppress it. In our work with people we've found that often, fear is not as big an issue as the fear of the fear. Most of us are deeply afraid that if we open up to experience our fear we will be overwhelmed by it, that it will be too intense for us to experience, that the very presence of fear will be seen as a sign of weakness or instability. We may believe that we should not have fear, or be afraid that to reveal that we feel it is tantamount to admitting failure. Thus, more than a few of us have concluded that fear is to be avoided in all circumstances. This only keeps it buried in our subconscious mind. It sits there generating a potent psychic force, roiling and boiling like the contents of a pressure cooker.

The unconscious fear bottled up within nearly all of us is not a tacit, benign presence. It affects our mental processes, causing us to make fear-based decisions, totally unaware that we are doing so. We think it's normal to avoid certain things or do others in order to evade the possibility of some perceived threat. But it is the fear-based mind that projects these threats from unresolved past, fearful situations, even though they may not really be there. It may seem reasonable to see fear everywhere, as the mind will remind us there is always a chance of things going wrong. *Bad things have happened before in circumstances like this,* it insists. Obviously, nothing is 100% safe on this planet since everything is impermanent, especially our health and our physical bodies. Everything involves a threat at some level. Yet life, for the most part, works. Things have a way of working out, despite ourselves.

Fear is a magnet for creating the very things we fear. When we hold deep fear of something, we are constantly projecting a fear-based picture out onto life. This is a creative act, albeit an unconscious one. Our world is a holographic mirror of what we hold as true, consciously or subconsciously. If we fear we will be abandoned, for instance, we will attract people who play into our unconscious, fear-based image of "my life story." That story becomes part of who we think we are, and keeps playing out until we awaken to the unconscious, fear-based images of ourselves and our lives.

In the days ahead, it is almost certain that in more and more moments, we will be catapulted out of our comfort zones by the breakdown of reality as we have known it. This could occur with little things, such as noticing that spring is abnormally early when the flowers blossom two months before they ever have, or on a summer day when we realize it has been extremely hot for weeks longer than usual. A knowing arises that this is almost certainly the result of climate change, and that it is the new normal, causing our bellies to rumble with fear. Or, it could come dramatically as we face a powerful hurricane, an inability to get gasoline, or the closure of our bank during a financial crisis. All these are possibilities, if not probabilities, that we will face in the days ahead.

We will need to respond to these very real Earth-plane challenges, even though we have no experiential framework or training to do so. Even more importantly, will we be able to respond to these crises as evolutionary drivers, fierce gifts of grace here to help us awaken to who we really are? This is the highest possibility in addressing them as necessary aspects of our life journey. As we awaken to who we truly are, the level of fear in our lives will diminish. We will find ourselves being led by the infallible guidance of our increasing soul-communion, resulting in greater peace, happiness, freedom and love. We will experience ourselves awakening at the end of time.

But first, we must face the results of our unacknowledged fear playing out in our multitudinous global crises. As we learned in Part Two, our identification and attachment to the body creates the existential fear that is assured with bodies that die. That fear has caused us to go to sleep to our true, eternal nature, and thus we suffer from the gnawing hole in the core of our being we attempt to fill, always unsuccessfully, with an excess of the things of the material world. We fear we won't have enough money, power, beauty, love, and on and on, while at the bottom sits the fear of death. This has caused us to consume and pollute to the degree that we face the very thing we fear the most.

When we are in unconscious fear, the mind is incapable of perceiving reality as it is. This is how we perceive problems and enemies where they do not exist. It's how we keep acquiring more, better, and different things of all kinds and still believe we don't have enough. Fear acts as a dark, opaque veil that distorts and narrows our scope of perception. When we are in fear, we are not experiencing what is really going on, but what the ego-mind projects. The ego's job is to keep us safe and secure, but unfortunately, its perceived threats often don't exist. Even when there is a real danger to our safety, it is not certain the ego will steer us to safety.

When we are in fear, the ego is projecting all of its various ideas, beliefs, and (mis)perceptions onto the screen of the mind. It is rapidly analyzing all the distorted perceptual input, looking for circumstances in the past that might closely match in order to develop strategies to solve the perceived problem. This makes sense when we believe the ego-mind is the only resource we have at our disposal. It also has some merit when we are facing something that is within the scope of our previous experience, so our past learning can be appropriately and effectively projected onto the current situation. But what do we do when we face a Category 5 hurricane for the first time, when the biggest threat we've ever experienced is a thunderstorm? We are thrown so far out of our comfort zone and into such deep levels of fear that we can become overwhelmed and paralyzed, because the ego is not capable of dealing with what is going on. We've all read many stories of people in such circumstances making poor decisions that resulted in their injury or death.

There is another source of guidance and information that is far more accurate and functional than the ego-mind. Our soul is always in communion with the infinite intelligence, omniscience and omnipresence of the Divine. The Ocean of God knows everything — past, present, and future — and each soul, as a drop in the Ocean of God, can immediately and continually access that infinite intelligence. When we go through and beyond our fear, we come to the clear guidance that only wants to shepherd us through any and every circumstance. This internal GPS doesn't rely on past experience or information to make decisions or create strategies. It sees the situation from a vast, overlighting perspective and knows exactly what must be done to transit whatever is occurring with maximum ease and grace.

If it is so readily available, why don't we all live from this level of guidance? What stands in the way is the ego-mind and its deep anchoring in the emotion of fear. To get in touch with our soul, we must pass through the charge of fear that is really what's behind the limited and illusory perception and chaotic chatter of the ego-mind. When that is running, it is very difficult to be in touch with our soul. That is why it is critical to learn to recognize that we are triggered, *as it happens*, and to learn how to feel and release the fear, which allows us to come back into communion with the true Self. We will touch on this briefly below, but for a more thorough exploration and training on how to gain self-mastery, we invite you to read our recent book, _Taking Off Overcoats: A Simple, Loving Approach To Awakening_ and utilize the recorded guided inner processes that you may download for free when you buy the book. Working with these over time will support you in developing the capacity to move through fear and ego resistance and deepen your soul communion.

Moving through and beyond the fear and distorted thinking of the ego-mind and accessing the soul's expanded input are critical skills for any of us to cultivate. They are important now, and will only become more crucial in the days ahead. Cultivating them may even determine whether your bodily existence continues, for living from fear creates completely different results from trusting the soul's guidance and acting on it.

A pivotal personal demonstration of the importance of inner guidance arrived during Hurricane Iniki on the island of Kaua'i in 1992. The essentials of that experience may provide a template for what many will go through in the not too distant future. On the morning of September 11th, the phone rang at 6 a.m., waking us from a deep sleep. We were taking care of the home of a woman who was on retreat in the mountains at the center of the island. When I picked up the phone, she immediately went right to the point: "A Category 5 hurricane is headed for Kaua'i and is expected to come onshore around one this afternoon. Category 5 hurricanes have sustained winds of 150 miles an hour with gusts up to 200 miles an hour. I send you prayers and blessings. May God be with you."

For a few seconds, the deepest survival fears pulsed through my body as images of what winds of this magnitude might cause flashed across the screen of my mind. There was an instant recognition that our physical lives were in immediate danger. A clear knowing arose that there was absolutely no time to do anything that would not directly support our survival. That meant not getting bogged down in a lot of mental processes, but instead dropping into deep contact with the soul so all guidance would come from it. With this realization, the fear subsided and the mind became absolutely quiet and still. All the years of inner work were paying off as never before.

I told Karen what our friend had said, and from that moment on, we were guided, step by step, into exactly what we should do. There was no thought involved; knowing and action were one unified movement. While we dressed, we filled the bathtub with water. Within moments we were in the car, headed to the local shopping center to pick up whatever would help ensure our safety and survival. As I drove, Karen made a list of the items we would need as they cascaded into our consciousness from our Higher Selves.

I had been guided the day before to take a trip to town to buy a large supply of groceries, although we had no immediate need of them. I had no idea a hurricane was on the way, although I did have a sense that something was unusual about the weather. For several weeks, both of us had felt something vaguely ominous lurking in the background of our everyday experience.

Recent National Weather Service bulletins had indicated this storm would track west across the Pacific, far to the south of Kaua'i. It was expected to make landfall somewhere on western O'ahu, far from the heavily populated areas of Honolulu and the North Shore. At the last minute, the swirling mass of air took an unexpected ninety-degree turn and headed north toward a bullseye hit on Kaua'i.

But that still lay in the near future. Now, as we drove into the shopping center, we first came to the grocery store, which had not yet opened. A long line of people snaked around the building and out into the parking lot. Deep feelings of gratitude arose that our souls had guided us, in advance, to secure the food we would need for what lay ahead. Instead of waiting in the grocery line, we could go directly to the hardware store to acquire the supplies to stormproof the house. We tore the list in half, grabbed two shopping carts, and rapidly filled them with hammers, nails, storm parkas, flashlights, rope, candles, matches and the numerous other things we were shown we would need.

Back at the house, I was guided to look beneath it. Stacked in the crawl space were large sheets of plywood, which we used to cover as many windows as we could reach. We were especially glad to find coverings for all the windows of one of the bedrooms, which we planned to use as a bunker during the storm. As we pounded in the final nails, the winds began to pick up. We gathered up the family dog, along with some water and food, and went into the bunker room.

What happened next is detailed in our first book, _Soul Awakening: The Journey From Ego To Essence_, in the chapter called "The Miracle Of Iniki." In summary, we transited a major hurricane, facing and surrendering into the possibility that we would not survive it, only to emerge unscathed. Even the house itself suffered very little damage, when any of a number of threats could have easily badly damaged or destroyed it.

The experience of Iniki became a pivotal chapter in our own journeys of awakening. If we hadn't been able to rise above the fear and panic in the ego-mind, there was no way that September day in 1992 would have unfolded in such a miraculous fashion. We were perfectly guided to do exactly what was needed, and when our preparations were complete, we lay down on the bed in the bunker room, holding hands.

What happened next was something neither of us could have made happen. Through Grace, we both completely surrendered into whatever the hurricane brought next. We gave our lives to the Divine, and were carried into a state of total peace and bliss. As the winds raged all around us, we felt utterly calm within. We rested in our souls and were aligned with whatever came next, knowing that it would resonate with our truest Selves.

This immense gift of Grace provides great solace going into the days ahead, for we know that impeccable guidance will always be available to us when we need it most. But the only way we can access that guidance is if we know how to move through and beyond our fear. Otherwise, we can easily be overwhelmed by the mental chaos that arises out of deep fear. Once we have turned the fear over to the Divine and asked for Its guidance, the soul steps forth and takes dominion over the bodymind. All we need to do then is still ourselves and listen within.

How do we go beyond the fear that can become paralyzing in extreme moments? The path to transcending fear is to face and embrace it where it arises within our own bodies. First, we become aware that we are starting to lose our center. Our mind starts to race and we feel disconnected from ourselves. We're up in our heads, looking out into the world at what we perceive as the source of the fear, and busy developing strategies to get rid of it as soon as possible. We are disconnected from our bodies and our souls, untethered in a sea of mentalizations.

But we don't have to stay in this disembodied, fearful state. The way through it is to come out of our minds, drop into our bodies, and feel the fear that is arising. We let our eyes close, focus on the breath, and turn within. Becoming aware of the feeling of the breath moving in the body is key, since it gives our awareness another point of focus other than the mind. As we stay in touch with our breath, feeling the sensations as it moves in and out of the body, the mind will quiet. That allows us to notice what is arising within the body — to get to know the sensations that go with fear. We may feel a tightness in the throat, or a knot of anxiety in the belly, or any of a thousand other sensations.

When we rest in the breath, we are simply present to the energetic charge and "feeling" of the fear wherever it is focused within the body. If we can breathe and feel that charge of fear, it will move through and dissipate, like a wave passing through the ocean. We do not have to do anything to get rid of it, to try to figure out what it's about, or to attempt to go beyond it. It is simply asking us to be present with it so it can pass through our emotional body without being blocked. Any and all thoughts and feelings will go through the same kind of process if we do not run from them or try to suppress them. When they receive the attention they require, they always dissolve on their own.

As the fear moves through us, we begin to hear all the reasons why we are afraid. The mind will tell us what it has been perceiving and believing — the ideas and concepts that justify the feeling of fear. As we bring consciousness to them, they almost always fade away as they are seen to be untrue. This automatically brings us into deeper communion with our true Self. Once again we are back home in our place of truth, knowing, and peace.

The ultimate foundation of fear is found in the illusion of separation. When we perceive that we are separate, mortal, physical beings, divorced from the eternal divinity of our souls, we experience fear. As an eternal, divine soul, nothing can really damage, harm, or destroy us. When the body ceases to function, we simply drop it and move on to another experience. There is no damage or loss to who and what we really are. To fully awaken to and remember this is to be completely beyond fear and egoism. The ego arises when we believe we are separate, ephemeral, mortal beings whose fate is synonymous with that of the body. Fear is always with us when we believe we are the ego-self, as the threat that we will be hurt or even cease to exist.

The fear that arises from the innate survival responses of the body does have some benefit. If we're walking across the street and became aware of a large truck bearing down on us, the survival response causes us to react suddenly and quickly to get out of the way. Unfortunately, the survival fear has been generalized and projected onto many circumstances in our everyday lives, distorting our perception. The root of every fear we experience, whether of getting fired from our job, not having enough money to pay bills, or that we will be found unattractive as the wrinkles of age appear on our face, lies in body identification and attachment. This the basis for the separate ego self sense. It is the core of the misperception of our true nature, and that is exactly what needs to be transcended to come into communion with and live as the true, eternal Self.

This is why fear may be the greatest doorway to awakening and Self-realization. Its presence is the sign that we are disconnected from our true Self. When we are aware enough to face and embrace it, we can see that the presence of fear is a gift. As fear arises and we recognize that it is not something to be afraid of or avoided, but something to be faced and embraced, we open the door to releasing the emotional charge of fear. That charge constricts, blocks and distorts our mental, emotional and etheric-physical bodies, veiling our communion with the radiance of our luminous, true Self. As we feel and release the energetic charge within the sensations of fear, more of the light that we are can shine out into our life, showing us the way through whatever challenges arise.

Dark Night of the Soul

If we are going to be reborn as a new, soul-awakened species, there must be a death of the self that we thought we were. This can happen gradually and gently over time, and it can also happen through a deep, dark descent into the unconscious realms that may last for months or even years. This has been called the Dark Night of the Soul, for we often experience it as being psychically submerged in interminable shadow-realms with no way out. We are thrown into an experience of deep loss, depression, and alienation from our souls, and no matter what we try, we can't seem to dig our way out from under it all. The Dark Night is a common passage in the journey of awakening, and will almost certainly be more present in our collective psychic landscape as we transit the awakening at the end of time.

Loss is often a major catalyst for and feature of the descent. In many Dark Nights we lose persons and things that are most important to us. Aspects of our life that give us passion and desire and spark are taken away. The Dark Night may present the greatest of challenges, as relationships and ways of being that are woven into the fabric our souls are now gone. These losses are far beyond the kinds of ego/personality attachments and preferences we are all asked to go beyond as we awaken. During the Dark Night, we may have to relinquish the most precious aspects of our lives that emanate from the core of our being.

This can cause us to try as never before to get our old sense of self back. We attempt to fix the things that seem to be going wrong in our lives, to get back to the light and happiness we once knew, but nothing works. Instead, we find ourselves being swallowed up in darkness, as if we were sinking into quicksand. Nothing we do seems to be working.

We question what is happening, and may even believe that God has abandoned us. We may feel like our soul is dying. Our usual sense of connection with the Divine can vanish, leaving us in a dark void that feels empty beyond comprehension. The pain and suffering may escalate to such a degree that we don't want to go on. The crucial moment in the Dark Night occurs when we realize that we would be happy to die, but even this isn't an option. We must even surrender this ultimate form of escape.

My own Dark Night of the Soul is a classic example of what this journey is like. I will relate it to you because many of you are already or will be experiencing something like it in the time ahead. It began slowly with the more overt aspects of my personal ego-identity being dismantled. The sense of self-esteem and pride that I had generated in earlier decades through success in the business world was completely crushed. Everything I tried to do to bring my life back into the pattern that I felt I deserved bore no fruit. All the magic I thought I possessed to create the life that I felt I deserved was gone. I had already given up all previously held hopes of being financially wealthy, but now a complete meltdown of my finances ensued, ending in bankruptcy. Even the availability of a car had been taken away, and I had to walk or ride a bicycle even on dark, stormy winter nights. For five years my sense of self, all that I thought of as who I was and what my life was about, dissolved. I even had to even give up what I thought was my divine soul purpose and destiny. Then I had to give up what I thought was core to everything this lifetime was about, the relationship with my twin flame.

With each loss the grief, sadness and despair went deeper — deeper than what most people would call classic depression. I didn't care enough to even be depressed. I was completely empty; there was a void in the core of my being. I withdrew from the world and could not bear to even walk into town to buy groceries. Many days, I just wanted to leave the planet, and Karen often wondered if I would come back from a simple walk through the neighborhood. I saw nothing to live for, no purpose to be here. I looked around and nothing attracted or inspired me, nothing gave me the desire to continue on. I had stopped asking God to bring me home, because I did not even feel a connection with God. This was quite troubling, as I had experienced many powerful realizations of Self and God during the previous six or seven years.

When it didn't matter whether I continued, I walked through what may be the most potent door of ego-death, facing the death of the body. In the middle of winter I found myself facing the fact that my life had become a black hole of desperation, which threatened to bring my beloved Karen down with me. I had no money, was bankrupt, and had lost my passion for everything, including what I knew to be my life's work. I was incapable of doing anything in the world to support myself. Karen was not able to make enough money to support us, and now her credit card debt was piling up. I felt that I could not pull Karen down with me and that the only truthful and honorable thing to do was to walk out the door.

One day, after another conflict over money, I grabbed my sleeping bag and prepared to leave our apartment, knowing that there was a great likelihood that the very tenuous connection I had with this human form would be lost under the extreme stress of living out in the cold and rain of winter. I saw myself dying of hypothermia in a cold, wet sleeping bag in a back alley. As I contemplated this as the end of this lifetime, there was no fear or sense of conflict, as I knew that even this would be okay. If that was the way God wanted to bring me home, then I knew it would be okay and would even be the highest and best for me, no matter what my mind and emotions might be telling me.

I fully surrendered my life, expecting I would be leaving my body very soon. All this occurred in but a moment, one of the most potent in this life. Something subtle but immensely powerful and pervasive shifted someplace deep within. An immense peace washed over me, something I had not experienced in years. I had fully left go. The lyrics from Janis Joplin's song "Me and Bobby McGee" popped into my mind: "Freedom's just another word for nothing left to lose," which spoke to me in a very deep way. There was a flicker of light and joy in my heart, something I had not experienced in years, as I knew that this was true. I had given it ALL up to God. There was absolutely nothing left to lose. I was finally free. Whether the physical body died in the cold, dark, wet alley didn't matter. For what I thought I was had died — finally, after half a decade of long, slow death, I was gone. And I was finally free.

I never went out on the street, and obviously I did not die. As I walked toward the door Karen called me back, telling me that she loved me and that no matter what happened we were supposed to be together. Her words were like a clear ray of light entering my being, and I knew she was speaking the truth.

The darkness began to lift, although who and what I thought I was before was gone. The emptiness that I perceived as a gnawing sense of loss of soul began to shift. There was no longer a sense of loss or absence, but a peaceful emptiness that was vast and light.

I saw that the personal ego sense of self that had lived in the dualistic world of the ups and downs of positive and negative experiences was gone. There was nothing anymore to seek for or run from. Instead, a sense of infinite expansion and oneness with everything was present. I entered a phase of rebirth which took me into a life I never could have conceived of or found my way into, a life full of joy and happiness the likes of which I had never experienced. Years later, I came upon these words from Joseph Campbell, which described exactly what I had been through. "The dark night of the soul comes just before revelation. When everything is lost, and all seems darkness, then comes the new life and all that is needed."

A new life did unfold for me, in which each year finds me living more and more fully in a heavenly experience of the earth-plane. I now know that this awaits us all as we transit the process of ego-death through whatever Dark Nights lie ahead. All will be gifts of grace, from a loving God who only wants us to awaken and come home to our true Selves. As we do so, the Earth around us will transform to reflect what we have realized within. As more and more of us awaken, it is impossible that anything could unfold except a new EarthHeaven, to be experienced by all who have entered that timeline through their own death and rebirth process, awakening at the end of time.

33

Facing Death as the Ultimate Doorway to Awakening

The specter of physically life-threatening events offers the opportunity to dive into the depths of our being, down to our bottom-most fears. Beneath all others is the one that forms the ground of our false identity: the fear of death and nonexistence. A primal false assumption lies below the conscious awareness of most human beings -- that when the body dies, something really bad happens to "me." In a nutshell, "I" cease to exist. It all goes dark forever. This fearful illusion is the heavy cloud that looms over every moment of human existence, for those of us who buy into it. We simply aren't aware of it, since we subconsciously suppress it. We carry on as if this life will go on forever, for we are too afraid to examine the alternative.

Much of the average, ego-centered human life is spent in an unconscious quest to quell the subterranean fear of death and nonexistence. This causes humans to seek externally for something, anything, to fill the void. Our ravenous consumption of the planet for all the material substitutes we worship is a prime means by which we deny the deepest of all fears. Until we begin to awaken, we have no idea that only rediscovering our eternal, whole, perfect nature will ever banish this deepest of fears.

As we saw in Parts One and Two, humans' rampant seeking, rooted in denying our true nature and the corresponding ignorance of the laws of life, has resulted in the avalanching karmic accumulation that is becoming a species-threatening crisis. As the law of cause and effect brings our mis-creations back to us, we are given the opportunity to experience the unconscious fears of lack, limitation and ultimately death and nonexistence that impelled our creating them. How loving, truthful and fair the laws of life turn out to be. Everything we think and do eventually comes back to us, perfectly mirroring whether our actions were based in truth or illusion.

The specter of physical death may be the most profound catalyst for awakening available to a human soul. It has the potential to strip away all that we thought we were, to the very bottom of our human, bodily identity. Understanding this, Tibetan Buddhists view preparation for death as the core of their spiritual practice. Each night, they end their day in the consciousness that this may be their last on planet Earth. After dinner, Buddhist monks turn their drinking glasses upside down, a symbolic gesture that is also used when a monk dies. This is not a gloomy practice for them, because they find that facing and embracing the reality of their bodily impermanence makes them even more happy and alive.

While some people do receive forewarnings of impending death, whether their own of that of a loved one, most human beings do not. The truth is, the next moment could be the last for any one of us. We can die before we die by facing this reality. This, in fact, is <u>the way Ramana Maharshi became liberated</u>. One day he felt the presence of death moving in his being, and he lay down and completely surrendered into what that journey would be like. He went all the way to the bottom of this great illusion, forcing his body to simulate death, letting go of the body, facing death fully. Here, this awakened being describes the ultimate confrontation:

> *I held my breath and kept my lips tightly closed so that no sound could escape, so that neither the word 'I' or any other word could be uttered. 'Well then,' I said to myself, 'this body is dead. It will be carried stiff to the burning ground and there burnt and reduced to ashes. But with the death of this body am I dead? Is the body 'I'? It is silent and inert but I feel the full force of my personality and even the voice of the 'I' within me, apart from it. So I am Spirit transcending the body. The body dies but the Spirit that transcends it cannot be touched by death. This*

means I am the deathless Spirit.' All this was not dull thought; it flashed through me vividly as living truth which I perceived directly, almost without thought-process. 'I' was something very real, the only real thing about my present state, and all the conscious activity connected with my body was centered on that 'I'. From that moment onwards the 'I' or Self focused attention on itself by a powerful fascination. Fear of death had vanished once and for all. Absorption in the Self continued unbroken from that time on.

Like Ramana Maharshi, we are all faced with the big questions: *What happens when the wave of death washes over me and these eyes close for the last time? Who and what will remain?* As all the fear that propped up the false, egoic self sense is faced and embraced, the very foundation of who we thought we were dissolves. We experience a personal apocalypse as the veils of illusion are shredded to reveal the truth that has always lain hidden under the layers of false self. When we have traveled to the bottom of the deepest layers of fear, we must eventually fall into the ground of our being -- the eternal soul, the true Self.

Awakened to who and what we really are, we transcend all sense of ourselves as separate human beings. We rest in the experience of being indestructible, eternal divinity.

Wonderful am I. Adoration to myself who knows no decay and survives even the destruction of the world, from Brahma (God/Creator) down to a clump of grass.
                                    Astavakra Samhita

34

The Coming of the Collective Avatar

The Divine has been descending directly onto this planet since the very beginning. History is blessed with numerous accounts of divine beings including Osiris, Moses, Zoroaster, Krishna, Buddha, and Christ. All were, to one degree or another, the fullness of the Ocean of God even while appearing temporarily as a drop. Each of these divine incarnations was an important part of the great journey of God realizing Itself within the realm of form.

Two thousand years ago, an epochal moment in this journey occurred. The being Jesus, or Yeshua, came to embody the fullness of the Godhead and proclaim, "I and the Father are One." His coming does not discount or diminish the divine incarnations who came before. This being was simply a culmination point in the long process of the Divine slowly coming into incarnation through a host of masters, saints and adepts throughout history.

The "First Coming" was the moment when the fullness of Source was able to fully incarnate into the human form, completely penetrating and breaking the material resistance and thick veils that had enshrouded the planet. The public crucifixion, resurrection and ascension were the crucial events that encoded or inseminated the Earth with the seed crystal of the totality of Source Presence or "The Father," as Jesus called it. This was the most important evolutionary event until this time, so crucial that humans continue to demarcate historical events as occurring before or after this coming. The seed crystal that was planted through the incarnation of God/One/Source through the being Jesus has been gestating, slowly growing during the last two thousand years. For much more on this, we invite you to read our third book, *We Are The Awakening Christ*.

The word **Christ** is, in a way, just a name, albeit a very spiritually powerful one. Most importantly, invoking the Christ gives us a way to connect to the full presence and manifestation of the second aspect of the triune nature of God, the Holy Son and Daughter, God incarnate within Its own creation. Avatars and divine incarnations in all spiritual traditions since the beginning are manifestations of the Holy Son and Daughter of God, the soul fully realized and one with Source. Yet this being we call the Christ stands apart from all others in profoundly unmistakable ways.

The story of the coming of Christ is not about religion or Christianity. In both positive and negative senses, Christianity has had an enormous influence on this planet. Unfortunately, the dark shadows it has cast often obscure the immense importance of the First Coming. It is important for us to understand the profound significance of what occurred in Galilee 2000 years ago, before the idea of a humanly created religion called Christianity ever occurred to anyone. Jesus was a divine incarnation, like those celebrated by other faiths and traditions, who come to Earth to plant divine seeds of Grace for humanity.

With the First Coming, the seed of the Tree of Life was planted in the fecund soul-soil of this earth. The transcendence of death and return to the divine, heavenly estate was seeded through the crucifixion, resurrection, and ascension. This story was recorded for all to experience through the most widely read sacred text in planetary history. It was known that the seed of Christ's unparalleled accomplishments would gestate, sprout and grow until it was ready to flower at the end of the 2000-year cycle of human soul-evolution.

As mentioned in Part Two, the great spiritual traditions contain prophecies that at the end of this age, a great avatar will come to Earth to liberate and awaken humanity. Hindus expect the tenth and final incarnation of their Christ figure, Vishnu, as the Kalki Avatar, who rides a white horse and carries a sword, just as the returning Christ does in biblical Revelations. The sword is used to destroy "evil" and liberate humanity. The Vedic tradition refers to this as the time Kali will dance, destroying fear, ignorance and egoism. Islam expects the Imam Mahdi, their Christic figure, who will come to awaken and save humanity. Jews await their Messiah, while Buddhists anticipate the incarnation of the Maitreya Buddha, their avatar of planetary awakening. These and others are the many faces of the One, descending as a collective avatar that is entering the psycho-sphere of this planet more rapidly with each passing day. The Galactic Superwave, the solar event, and the declining geo-magnetic field are all symptoms of this greater causal impulse.

The light of any solar event is but the third-dimensional manifestation of an infinitely unfathomable luminescence that is enfolding this planet on the higher-dimensional levels. This is the real story, above and beyond any destructive manifestation that may occur as a byproduct. It's important to note that no destruction at all would occur if the planetary, physical base frequency were raised to at least a fourth-dimensional level, in which the trapped entropy and chaos that precipitate destruction are considerably smaller. We are not there yet, and we may not be when the light event occurs. How close we will be remains to be seen, and that will dictate how much destruction needs to occur.

The light of the descending collective avataric presence is also awakening in the center of the soul of everyone, especially those who are choosing to turn within and embrace it. There has never a time when spiritual awakening and soul evolution have been possible on such an immense scale. It is a time of tremendous grace, bestowing blessings that are unfathomable to most sleeping human beings. We need do so little now, spiritually, to grow so much. If we take one step toward God, God will take ten back toward us.

Turn within and feel the light; feel the building divine presence within you. Even as the great "harvest" happens, in which some beings seem to go deeper into density and darkness while others awaken, it is the light of the descending collective avatar that is fueling this process. In truth, no one is being lost in this harvest. Spiritual evolution is accelerating to such a degree that some souls are unable to keep pace and seem to be going backward. It's as if the planet is moving ahead at a thousand miles an hour, while some beings are only able to go five hundred; relative to the progression of the Earth, they seem to be falling behind. Bless them, for they, too, are held in God's all-loving grace.

The collective avatar of awakening humanity is descending as the Kalki/Maitreya/Christ. Each of us will experience this as the face that is most resonant with our soul evolution. There is no conflict between religions or traditions, for behind them all is one being, one presence with many faces. And it is waking up in each of us as our true, essential nature. We are each an inextricable part of the Second Coming. We are the awakening Kalkis, Buddhas and Christs. Someday, sometime beyond time, we will all realize what these great beings did. In the core of our being, the seed of this awakening is gathering momentum toward blossoming. The light is expanding within our third-dimensional, caterpillar nature more rapidly with each passing day, calling us to turn within and enter the chrysalis. We are asked to release all previous identities — to die to who and what we have been — so our luminous, divine soul nature can be born.

Our little, human selves are incapable of controlling this metamorphosis. The Descent of the Divine is doing it all, as the Ocean of God is arising within the drop of our soul. All that is asked of us is to relinquish our sense of being drops separate and apart from the ocean, to die to this third-dimensional, physical sense of self, and to fully realize that we are infinite, eternal, divine souls. We embrace that as our true identity as we turn within to the light of our Source in the core of our being. Remembering and reuniting with That in which our soul has its foundation and being, we feel all sense of separation dissolve. As we surrender into this, the illusion of separation itself likewise melts away, with as much ease and grace as we can allow. If things become more difficult in the future, if we face trials we are not sure we will be able to weather, we can remember that the Divine is there, reaching down to embrace us — to lift us up as never before.

Long ago, during a time of overwhelm with the revelations of the future that were cascading into consciousness, Christ Jesus, the face of the collective descending Avatar that we most deeply relate to, delivered a message to which I often return. It has provided a touchstone of truth that always reorients me to peace and trust whenever facing what may unfold agitates my heart and soul. Now, I offer this message to you. Christ's message contains all that we really need to know to align with the path of grace into the new EarthHeaven. Here is what he said:

I achieved the path of salvation which everyone now must walk. Come to the Christ/God and receive this gift. It is done. Can you receive that much? Can you surrender that much? Can you let go of all the ideas that you need to do and achieve this? For it is I, in truth, who achieved nothing. It simply occurred as the walk of my journey. I of myself did nothing, as I stated at the time. It was pure grace. All that was required of me was to do my best to bring the fullness of myself to my experience, to continue to have the courage to, as you say, Barry, "show up" and take the next step that was laid out before me.

I walked those steps, the path through death and beyond. It is done. Can you hear that? Can you feel that? Can you allow that? I place this gift now in your heart. It is this simple.

Release all your ideas of self-hatred, inadequacy, worthlessness, and evil. Drop them for the illusions that they are, for you are the holy son, the holy daughter. The Father's plan for your salvation was written before time began, before you took this sojourn in matter. I came simply as a harbinger to tear aside the veils of your illusion and instill the remembrance and truth of your destiny.

Grace is now raining down upon you -- free, flowing everywhere. Try as hard as you will, you cannot run between the raindrops, you shall get wet in this torrent of grace which will drown your sense of separation...forever.

Why not look skyward and receive the full torrent and be free? This is my gift. That was the gift of Christ Jesus/God. And it is yours. Resist as you will, surely you will be swept away by it. This I guarantee. For this river of light flows rapidly to the sea of oneness with the Father and the Mother and the Kingdom. It goes faster every day.

Can you feel this stream of light? Let go and receive my grace. I lift you up, I carry you. I walk for you when you cannot walk. Remember those times when you thought you could not even crawl? I crawled with you and for you. That is how much I *love you, how much I am with you, how much we care.*

Your salvation is assured. It is done, from the beginning to the end, always an assured fact. This is the truth, the song that I offer you. Rest in this and experience the peace that truly passeth all understanding.

The Christ

Afterword

Resources for Awakening

How to personally navigate the death of the human caterpillar self and the birth of the luminous, divine, butterfly Self is a subject far too vast to even begin to dive into in this book. As you consecrate your life to this journey and turn it over to the Divine, you will assuredly be taken on the perfect path for you.

If you feel resonant with what we have presented, you may want to explore some of the many resources we offer, all designed to assist you to more easily die to the limited, false self sense and realize the true, eternal Self.

Our website, https://www.luminousself.com/, is a good place to start, since it the connecting-point for all the various resources we offer. There, you will find considerable evolutionary stimulation to support your journey of awakening, and to explore whether you feel drawn to go deeper into our offerings. An abundance of free content is offered to support your journey into full Self-realization and freedom. You can also sign up for our occasional Newsletters.

The **Birthing the Luminous Self Trilogy of books** offer a compendium of what we have learned during our journeys of awakening, and in assisting many others to go beyond suffering and awaken to the grace and peace, the wisdom and love, of who they truly are. We've devoted 30 years to facilitating awakening, and we've been blessed with an ever-deepening understanding of what is involved in waking up to who and what we truly are and releasing all that we are not.

Everything in these books is derived directly from our own experiences of awakening and supporting others as they awaken. There is no hearsay or abstract spiritual theory here! You will not find spiritual platitudes, naive assumptions, or empty promises cluttering up these books. Here's a brief summary of each book:

<u>Soul Awakening: The Journey From Ego to Essence</u> contains potent information about and experiences of the journey of awakening, as well as a transmission of what goes on during the soul-awakening journey. This book also shares a wealth of direct experiences of the divine essence that lives within the Soul Lotus, in the many ways that manifests to awakening souls.

<u>Agents of Grace: Fulfilling Our Destiny, Blessing the World</u> is a manual designed to assist those awakening souls and light workers who know they are here to fulfill their soul destiny as agents of awakening. The three soul centers — head, heart, and belly — are discussed in depth, along with the Transmissions of Grace that activate each center. As the Transmissions of Grace are experienced and integrated, they can be shared with others in a neverending "Pay It Forward" of awakening.

<u>We Are The Awakening Christ: The Birth of the Luminous, Divine Human</u> is a powerful transmission to catalyze the realization of the luminous, Christed Self, the ultimate destiny of all souls. What does it mean to walk this Earth as an awakening Christ? What kinds of extraordinary experiences might we be blessed with as we recognize that the Christ lives within us as our truest nature? This book discusses these questions and much more.

Our most recent book, <u>Taking Off Overcoats: A Simple, Loving Approach to Awakening</u> is a hands-on, self-guided manual on how to let go of the "overcoats" of the false self in order to reveal the luminous, divine Self hidden within. It is a step-by-step, progressive journey through the various levels of the awakening process. Each chapter contains essential information and inner processes to catalyze awakening. *Overcoats* was written for us all — from spiritual beginners to those who have been on a path of awakening for decades. When you buy a copy of *Taking Off Overcoats*, you receive a link to free MP3s of the 20 guided inner processes that form the core of the book's journey of awakening, as our gift to you.

We have also created an integrated series of inner process Modules that catalyze direct experiences of awakening. Each Module contains one or more MP3s that present in-depth information and guided inner processes. Many people tell us it is comforting to hear our voices as they work with these Modules, and some like to fall asleep to the soothing vibrations of the guided inner processes.

We also offer three Transmissions of Grace, which awaken the three soul centers. Each center focalizes a primary aspect of the soul's three dimensions of being. In a Self-realized being, all three centers are fully functioning and realized. The head center is where we experience En-Light-enment, the heart center is the home of En-Love-enment, and the belly center is where we get in touch with En-Life-enment. The three soul centers are different from, more causal to, and thus superior in their role in awakening to the chakras. When all three are activated and present in our conscious awareness, awakening occurs in a balanced, integrated way.

Our YouTube Channel is another fountain of information on the journey of awakening, and speaks to many subjects of interest to awakening souls, such as Twin Flames and the Universal Christ. Many of our videos also contain short guided inner processes at the end, so be sure to watch all the way through. Subscribing to our channel will automatically alert you to new videos as they are released. We welcome your comments and suggestions about future topics you'd like us to discuss.

The most direct and powerful way to tap into our consciousness resources and extensive experience with awakening souls is to work with us over time through a series of sessions. We offer sessions by phone, in person, or via Skype. We invite you to contact us for a free, 20-minute consultation to explore whether our approach to awakening resonates with you. Walking alongside those who are awakening to who they truly are and releasing what they are not is our greatest joy. We would love to share the adventure of awakening with you, and we know that your unique pathway Home will beautifully reveal itself as we drop into the sacred space of the soul together. Our work is unique in that it completely respects the inner flow and divine guidance that is unceasingly pouring through your eternal essence. Our deepest joy is helping you to get in touch with and live from That!

Blessings to you on your journey. Remember that the ultimate outcome is known, and that none of us can fail to realize our true nature. While the journey may have its moments, it will all be worth it in the end. One day in the future, out beyond time, we will remember our Earth days with fondness as a long-ago dream, while we experience a blissful, love-infused, luminous life on a higher-dimensional Earth and beyond.

www.ingramcontent.com/pod-product-compliance
Lightning Source LLC
Chambersburg PA
CBHW062157080426
42734CB00010B/1719